STOCK MARKET TRADING SYSTEMS

STOCK MARKET TRADING SYSTEMS

By
GERALD APPEL
W. FREDERICK HITSCHLER

TRADERS PRESS, INC.
P.O. Box 10344
Greenville, S.C. 29603

Publications of TRADERS PRESS, INC.:

Commodity Spreads: A Historical Chart Perspective (Dobson)
The Trading Rule That Can Make You Rich* (Dobson)
Viewpoints of a Commodity Trader (Longstreet)
Commodities: A Chart Anthology (Dobson)
Profitable Grain Trading (Ainsworth)
A Complete Guide to Trading Profits (Paris)
Trader's Guide to Technical Analysis (Hardy)
The Professional Commodity Trader (Kroll)
Jesse Livermore: Speculator-King (Sarnoff)
Reminiscences of a Stock Operator (Lefevre)
Understanding Fibonacci Numbers (Dobson)
Study Helps in Point and Figure Technique (Whelan)
Winning Market Systems (Appel)
Wall Street Ventures and Adventures (Wyckoff)
Commodity Spreads: Analysis, Selection and
         Trading Techniques (Smith)
Stock Market Trading Systems (Appel & Hitschler)
Comparison of Twelve Technical Trading Systems
         (Lukac, Brorsen, & Irwin)
Day Trading with Short Term Price Patterns and
         Opening Range Breakout (Crabel)

Reprinted by special arrangement with the authors, Gerald Appel
    and W. Fred Hitschler, April, 1990.
Original edition published by Dow Jones-Irwin, 1980.

ISBN: 0-934380-16-3

TRADERS PRESS, INC.
P.O. Box 10344
Greenville, S.C. 29603

Books for Stock
and Commodity
Traders

Preface

We have written this book to improve both your market timing and the profits you are able to take out of the stock market.

In preparing this work, we have had two simple objectives in mind:

1. We have attempted to isolate what stock trading strategies work and what does not work.
2. We have sought to derive certain basic trading strategies that do work, that are relatively simple to carry out—requiring little time each day—and that are effective. Moreover, we have attempted to create market strategies that involve a minimum of mathematics, a minimum of emotion, but a maximum of objectivity. In other words, as far as possible, we are trying to eliminate those bugaboos of investment success, fear and greed, from your investment decisions.

Our approach is obviously technical in nature. We recommend that aggressive traders pay a minimum (if any) attention to fundamental data such as news of corporate earnings, interest rates, balance of payment deficits, oil prices, unemployment figures, and auto sales. Heresy? Perhaps. To the technician, all of these factors, and myriads of others, have already been and are currently being reflected in the action of the stock market itself. What you read each day in *The Wall Street Journal* has already been read and digested by millions of investors, its implications already reflected in the action of the stock market.

Nor are we going to concern ourselves with the vast majority of indicators generally employed by technical analysts—indicators such as margin debt, credit balances, secondary offerings, bellwether stocks, and Dow Theory. This book is *not* the usual compendium of technical indicators. In our experience, the majority of technical indicators have proven contradictory.

The trading systems we will present for your use will involve mainly four basics—trend, time, reversal areas, and excessive swing. The actual movement of the market itself will be our major barometer. Tracking methods will be clearly explained, based upon computer derived data and research and based upon our own trading experience and study of many years of stock market history.

The research which has gone into this book has been largely derived from a computer study (involving *thousands* of computations) of the stock market of the period 1966–79. Many of our systems have been back-checked for periods of up to 12 and 13 years of daily and weekly market and stock history.

It should go without saying that no single technical indicator is perfect, or even nearly perfect, and that no system or systems of trading can eliminate the risks involved in active stock market investment. Our research has, for the most part, been hypothetical in nature and in no case have the authors, or anyone to our knowledge, traded for any extended period of time upon any of the systems we will be discussing. There is no assurance, implied or intended, that the future results of any system employed will equal past hypothetical results.

February 1980   Gerald Appel
                                                         W. Frederick Hitschler

Special acknowledgment

The computer simulations for the research for this book were run on the time-sharing services of Remote Computing Corporation of Palo Alto, California, utilizing their Merlin Systems extensive financial data base and library of trade testing and optimizing model programs created for them by W. Frederick Hitschler. Mr. Hitschler wrote other programs specially devised for this book as well as programming the ideas suggested by Gerald Appel.

For those who wish to explore further the technical trading methods described in this book, the same programs we used as well as others are available on Remote Computing.

A word to the reader

The research, data, and results presented herein have been prepared with every effort at accuracy, but nonetheless complete accuracy cannot be guaranteed, given the thousands of calculations that took place in the preparation of this work.

Furthermore, although the authors have made every effort to present results of research fairly, thoroughly, and without bias, no intent should be implied on the part of the authors or the publisher to suggest that any stock trading system—or combination of systems—can be guaranteed to produce profit. Risk is always inherent in stock market speculation, and particularly so in the aggressive trading systems suggested by the research presented.

Nor should any intent be implied to recommend any particular stock or group of stocks for purchase or sale. Issues discussed within this book are discussed as examples only, and not as specific recommendations for future action.

G. A.
W. F. H.

Contents

How to compute the cats and dogs relative strength indicator. The zero balance trading system—Anticipating intermediate turns before they take place. How to compute zero balance points. Results of trading via zero balance. How to deal with certain zero balance patterns which can mislead the unwary.

An averaging method for stock options that should produce large profit even on an issue that declines in price. Option scale trading. How to make favorable use of option leverage. Those very deep discount houses. The telephone switch funds. One final trading system for calling the direction of the next day's market.

STOCK MARKET
TRADING SYSTEMS

FOREWORD

This classic work on technical analysis was brought to my attention so often by traders wanting to acquire it after it went out of print several years ago that I felt that reprinting it was a project which fit right into the **Traders Press** philosophy: make the best educational material on trading available to the trading public and, if unavailable, to take the necessary measures to make them available again.

TRADERS PRESS periodically publishes a **Traders Catalog** which lists and describes over 200 books, tapes, courses, and systems of interest to the stock, option, and commodity trader. (Current edition is 48 pages in length!) Write today for your free copy: **Traders Press, Inc.**, P.O. Box 10344, Greenville, S.C. 29603.

Edward Dobson

Edward D. Dobson
Greenville, S.C.
March, 1990

1

How to determine
the true trends of the stock
market with moving and
exponential averages

Trend (the general direction of stock prices) is a major component of our "Time-Trend-Momentum Trading System," the integrated market system that we believe to be our best trading technique. This system will be described in full in Chapter 12. Trend also happens to be a prime, if not the sole, ingredient of a number of more basic trading systems, several of which we shall describe shortly. Therefore, let's take the time right now to define and to develop means of measuring true stock market trend.

The basic definition of market trend

Trend, as we noted above, refers to the direction of market prices. The stock market may be considered to be in an uptrend whenever stock prices etch out a series of higher highs and higher lows—each peak in the market averages higher than the preceding peak and each trough or low point higher than the preceding low point. The stock market may be considered to be in a downtrend whenever stock prices trace out a series of declining highs and declining low points. (See Figures 1–1 and 1–2 for examples.)

The classic Dow Theory is based on such configurations. According to the Dow Theory, a major bull market signal is rendered whenever both the Dow Industrial average and the Dow Transportation average surpass previous intermediate high points, following failures by both averages to fall beneath previous intermediate low points. Bear market signals are rendered whenever both the Dow Transports and the Dow Industrials etch out declining intermediate formations. In general, Dow Theory signals have proved

FIGURE 1-1
El Paso rose in a classical uptrend between October 1978 and June 1979

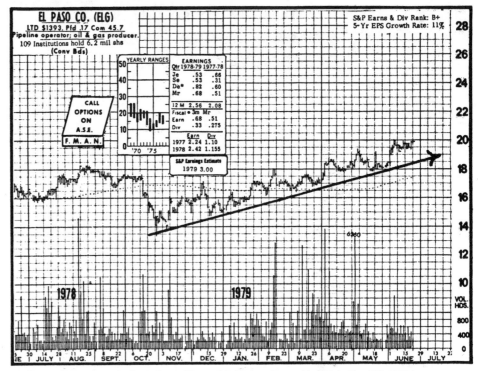

Source: *Trendline Daily Basis Stock Charts*, 345 Hudson Street, New York City, N.Y. 10014.

profitable on balance, although they often do occur several months and approximately 100 Dow points from major bear market bottoms or bull market peaks.

We will be evaluating market trading systems based on the market averages' surpassing previous high points and falling below previous low points, but for now let's just consider some of the problems encountered in the determination of true market trend via such an approach. For example,

The market, in its daily and weekly fluctuations, constantly etches out various series of minor uptrend formations and minor downtrend formations. It is often difficult to determine which of these formations truly signify a change in major trend, and which measure to employ to separate minor trend reversals from more significant intermediate and major trend reversals. As a result, many Dow theorists find themselves in disagreement as to just when Dow Theory signals have in fact been rendered.

There are many periods of apparently neutral market action when trends defined by price fluctuation are particularly difficult to ascertain. Prices seem to move for periods of time in a very random fashion.

FIGURE 1–2
**Denny's major downtrend continued from 1978 well
into 1979.**

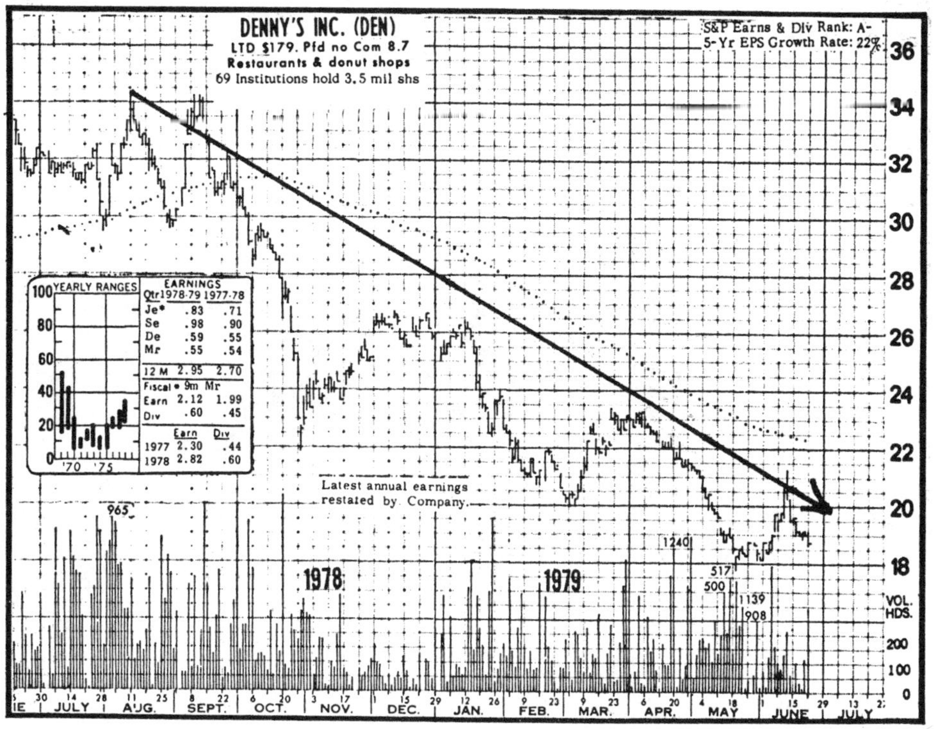

Source: *Trendline Daily Basis Stock Charts*, 345 Hudson Street, New York City, N.Y. 10014.

**How moving
averages
can be used
to define market
trend for the period
you wish defined**

Moving averages are statistical devices that may be employed to smooth out stock market and other data in order to reveal more clearly the true underlying trend of the stock market and of individual stocks. The *direction* of the current trend may be determined by noting whether the pertinent moving average is rising or falling. The *strength* of the current trend may be determined by the *slope* of the moving average—the rate at which it is rising or falling.

Figure 1–3 shows the Dow Industrial average for a period of time with its 10-week and 30-week moving averages, which, in this case, are front weighted to provide more weight to recent than to past readings. A 10-week moving average is the average reading of the most recent ten closing weekly postings of the Dow. A 30-week moving average would average the most recent thirty weekly closings.

The 10-week moving average may be taken as a measure of the stock market's *intermediate* trend, which may be considered to be rising for as long as the 10-week moving average is rising and declining for as long as the 10-week moving average is declining. The 30-week moving average may be taken as a measure of the longer-term trends of the stock market. The *major*

4

FIGURE 1–3
The 10-week moving average of the Dow Jones
Industrials defines the intermediate trend and the
30-week moving average defines the major trend

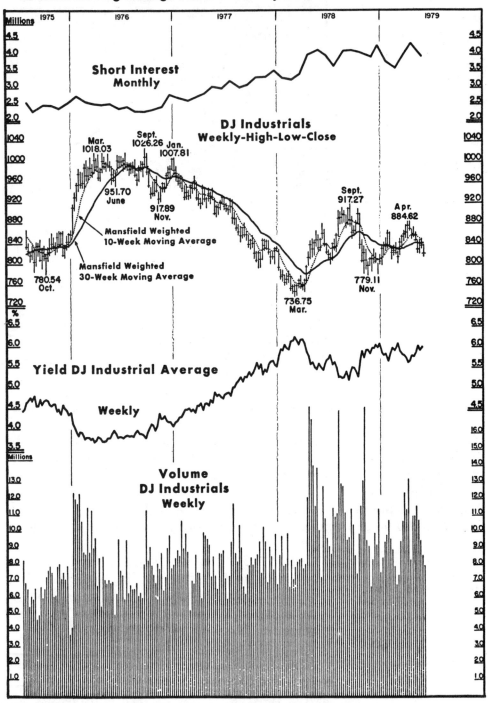

Source: *Mansfield Stock Chart Service*, 26 Journal Square, Jersey City, N.J. 07306.

term trend will be considered up for as long as the 30-week moving average is rising. It will be considered to have turned down when the 30-week moving average turns down.

You can see that the Dow Industrials were in a major uptrend from late 1975 into mid-1976. The uptrend reversed in mid-1976 and, with minor interruptions, this downtrend continued into 1978, when the trend once again turned up.

Intermediate trend reversals occurred much more frequently. Longer term trend followers could have remained in the market in long positions throughout 1975, despite intermediate trend reversals, and would have remained out of the market throughout 1977, presuming that sales and purchases were made upon changes in direction of the longer term moving averages. Intermediate term traders would have probably entered and left the market with much greater frequency, since intermediate trends, reflected by the direction of the 10-week moving average, changed direction at many points, in conflict with the longer term trends of the market.

Matching the moving average to the trend in question

You may adopt the following lengths of moving average to match the trend you wish to follow:

1. Very short term market trends may be tracked with moving averages that span from 5 to 13 days.
2. Short term market trends may be tracked with moving averages that span from 14 to 25 days.
3. Minor intermediate trends may be tracked with moving averages that span periods of from 26 to 49 days.
4. Intermediate market trends may be tracked with moving averages that span from 50 to 100 days.
5. Long term trends may be tracked with moving averages that span from 100 to 200 days.

Any moving average will smooth out market fluctuations and trends that are shorter in period than the period of time reflected by the length of that particular moving average. For example, a 50-day moving average will smooth out any data lying within a period of 50 days but will not affect longer term trend measurements.

A number of our trading systems involve moving average spans of up to 50 days. Aggressive market traders will probably not wish to employ longer term moving averages, which provide market results more closely approximating buy and hold strategies.

The computation of various forms of moving averages and which forms of moving averages serve the most useful purposes

Many readers are, no doubt, already familiar with basic methods of computing moving averages. However, since moving averages play so significant a role in a large number of effective trading systems, let's take the time to review the construction of some forms of moving average.

The straight moving average. A straight or simple moving average is calculated by simply adding up the data for the most recent series of units you wish averaged and then dividing by the number of units involved. For example, suppose you wanted to secure a 10-day moving average of the most recent 10-day action of the NYSE Index. First, you add up the most recent 10-day total of the data to be averaged—for our purposes, market averages, stock prices and/or indicator data. The result so derived is referred to as the *moving total,* which for many purposes is sufficient in itself. If the moving total is divided by the number of entries, the result is the *moving average.*

Day	NYSE Index	10-Day moving total	10-Day moving average
1	53.00		
2	52.50		
3	52.00		
4	52.35		
5	52.75		
6	53.00		
7	54.00		
8	54.25		
9	54.25		
10	54.45	532.55	53.26
11	54.35	533.90	53.39
12	54.30	535.70	53.57

A simple way of maintaining your moving total would be to calculate a 10-day moving total for an initial 10-day period. On the 11th day, add in the 11th day's data and subtract the data from the 1st day. On the 12th day, add in that day's data and subtract, again, the 11th day back from the most recent posting. For example, on day 11 in the above table, you would add 54.35 to your moving total and subtract 53.00.

Notice that the 10-day moving average in the above table is rising. This would indicate a rising short term trend to the market, even though the most recent two trading days have shown minor declines.

The front weighted moving average. The front weighted moving average is designed to render the moving average more sensitive to recent price changes by providing more weight to recent than to past data. The straight moving average provides equal weight to all of its data inputs.

To compute a weighted moving average, you multiply the most recent data by some predetermined factor before adding it to your moving total. The next most recent data input is given a somewhat lower factor, and so forth. The moving total consists of the sum of all the weighted inputs. The moving average results from dividing this sum by the sum of all the weights. One example should suffice to illustrate the point.

Day	NYSE index	× Weighting factor	= Weighted data	Moving total	Moving average
1	53.00	1	53.00		
2	52.50	2	105.00		
3	52.00	3	156.00		
4	52.35	4	209.40		
5	52.75	5	263.75		
6	53.00	6	318.00		
7	54.00	7	378.00		
8	54.25	8	434.00		
9	54.25	9	488.25		
10	54.45	10	544.50	2949.90	53.63 (2949.90 ÷ 55)
		55	2,949.90		

We have used, in this example, the same data that went into the computation of the straight 10-day moving average. Notice that at the end of day 10, the straight moving average produced a reading of 53.26 while the weighted 10-day average came to 53.63, more closely approximating the final reading of the daily data, 54.45.

Although many programmable hand calculators are available with software programs for computing weighted moving averages, you can see that the calculations of such averages can prove quite cumbersome. Fortunately, our research has indicated that weighted moving averages, while more responsive than straight moving averages, provide no advantage over exponential averages, which are much simpler to compute and to maintain.

The exponential moving average. Exponential moving averages, like straight moving averages and weighted moving averages, smooth trends and, like weighted moving averages, provide more weight to recent than to past data. Our research has shown that exponential averages are at least as useful in the establishment of trading systems as either the straight or the weighted moving average. In addition, exponential averages are simpler to compute. To compute an exponential average, you take the following steps:

1. Derive a *smoothing constant* for the exponential average you will be employing. The constant is derived by dividing the number of days you wish averaged plus one into two. This procedure may be described by the formula

$$\text{Smoothing constant} = \frac{2}{(N + 1)}$$

where

N = the number of days to be averaged.

Examples. You wish to derive a smoothing constant for an exponential average that will roughly approximate a 10-day weighted moving average. Divide 2 by (10 + 1) for a smoothing constant of 0.18.

You wish to derive a smoothing constant for an exponential average that will roughly approximate a fifty-day moving average. Divide 2 by (50 + 1) for a smoothing constant of 0.039.

  2. The exponential average is derived by the following formula:

New exponential average = [(A − B) × smoothing constant] + B

where

  A = Today's data
  B = The most recent exponential average.

Example. Let's assume that the most recent 10-day exponential average of the NYSE Index came to 53.00. Today's close came to 53.50. A smoothing constant of 0.18 is being employed.

The new exponential average would be computed by the formula:

New average = [(A − B) × smoothing constant] + B
[(53.50 − 53.00) × .18] + 53.00
(.50 × .18) + 53.00
.09 + 53.00
or 53.09

Let's suppose now that on the following day, the NYSE Index declines to 52.75. We would compute the new exponential average based on our usual formula:

New average = [(A − B) × smoothing constant] + B
[(52.75 − 53.09) × .18] + 53.09
(−.36 × .18) + 53.09
−.065 + 53.09
or 53.025

Notice how the negative number involved was handled in the equation. Also notice that *since today's closing data stood below yesterday's exponential average, the exponential average turned down*. This is a significant quality of exponential averages. They will reverse direction if the most recent data input crosses from below to above the previously computed exponential average or if today's data entry crosses from above to below the most recently computed exponential average. Exponential averages are very sensitive to changes in the direction of the data that enter into their construction, and themselves reflect changes in trend very sensitively.

  3. You must stabilize the data for a period of days equal to the number of days included in your exponential average. If you are employing the 0.18 smoothing constant, covering ten days, you stabilize your average by running the exponential for ten days. On the eleventh day, your exponential average will become valid.

To stabilize your average you do the following, starting with your initial daily posting of the data:

1. Take your first data entry as the most recent exponential average, although, of course, it will not be so.

2. Continue for ten days thereafter. On the eleventh day, your average will be accurate.

Example. You are starting to maintain an exponential average. On the first day, the NYSE Index stands at 53.00. You assume that that is your first reading of your exponential average, B in our formula. On the second day, the NYSE Index closes at 52.50. You apply the formula, employing a 0.18 smoothing constant, securing a new exponential average reading of 52.91. Continue in this manner for ten more days, at the end of which time you will have secured a stabilized exponential average.

Day	NYSE index	Exponential average (assumed)
1	53.00	53.00
2	52.50	52.91
3	52.00	52.75
4	52.35	52.68
5	52.75	52.69
6	53.00	52.74
7	54.00	52.97
8	54.25	53.20
9	54.25	53.39
10	54.45	53.58
11	54.35	53.72

Your data is now stabilized and your exponential average is now accurate.

Further observations

1. Notice how the exponential average turned upward on day 5 as the most recent data crossed from below to above the exponential average.

2. In maintaining exponential averages, you do not have to keep and maintain extensive past data. Your only requirement is to keep the most recent posting of the exponential average you are using, once it is stabilized. In computing other moving averages, you must maintain back data of at least the length of the moving average you are employing.

3. Once you become familiar with the procedure, exponential averages are very simple to compute. Programs can be readily set up on programmable calculators so that you can run a long series with little trouble. The Texas Instruments SR-58 and SR-59 and certain Hewlett Packard calculators serve very well for this.

Figure 1–4 shows the NYSE Index, plotted for a period of three months on a daily basis, with its 10-day moving average and 0.18 exponential average, approximately equivalent to a front weighted 10-day average. You can see how the differing formats each reflect the short term trends in their own way.

10

FIGURE 1–4
The 0.18 exponential average will track market movements somewhat more closely than the 10-day moving average

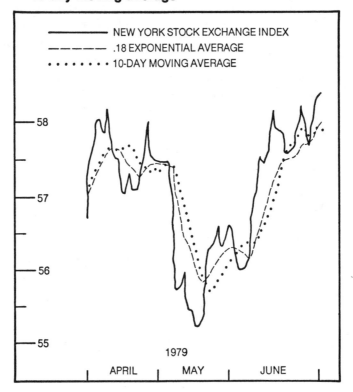

2

The moving average trend-following systems: How moving averages can show you when to buy into strength

Before we proceed further into the ingredients that comprise our basic Time-Trend-Momentum trading system, let us examine a variety of trading systems based on moving averages alone. Some of these are excellent systems in themselves for certain purposes—fully automatic, reliable, easily verified and carried through, and highly profitable with certain investment vehicles. In the process, we will come to understand the qualities of moving averages, their assets and limitations, all of which will prove useful to you as we enter into our more complicated systems.

A viable stock trading system should provide the following features:

1. You should be able to establish over a period of hypothetical (and we hope also real life) study that the system is clearly profitable on balance.
2. Losses should be sufficiently small so that even a string of losses does not seriously erode your capital base.
3. Decision making should be as close to "automatic" as possible. Signals rendered by the system should be clear, subject to a minimum of interpretation.
4. The mechanics of the system should be sufficiently simple to encourage rather than discourage use of the system.
5. Profits per transaction should be of sufficient size on average to cover all transaction costs. The net results of the system should prove sufficiently profitable to outperform a buy and hold approach to the market, even given the extra transaction costs resulting from active trading and possible adverse tax consequences.

These are not minor demands on any trading system, and we can readily comprehend why the random walkers are often so vociferous in their insistence that the market cannot be beaten by trading. For example, if we were to present to you a trading system that has had a history of positive results on half the trades and negative results on half the trades, with the positive trades producing an average of 7 percent profit and the losers only a 3 percent loss, would you consider that a viable trading system? With the profitable transactions more than twice the size of the unprofitable on balance, we would ourselves consider such a system viable—for certain trading vehicles. However, since the average percentage gain per transaction would be only 2 percent (7 percent − 3 percent, divided by 2), this system would not be valid for all investment vehicles. Commission costs would, in the end, prove to be the decisive factor.

You should evaluate all trading systems presented here in terms of those vehicles you trade yourself. Certain systems will not prove sufficiently profitable on a trade-to-trade basis for high commission vehicles, but may provide excellent entry points, for example, into stock positions, while other means are employed for liquidating positions. We will be providing some suggestions regarding capital management, which should serve to expand the usefulness of many otherwise borderline trading systems. More regarding that later, but in the meantime, do keep in mind the fact that at certain brokerage houses you can trade 100 shares of Superior Oil (a $300 stock at the time of this writing) for a piddling round trip commission cost of only $25, or for less than 1/10th of 1 percent of the total stock price. That sort of execution cost should give even the random walkers some pause for thought.

Enough of meandering for the moment. Let's get down to our real business, the evaluation of some actual stock trading systems.

The basic moving average crossing method

This is the simplest of the moving average systems and, for some purposes, it is quite effective. There are only two basic signals, each of which should be followed on a fully automatic basis.

1. Buy signals are rendered whenever the price of the stock (or the level of the stock market index employed) rises above the level of the moving average employed.
2. Sell signals are rendered whenever the price level of the stock (or the level of the market index employed) falls below the level of the moving average employed.

Some traders employ intra-day crossings as triggers, which do provide more sensitive signals, but which also involve a good deal of additional trading. In general, you will probably want to employ end-of-day readings for your signals or, if you prefer slower trading, end-of-week readings which are compared with weekly-based moving averages.

Steps in employing the basic moving average crossing method

The methodology of the basic moving average system is simple and straightforward.

1. You maintain the moving average that you are employing as your measure of basic trend. The shorter the term of the moving average, the more sensitive will be your system to minor market moves, and the more transactions you will incur. This provides both advantages and disadvantages, which we will study as we analyze results of such systems.
2. The stock price itself (or the market index you are employing) acts as the trigger to activate buy and sell signals.

In employing the basic moving average system, you are presuming that the market is showing strength when the market averages rise from below to above their own moving averages, which, again, measure average strength for the period of the moving average.

In other words, if a 10-week moving average reflects the average market strength for a period of the last ten weeks, the market, in rising above this moving average, is indicating (theoretically at least) that its strength is improving from below the 10-week average strength of the market to above the average strength of the latest ten weeks. Therefore, investors may take long positions. If the market averages fall from above to below the 10-week moving average, indications are that near term strength has fallen below intermediate strength and that sales are in order.

Some further thoughts on the rationale of the system

Figure 2–1 shows the typical pattern of a moving average buy-sell sequence, and reveals the strengths as well as the weaknesses we might anticipate in such a system.

The primary strength of moving average systems lies in the profit-loss ratio you may anticipate for each trade. Since you are employing the moving average itself as your stop loss point, your losses, upon taking a position, are theoretically limited to the distance between your entry point and the moving average itself (plus some overshoot, if you are using closing prices). Losses, in practice, tend to be quite small.

Your gains, on the other hand, are theoretically unlimited; your positions are held until the moving average is recrossed. From time to time, during strongly trended market periods, you will achieve excellent profit. With profits theoretically unlimited, and the size of losses more or less fixed, the basic moving average system should produce much larger gains on average than losses, and does, in practice, tend consistently to do so. Given a clear market trend, the basic moving average system does, indeed, figure to perform very well.

The major weakness of the basic moving average system lies in the amount of whipsawing that occurs during narrow trading ranges—these whipsaws resulting in minor gains or losses, but in high commission costs. As we men-

14

FIGURE 2–1
A typical moving average system pattern

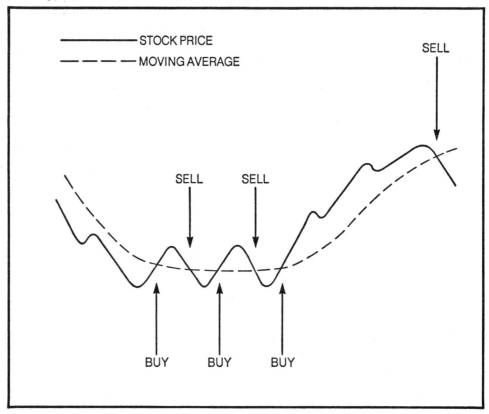

tioned above, in the end, the efficacy of the basic moving average system lies in your ability to keep commission costs to a minimum.

We have also found, in our research, that crossings of moving averages actually carry *little* predictive value. The moving average is just about as likely to be recrossed without profit within a short time as the move is likely to show a profit. Nonetheless, risk-reward ratios do remain favorable because of the quick losses taken on unprofitable trades balanced against the potentially larger gains secured when the market moves in your direction. What the system does do is force you to trade properly, which means cutting losses quickly while letting profits run. Since your moving average will gradually move in the direction of the market move in progress, your stop loss point will continuously move in the direction of your trade, locking in profits already achieved—or at least a good portion thereof.

Our computer tested results of the basic moving average crossing method

By use of computer, we were able to measure the effects of basic moving average signals for moving averages of varying length and character for the period 1970–78. A buy signal for the NYSE Index was presumed to have

TABLE 2–1

A breakdown of results of trading the New York Stock Exchange Index during 1970 according to basic moving average buy and sell signals, for moving average spans of 1–60 days

```
NAME = N.Y. INDEX
SIMPLE MA NYE   4                        FROM 700101 TO 710101 NYE
*********************************************************************
```

AV	C.P/L	LGLOSS	RATIO	GR.PFT	GR.LOS	RATIO	TR	PR	LS	AVES	PS	LS
1	32	-2	16.06	42	-9	4.40	95	46	49	0	1	0
2	30	-2	14.94	40	-10	4.02	78	38	40	0	1	0
3	20	-3	6.54	32	-13	2.53	59	23	35	0	1	0
4	22	-2	11.03	32	-10	3.23	45	22	23	0	1	0
5	20	-2	14.37	34	-5	6.79	33	19	14	1	2	0
6	29	-1	28.49	32	-4	8.23	31	19	12	1	2	0
7	27	-1	27.23	30	-3	9.95	26	19	7	1	2	0
8	26	-1	26.01	29	-3	10.16	24	18	6	1	2	0
9	22	-2	10.92	25	-3	8.45	22	15	7	1	2	0
10	19	-1	19.03	24	-5	4.92	24	13	11	1	2	0
11	17	-1	17.35	23	-6	4.15	22	11	11	1	2	-1
12	16	-2	8.09	21	-5	4.11	20	11	9	1	2	-1
13	14	-3	4.63	20	-6	3.36	20	11	9	1	2	-1
14	13	-3	4.29	19	-6	3.07	22	11	11	1	2	-1
15	13	-3	4.30	19	-6	3.25	20	11	9	1	2	-1
16	12	-3	3.87	18	-6	2.92	20	10	10	1	2	-1
17	10	-3	3.40	17	-7	2.51	18	8	10	1	2	-1
18	8	-2	3.05	17	-9	1.89	22	8	14	0	2	-1
19	10	-3	3.28	17	-7	2.38	18	7	11	1	2	-1
20	11	-3	3.67	17	-6	2.84	16	7	9	1	2	-1
21	9	-4	2.28	16	-7	2.27	18	7	11	1	2	-1
22	9	-3	3.04	16	-7	2.25	16	7	9	1	2	-1
23	8	-3	2.52	15	-7	2.06	16	5	11	0	3	-1
24	8	-2	3.87	15	-7	2.12	18	5	13	0	3	-1
25	8	-2	3.88	15	-7	2.11	18	5	13	0	3	-1
26	8	-3	2.74	15	-6	2.25	18	5	13	0	3	0
27	9	-2	4.59	15	-6	2.61	16	6	10	1	2	-1
28	9	-2	4.55	15	-6	2.57	16	6	10	1	2	-1
29	9	-2	4.52	15	-6	2.55	16	6	10	1	2	-1
30	8	-4	1.97	15	-7	2.09	16	6	10	0	3	-1
31	8	-3	2.81	15	-7	2.27	16	6	10	1	3	-1
32	6	-3	2.14	15	-8	1.78	18	5	13	0	3	-1
33	7	-3	2.28	15	-8	1.87	18	4	14	0	4	-1
34	9	-3	3.15	15	-6	2.58	16	4	12	1	4	0
35	10	-2	5.04	15	-5	2.94	17	4	13	1	4	0
36	9	-2	4.73	15	-6	2.67	17	4	13	1	4	0
37	10	-2	4.78	15	-6	2.66	17	4	13	1	4	0
38	12	-2	5.75	16	-5	3.42	17	5	12	1	3	0
39	11	-3	3.64	16	-5	3.10	17	5	12	1	3	0
40	12	-2	6.06	16	-4	3.99	15	5	10	1	3	0
41	13	-2	6.25	16	-4	4.19	15	4	11	1	4	0
42	13	-2	6.45	16	-3	4.88	13	4	9	1	4	0
43	13	-2	6.74	16	-3	5.62	10	4	6	1	4	0
44	14	-2	6.78	16	-3	5.75	10	4	6	1	4	0
45	13	-2	6.54	16	-3	5.21	10	4	6	1	4	-1
46	13	-1	12.86	16	-3	4.86	10	4	6	1	4	-1
47	11	-2	5.65	15	-4	3.78	12	3	9	1	5	0
48	11	-2	5.52	15	-4	3.51	10	3	7	1	5	-1
49	12	-2	5.95	15	-3	4.44	10	3	7	1	5	0
50	12	-2	6.02	15	-3	4.61	10	3	7	1	5	0
51	13	-2	6.47	16	-3	5.51	8	3	5	2	5	-1
52	13	-2	6.36	16	-3	5.12	8	3	5	2	5	-1
53	13	-2	6.35	16	-3	5.07	8	3	5	2	5	-1
54	13	-1	13.18	16	-3	6.01	8	3	5	2	5	-1
55	14	-1	13.83	16	-2	7.08	7	3	4	2	5	0
56	14	-1	14.06	16	-2	8.40	7	3	4	2	5	0
57	14	-1	14.21	16	-2	9.12	7	3	4	2	5	0
58	13	-1	12.80	15	-2	6.22	7	3	4	2	5	-1
59	13	-2	6.29	15	-3	5.69	7	3	4	2	5	-1
60	13	-2	6.37	15	-3	6.03	7	3	4	2	5	-1

```
SIMPLE MA NYE   4                        FROM 700101 TO 710104 NYE
*********************************************************************
NAME = N.Y. INDEX
```

taken place whenever the level of the index rose on a daily closing basis from below to above the moving average employed. A sell signal was presumed to have been rendered whenever the NYSE Index fell from above to below the moving average employed.

Table 2–1 illustrates the computer printouts we secured during our test runs of alternate trading systems. Let's go through the columns, step by step, for the year 1970.

1. On the left are the numbers of days included in the moving average for the test, which was in this instance the straight moving average with lengths of from 1 to 60 days.
2. The next column, C.P/L, shows the total profit or loss if that span of moving average had been employed during 1970. (Results are rounded off to whole numbers.) For example, had you purchased whenever a 2-day moving average was crossed to the upside and sold short whenever a 2-day moving average was penetrated to the downside during 1970, you would have gained approximately 30 points on the NYSE Index during that year.
3. The LGLOSS column shows the maximum number of points you would have lost in any consecutive losing streak. The first RATIO column shows the ratio between your total points gained and the losses that would have theoretically accrued during your longest losing streak that year. This relationship may be taken as a measure of the capital preservation qualities of the system.
4. GR.PFT shows the total points gained on winning trades. GR.LOS shows the total points lost during the year as a result of losing transactions. The RATIO column immediately to the right shows the relationship of these to each other. 1970 was a good year for moving average systems. All moving average lengths produced profit.
5. The next three columns show the number of trades each year (TR), the number of profitable trades (PR), and the number of unprofitable trades (LS). You can see that for most moving average lengths, the majority of trades are likely to prove unprofitable; but as you can also see in the next series of columns, the average profit per profitable trade is likely to be much greater than the average loss per unprofitable transaction.
6. The final three columns show the average gain or loss per trade (AVE $), the average gain per profitable trade (P$), and the average loss per unprofitable trade (L$).

Which moving average is really the best for trading?

We will in future cases be summarizing our results rather than listing the full workouts, but for now, at least, let's take a look at the printout to see what results you might expect from using the basic moving average system with a straight moving average.

1. The use of a simple penetration of a straight moving average proved theoretically profitable in 1970 with moving averages of all lengths from 1–60 days. These results were consistent with results generally obtained over the

years 1970–78, with the exception of 1977, when the majority of moving averages applied in this manner produced losses.

1977 was a year in which the NYSE Index showed gradual erosion—the worst pattern for moving average system players. Systems of this sort do well during strongly trended market periods. Gradual erosions tend to trigger signals frequently but, unfortunately, usually right at the peaks of short term market advances.

2. In general, the very shortest moving average spans produced the greatest cumulative profit. This result has also been consistent over the years.

3. However, the average profit per transaction proved quite low for trades based on short term moving averages. For example, trades based on a crossing of the 5-day moving average during 1970 would have theoretically produced a profit of approximately 0.88 per transaction, or somewhat less than 2 percent per trade. This rate of return per trade would be sufficient to cover trading of no-load mutual funds very well, and might have been sufficient to cover multiple lot transactions at discount brokerage houses. It would not have been suitable for trading 100-share lots at usual Merrill Lynch commission rates throughout 1970.

4. Intermediate moving average lengths, those spanning periods of from 15 days to 45 days, provide relatively little benefit as compared to the shorter term moving averages and somewhat longer term moving averages. If you are not going to trade very rapidly, you are as likely, based on our research, to produce equal cumulative gain by moving out to a 50-day moving average. In 1970, trading via the 50-day moving average would have produced an average gain of approximately 2 percent per trade over five round trip transactions.

5. Longer term moving averages, spanning lengths of from 70–200 days, turn out upon computer examination to be far less useful as trading tools than many market letter writers would have you believe. However, trading even on longer term moving averages would far outperform a buy and hold approach to the market, especially for commission free vehicles.

The myth of the 30-week moving average

Let's consider just one such moving average, the 30-week moving average, popularized, no doubt, because such chart services as TRENDLINE carry its posting each week. Given the credence afforded this moving average in the general market literature, you should, at least theoretically, be able to produce fine profit by buying when the market averages lie above their 30-week moving averages and selling when the market averages fall below their 30-week moving averages. Let's see what the actual results of doing so would have been for the period 1970–78, in Table 2–2.

Sad—but true. Had you purchased the Dow Industrial average each time that the market index rose above its 30-week moving average from 1970–78, and had you sold the Dow short each time it fell below its 30-week moving average, you would have shown a total gain of 428 Dow points over a nine year span, the results of 77 trades, averaging a 5.6 Dow point gain per trade.

So much for one myth.

18

TABLE 2–2
Results of trading the Dow industrials on penetrations of its 150-day moving average

Year	Number of trades	Profitable trades	Unprofitable trades	Total points Gained	Lost	Average per trade	
1970	2	1	1	65		33	
1971	15	4	11		−34		−2
1972	13	3	10	43		3	
1973	10	2	8	1		0	
1974	7	2	5	149		21	
1975	14	4	10		−19		−1
1976	9	2	7	114		13	
1977	4	2	2	106		27	
1978	3	3	0	3		1	
Average	8.6	2.6	6.0	+68.7	−26.5	+14	−1.5

If you are going to trade via moving average systems, you might as well opt for somewhat more sensitive moving averages, which will not necessarily produce greater profit per trade but which will, at least in the right vehicles, pile up a goodly number of points along the way.

The problem with long term moving averages, of course, lies in their relative unresponsiveness to market fluctuations. 1978 is a good case in point. The stock market rose from Dow 736 in February to a high of 917 in September, before plummeting sharply in October. Followers of the 30-week moving average would have purchased the Dow in April at approximately Dow 800, but would not have been triggered out of the market until nearly all of the October decline had happened, selling out at approximately Dow 845. The bulk of the fine 1978 rise would have been lost prior to the 30-week moving average sell signal. Shorter term moving averages were able to claim a much larger portion of the move.

To some extent, the sharpness of the October 1978 decline added to the relative inefficiency of the 30-week moving average during 1978. This particular average produced excellent results during 1977, keeping the Dow on a sell from March (at approximately Dow 960) all the way into April 1978 (at Dow 800). Much depends on the velocity of the market. During periods of sharp market swings up or down, shorter term moving averages will tend to outperform longer term moving averages. Where trends are more gradual, longer term moving averages often perform more profitably.

Many individual issues, incidentally, will track better than the market averages when traded via moving average systems of this sort, if longer term moving averages are employed. If you do trade individual stocks via this method, we suggest that you emphasize volatile, high priced issues. IBM, for example, traded on penetrations of its 30-week moving average from 1970–78 showed an average gain per trade of approximately two points, roughly equivalent to the gains achieved by trading IBM via its 10-week moving average.

How to improve the basic moving average system by weighting your moving averages

We discussed, in Chapter 1, some methods of weighting moving averages to provide measures of trend that give greater weight to recent than to past data. The methods we described included the linear weighted moving average and the exponential average. Both will track more closely to recent market data than the straight moving average, and both will generally improve your results vis-à-vis the straight moving average if you are employing the simple penetration system.

For purposes of comparison, let's consider some representative short term, intermediate term, and long term straight, weighted, and exponential moving averages and their results with the Dow, 1970–77, in Table 2–3.

Comments

We can see that overall results are improved somewhat with the basic moving average system if statistical tools are used that provide some form of front weighting to the smoothed curve. However, results are not consistent and tend to be more apparent when the longest term moving averages are employed. Front weighting the shorter term moving averages does result in a considerable increase in number of transactions, with little increase in profitability per transaction. Total points gained, however, are increased, which may be very useful for the trading of certain vehicles such as no-load switch funds and even, perhaps, high priced stocks if you are dealing at very low commission rates.

Front weighting the longer term moving averages, particularly via exponential smoothing, does seem to add not only to total points gained but to the average gain per trade as well. Apparently, as we noted above, straight long term moving averages respond too slowly to protect gains achieved following signals. Exponential averages move your stop loss points more closely in tune with market movements.

The best of the moving averages to employ if you are using the basic moving average system

Although the gain per trade might seem small, there is little doubt that any moving average system—with the proper investment vehicle—will almost certainly outperform a buy and hold approach to the market over the long run. In this regard, for example, you might want to consider the fact that the 150-day exponential average produced a gain of 556 points between 1970 and 1977, a period in which the Dow managed to tack on a gain of only 26 points.

Even a longer term investor would have greatly increased his returns over this period by buying and selling high volatility mutual funds on penetrations of the 150-day exponential average. By following this procedure, you would have participated in every bull market, avoided most bear markets, and

TABLE 2–3
Comparisons of straight, weighted, and exponential
moving averages of different time spans: Simple moving
average penetration system using the Dow industrials

Year	Straight			Weighted			Exponential		
	Total points gained or lost	Number of trades	Average per trade	Total points gained or lost	Number of trades	Average per trade	Total points gained or lost	Number of trades	Average per trade
Moving average period = 10 days									
1970	+ 294	22	+13.4	+ 205	35	+ 5.9	+ 269	28	+ 9.6
1971	+ 287	23	+12.5	+ 338	29	+11.7	+ 317	27	+11.7
1972	+ 137	33	+ 4.2	+ 166	39	+ 4.3	+ 145	39	+ 3.8
1973	+ 170	35	+ 4.9	+ 272	39	+ 7.0	+ 247	39	+ 6.3
1974	+ 144	33	+ 4.4	+ 247	43	+ 5.7	+ 163	39	+ 4.2
1975	+ 17	43	+ 0.4	+ 114	49	+ 2.3	+ 110	45	+ 2.4
1976	+ 23	45	+ 0.5	+ 69	57	+ 1.2	− 27	53	− 0.5
1977	+ 97	36	+ 2.7	+ 143	44	+ 3.3	+ 136	36	+ 3.8
	+1,169	270	+ 4.3	+1,554	325	+ 4.8	+1,360	306	+ 4.4
Moving average period = 50 days									
1970	+ 105	12	+ 8.8	+ 139	14	+ 9.9	+ 116	16	+ 7.3
1971	+ 143	9	+15.9	+ 165	19	+ 8.7	+ 134	15	+ 8.9
1972	+ 114	13	+ 8.8	+ 65	17	+ 3.8	+ 90	17	+ 5.3
1973	+ 92	16	+ 5.8	+ 141	19	+ 7.4	+ 73	24	+ 3.0
1974	− 17	20	− 0.9	+ 57	23	+ 2.5	− 79	29	− 2.7
1975	+ 147	16	+ 9.2	+ 62	23	+ 2.7	+ 162	18	+ 9.0
1976	+ 39	29	+ 1.3	+ 79	31	+ 2.5	+ 73	23	+ 3.2
1977	− 74	26	− 2.8	− 41	28	− 1.5	− 53	26	− 2.0
	+ 549	141	+ 3.9	+ 667	174	+ 3.8	+ 516	168	+ 3.1
Moving average period = 150 days									
1970	+ 65	2	+32.5	+ 85	3	+28.3	+ 74	2	+37.0
1971	− 34	15	− 2.3	+ 24	9	+ 2.7	+ 30	9	+ 3.3
1972	+ 43	13	+ 3.3	+ 83	15	+ 5.5	+ 76	11	+ 6.9
1973	+ 1	10	+ 0.1	− 10	10	− 1.0	− 15	12	− 1.3
1974	+ 149	7	+21.3	+ 142	9	+15.8	+ 176	9	+19.6
1975	− 19	14	− 1.4	− 27	24	− 1.1	+ 16	10	+ 1.6
1976	+ 114	9	+12.7	+ 61	19	+ 3.2	+ 126	7	+18.0
1977	+ 106	4	+26.5	+ 73	6	+12.2	+ 73	6	+12.2
	+ 425	74	+ 5.7	+ 431	95	+ 4.5	+ 556	66	+ 8.4

would have had to make only 33 round trip transactions over the eight year period. (Although 66 trades are shown for the 150-day exponential average, you would have made only 33 trades had you traded mutual funds, since mutual funds cannot be sold short.) Moreover, had you followed this simple procedure, and this procedure alone, your capital would have lain in cash for the majority of the bear market periods, earning the high interest rates that prevailed during 1973–74 and again during 1976 and 1977.

More aggressive investors can, again, employ the basic systems for the trading of no-load mutual funds. Although the shortest time spans tend to produce the greatest total gains, your choice of moving average will necessarily represent a compromise between the highest theoretical profits (gained by selling on any day that the market declines and buying on any day that the market rises, believe it or not) and the realistic viability of switching back and forth into and out of mutual funds. We would suggest a moving average length for the purpose of trading mutual funds that would result in no more than 15–17 round trip transactions per year. A moving average length of somewhere between 10 and 15 days would seem the most likely choice. If your fund (or your temperament) insists on a lower frequency of trading, then we suggest that you move out to the 50 to 55-day moving average spans.

We have found in our research, incidentally, that buy signals based on trading systems tend, generally, to produce better results than sell short signals. Since you can only purchase mutual funds—and cannot sell them short—your profit per transaction is likely to prove somewhat higher than you might anticipate from the results shown in Table 2–3, which include short sale results as well as hypothetical results from long purchases.

The basic moving average system is a system for the investor who will put up with the absolute minimum in computation, fuss and bother. Next, let's examine some of the variations of the basic moving average system, including some that require very little additional effort but that do improve trade-by-trade performance.

3

Moving average systems:
Some variations on a theme
to improve the basic moving
average system

Let's see where we stand at this point. We have considered some of the basic methods of computing moving averages and explored some of the ramifications of the basic moving average trading systems, reaching the following conclusions:

1. Moving average systems will almost certainly outperform basic buy and hold strategies for many stock market vehicles, and particularly for those in which commission costs can be kept to a bare minimum.
2. Shorter term moving averages will achieve the greatest gain in total points, but at the cost of what may prove to be excessive trading.
3. All moving average systems perform best during strongly trended market periods, but create problems during narrow trading ranges as the moving average is crossed and recrossed over short periods of time. We will be examining some trading systems that perform very well within such trading ranges, but since we have by no means exhausted the potential of moving averages alone, we will in this and subsequent chapters examine some of the methods employed by "moving average systems players" to offset some of the disadvantages of moving averages while retaining many of their advantages.

Some of these methods will, indeed, improve the performance of moving average systems. Others will unfortunately, upon examination, have to be relegated to the world of myth and fantasy.

Reducing the number of whipsaws in moving average systems by means of a penetration filter

Moving average traders frequently employ some form of filter to eliminate at least a portion of the "noise"—false signals created by minor whipsaws within trading ranges—that tends to plague the basic moving average system. These filters assume many forms, including the creation of a short term moving average of the basic data. This can then be used instead of the raw price level alone as the trigger.

Another filter requires that certain additional conditions are met before signals are generated. One such condition involves a certain requirement of penetration before a basic moving average signal is recognized. In other words, before a basic moving average signal is generated, the stock price or the market index must penetrate the moving average by a certain amount. Insignificant penetrations are disregarded.

Anticipated effects of the penetration rule

If a certain amount of penetration is required before a moving average signal can be rendered, we might anticipate the following results:

FIGURE 3–1
The use of filter bands around moving averages delays entry and exit action, but reduces the number of whipsaws you would otherwise encounter

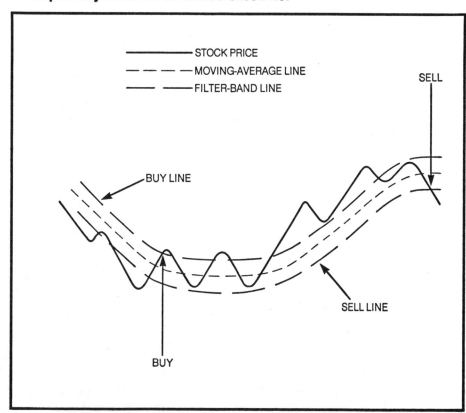

1. There will be somewhat fewer signals, since certain minor penetrations that result in whipsaws will be filtered out.
2. However, the risk–reward ratio of each individual transaction will suffer slightly, since this method establishes a greater distance between your entry point and your potential stop-loss point.

   In the basic moving average system, the initial entry point and the stop-loss point are theoretically virtually identical at the onset of the trade, although in actual practice you will probably be buying at at least some distance above the moving average employed and selling at at least a slight distance below.

   When penetration conditions are employed, your risk immediately becomes larger as a proportion of your anticipated reward. If you were to employ, for example, a 1 percent penetration requirement, you would not take a long position until the moving average employed was penetrated by at least 1 percent to the upside, and you would not sell until that moving average was repenetrated by at least 1 percent to the downside. Your initial risk per trade, therefore, amounts to at least 2 percent.
3. We would hope that the gain per transaction improves sufficiently to offset the disadvantages incurred by employment of the penetration filter.

Sampling the penetration method on one short term trading average

The 8-day exponential average happens to be one of the strongest of the short term moving averages for catching minor term market fluctuations, and may be employed by very active traders for the trading of certain stock options and/or no-load mutual funds. Conceivably, given a cheap enough discount house, and close attention, you might even be able to trade shares of common via this system as well.

For purposes of comparison, let's examine the results of trading the NYSE Index based on crossings of its 8-day exponential average (using closing levels), and based on crossings of the 8-day exponential average with a 0.15 penetration required before a signal is generated. Table 3–1 compares workouts. Only long positions (buy signals) have been considered; short sales are not included.

Comments

It seems clear, from the results shown in Table 3–1 at least, that applying a penetration filter to the short term trading of the market averages adds little either to total profitability or to per transaction profitability of market based short term signals. If you are going to be trading mutual funds via such signals, you will probably achieve greater profit if you avoid using any filters. Do notice the power of the 8-day exponential signal. It produced no annual losses, even on the buy side alone, in any single year, not even in the severe bear market years of 1973 and 1974. Many mutual funds, however, will not allow the frequency of trading generated by the basic 8-day system. If that is the case with funds in which you trade, you might employ a 0.15 filter, which does reduce the frequency of such trades from an average of 19 transactions per year to 15—a rate more generally acceptable to fund managements.

TABLE 3-1
Comparison of results of buy signals on the NYSE Index based on the 8-day exponential average and on the 8-day exponential average with a filter of a 0.15 penetration

Year	*0.15 penetration required*			*No minimum penetration*		
	Total points gained or lost	*Number of transactions*	*Average per trade*	*Total points gained or lost*	*Number of transactions*	*Average per trade*
1970	11	11	1.00	12	12	1.00
1971	11	11	1.00	16	14	1.14
1972	8	13	.62	10	19	.53
1973	− 1	18	− .06	3	19	.15
1974	0	17	.00	3	20	.52
1975	10	18	.57	12	23	.52
1976	10	16	.63	10	24	.42
	48	118	.41	69	152	.45

Ratio of profitable to unprofitable trades: The use of a 0.15 filter, applied to an 8-day exponential average, produced 50 profitable and 68 unprofitable trades. The use of an 8-day exponential with no filter produced 69 profitable and 83 unprofitable trades.

Stocks, of course, can be traded via their listed stock options based on short term trading signals. How would IBM have fared had we traded the issue based on its 5-day exponential average, using a 1 percent penetration filter? In this case, no signal would be generated unless IBM penetrated its five-day exponential average by at least 1 percent. The workout in Table 3–2 assumes both long and short signals; a full reversal is presumed at each signal.

Comments

Impressed? Well, neither were we, although the potential of the system, traded carefully, is probably far greater than the results shown in Table 3–2 suggest. The structure of this book, if the truth be told, reflects to some degree the process of our research—beginning with the obvious, for the most part discarded along the way as insufficient for our purposes—and ending, we hoped, with at least one sound, profitable trading system that could be applied to virtually any stock market vehicle. We knew that along the way we would be encountering many total misses and some near hits. This penetration approach is, we believe, in the latter category.

The rub, of course, in trading IBM via a 5-day exponential average with a 1 percent penetration lies in the average gain per transaction, only slightly above one point per trade. This rate of gain is, on the surface, far from sufficient to cover transaction costs. However, there just might be one way to turn this system, given these results, into a highly profitable device.

TABLE 3–2
Hypothetical results of trading IBM on signals generated by a 1 percent penetration of the stock's 5-day exponential average, using closing prices for signals

Year	Total points gained or lost	Number of transactions	Profitable transactions	Unprofitable transactions	Average gain or loss per trade
1970	133	41	18	23	3.24
1971	27	40	12	28	.68
1972	66	32	16	16	2.06
1973	− 2	54	22	32	− .04
1974	37	58	19	39	.64
1975	48	53	17	36	.91
1976	51	33	14	19	1.55
1977	31	27	12	15	1.15
	391	338	130	208	1.16

How to convert even a mediocre trading result into a highly profitable system

Simple enough! Instead of trading the IBM common, trade in-the-money put and call options on the stock, dealing with one of the discount brokerages that cut option commissions to the bone.

We recommend in-the-money options for the following reasons:

1. In-the-money options will tend to rise at virtually the same rate as the underlying common, and are therefore likely to provide sufficient movement per transaction to cover commission costs.
2. If you trade near term, in-the-money options you will be dealing with a highly fluid market. There should be little problem in executing your trades rapidly.

There are a number of discount brokerages, advertised regularly in media such as *Barron's,* which charge as little as $5 commission per option, provided you trade at least seven or so at a time. If you are a regular customer, some of these houses will even allow you to trade five and still provide a $5 charge per option. Your total commission then per transaction can be held to $10, so an average gain of one point per trade, representing perhaps 10–15 percent of your option cost, can add up to quite an annual profit, especially considering the number of transactions involved.

Still another means of possibly maximizing profit

Here, you do have to add a bit of artistry to automatic trading. Our figures are based on closing prices, and there will be occasions when a closing price will overshoot your signal level by several points. Assuming that you keep fairly close contact with the market, there will be many occasions as well when you will be able to anticipate a signal during the middle of a day, and when you will be able to take action at prices somewhat more advantageous than closing prices.

For the most part, the issue will probably lie in doubt and, if you can keep your costs down, you should be able to make out in certain stocks based on closing prices alone. However, again, do keep alert to days when it will obviously pay to act before the close.

Stock options are one way to play the commission game to your advantage. Convertible bonds are another. There are a number of very fluid convertible bonds, bonds that can be converted into common shares, usually of the underlying company. A number of these bonds trade at conversion value (sometimes even at a discount) and represent a very low-commission means of trading the underlying common indirectly. Commission costs at many houses for such bonds run as little as $2.50 per bond or $5.00 round trip. Why not check with your brokerage or with some market advisory service that specializes in convertible issues to see which actively traded bonds happen to be available? Some pretty lively trading issues have sported convertible alternatives in the past—issues such as Bally, UAL, Pan Am, ITT, Avco and Digital.

A brief comparison of the filter penetration method with basic moving average systems

Incidentally, just in case you've been wondering, the 5-day exponential trading of IBM with a 1 percent penetration does handily beat out any of the straight short term moving average systems for the same period of time. We'll spare you the gory details, but take our word: it wasn't even close.

In any event, have no fears. We have far from exhausted our repertoire of trading systems.

4

How to upgrade
the basic moving average system
by using more than
one single moving average

The use of crossovers of moving averages as a simple device for the determination of buy and sell points for stocks and the stock market appears, under the computer's scrutiny, to produce considerable cumulative profit, but only minor profit per trade. The profit-loss configurations of the basic systems, as we have seen, are quite suitable for certain investment vehicles, less suitable for others. Let's continue now with our examination of variations on the basic theme to see if we can develop systems that produce greater per trade profit with relatively little sacrifice in total profit. Along the way, we shall again find that while certain improvements are indeed possible, certain popular techniques simply do not stand up in actual use. The realities of result do not match general theory.

The basic multiple moving average crossing system

The basic multiple moving average crossing system employs two or more moving averages. If two moving averages are employed, *a buy signal is rendered when the shorter term moving average crosses above the longer term moving average,* indicating that shorter term trends are becoming more powerful than longer term trends. *Sell signals are rendered when shorter term moving averages cross from above to below longer term moving averages,* indicating that shorter term trends are weakening relative to longer term trends.

Since moving averages, rather than daily prices, are employed as crossover triggers, such systems are expected to create fewer whipsaws than systems that rely on daily prices as the crossover trigger since moving averages will be less likely to change direction rapidly within narrow trading ranges than single daily price entries.

In exchange for the reduction in whipsaws, as compared to the use of crossovers employing daily price data and one moving average, the user of two moving averages must sacrifice some timeliness—early entry and exit from stock positions. For example, let's consider the pairing shown in Table 4–1.

TABLE 4–1

Day	Price	10-Day moving average	3-Day moving average	10-Day moving average
1.......	50.00			
2.......	51.25			
3.......	51.15		50.80	
4.......	51.75		51.38	
5.......	52.00		51.63	
6.......	52.15		51.97	
7.......	51.75		51.97	
8.......	52.35		52.08	
9.......	52.50		52.20	
10.......	52.40	51.73	52.42	51.73
11.......	52.00	51.93	52.30	51.93
12.......	51.90	52.00 (sell)	52.10	52.00
13.......	52.10	52.09 (buy)	52.00	52.09 (sell)
14.......	52.28	52.14	52.09	52.14
15.......	52.10	52.14 (sell)	52.06	52.14
16.......	51.75	52.14	51.98	52.14

Comparison of single moving average crossover system (buy and sell when daily price crosses 10-day moving average) with system where buy signals and sell signals are rendered when 3-day moving average crosses above and below 10-day moving average.

You can see that use of single-day action provided more sensitive signals than use of the multiple crossing system, even when such a short term moving average as the 3-day average was employed as the trigger. The 3-day over the 10-day system provided better signals than the single-day over the 10-day in the above example. However, had the sell signal on day 12 for the single-day trigger not been followed by a market advance the next day, then the single-day system would have exited you from the market in better position than the slower responding 3-day versus 10-day system (a favorite, incidentally, among some commodity players and also used by certain stock advisory services which claim to provide "automatic" buy and sell signals to subscribers).

FIGURE 4–1

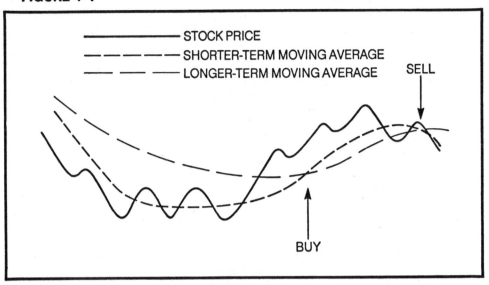

Buy signals in the crossover method are rendered when the shorter term moving average crosses over the longer term moving average, and sell signals are rendered when the shorter term moving average falls below the longer term moving average.

Combinations evaluated by computer

We evaluated the results of buying when a short term moving average crossed a longer term moving average and selling short when the same short term moving average crossed from above to below the longer term moving average for the period 1970–77. For the shorter term moving average, we considered periods of from 1–9 days, crossing over longer term moving averages of from 2–50 days. In addition, we employed short term moving averages of from 1–9 weeks, crossing over longer term moving averages spanning 2–40 weeks. In general, the best results were achieved when short term averages of from 5–8 days were crossed over longer term moving averages of from 40–55 days. Results from year to year were inconsistent, and no particular array stood out above the rest.

The results shown in Table 4–2 are typical of what you might expect from such systems.

Discussion

It appears plain that the 3-day versus the 50-day moving average combination produced the best results in these examples, although none of the combinations managed to produce the sort of gains we are seeking—approximately 3–5 percent on average per trade, sufficient to cover discount commissions with some room to spare. That will have to await our more sophisticated trading systems.

TABLE 4–2
Hypothetical results of buying when 3-day moving average crossed above 10-day, 30-day and 50-day moving averages, and selling short when 3-day moving average crossed below the longer moving averages

Year	3 versus 10-day		3 versus 30-day		3 versus 50-day	
	Cumulative points	Number of trades	Cumulative points	Number of trades	Cumulative points	Number of trades
New York Stock Exchange Index						
1970	+15	21	+ 1	17	+ 8	11
1971	+13	19	+11	11	+ 7	9
1972	+ 7	27	− 2	17	− 1	13
1973	− 8	30	+ 9	16	+ 6	8
1974	− 7	31	+ 2	11	+ 0	11
1975	+ 0	29	+ 5	16	+ 7	8
1976	− 3	29	+ 1	17	+ 3	11
1977	− 4	27	− 8	15	− 8	17
1978	+ 7	27	+ 4	15	+ 7	9
Averages:	+ 2.2	28.7	+ 2.6	15	+ 3.2	10.8
Honeywell						
1970	+49	29	+49	11	+53	5
1971	+ 6	32	− 8	19	+14	13
1972	+27	27	+15	13	+16	13
1973	+64	22	+40	8	+12	14
1974	+ 1	34	+17	16	+ 6	13
1975	+20	23	+19	14	+16	7
1976	+11	29	+30	11	+12	10
1977	+ 4	30	− 1	14	− 1	12
1978	+20	20	+18	16	+12	14
Averages	+22.4	28.3	+19.9	13.6	+15.6	11.2
International Business Machines						
1970	+50	27	+ 7	17	+88	3
1971	+24	32	+29	13	+47	9
1972	−17	30	−27	17	+ 7	13
1973	−94	34	+74	12	+70	8
1974	−54	33	+ 1	13	−20	11
1975	− 8	32	+44	12	+39	8
1976	−14	33	+26	21	+11	11
1977	−12	31	−27	19	− 9	15
1978	+68	23	+47	13	+52	7
Averages	− 6.3	30.6	+19.3	15.2	+31.7	9.4

TABLE 4–3
Hypothetical results of buying when the 10-day moving average crosses above the 30-day and 50-day moving averages and selling short when the 10-day moving average crosses below the 30-day and the 50-day moving averages

Year	10-day versus 30-day		10-day versus 50-day	
	Cumulative points	*Number of trades*	*Cumulative points*	*Number of trades*
New York Stock Exchange Index				
1970.................	− 5	13	+ 5	9
1971.................	+ 6	7	+ 7	7
1972.................	− 2	12	− 1	7
1973.................	+ 8	9	+ 2	6
1974.................	− 2	11	+ 4	9
1975.................	+ 6	8	+ 3	5
1976.................	+ 1	16	− 2	10
1977.................	− 9	12	− 3	7
Averages	0.3	9.8	+ 1.7	6.7
Honeywell				
1970.................	+36	9	+39	5
1971.................	+ 4	11	+37	11
1972.................	−12	11	+ 4	9
1973.................	+26	8	+ 2	8
1974.................	+21	9	+ 2	9
1975.................	+30	11	+12	7
1976.................	+ 9	10	+10	8
1977.................	− 2	10	− 3	6
1978.................	+12	21	+14	8
Averages	+13.8	11.1	+13	7.9
International Business Machines				
1970.................	+60	15	+74	3
1971.................	+36	9	+37	5
1972.................	− 9	11	+19	7
1973.................	+40	10	+83	6
1974.................	−46	11	−13	9
1975.................	+37	10	− 3	6
1976.................	+21	13	+ 6	7
1977.................	+20	11	+10	7
1978.................	+37	9	+43	7
Averages	+21.8	11	+28.4	6.3

It is also noteworthy that the popular 3-day versus 10-day system produced the least total gains, generally speaking, as well as the lowest rate of gain per trade. We may assume, right from this point on, that trading systems that involve more than 8–10 transactions per year will simply not be able to produce high per transaction profit; for those really good average rates of return you will have to concentrate on slower trading tracks, leaving the faster action for strictly no-commission vehicles.

Let's consider two of those slower trading devices right now, the combination of 10-day moving average and 30-day moving average, and the combination of 10-day moving average and 50-day moving average (Table 4–3). Since the 10-day moving average will be much slower to change direction than the 3-day moving average, we can anticipate fewer crossovers and consequently fewer transactions. Let's hope that the average profit per trade increases concomitantly.

Discussion

This trading system does seem to offer more promise than more sensitive systems. The longer term pairings did *not* seem impressive in terms of signaling turns in the market averages, but they *do* seem to produce profitable results when applied to fairly high priced and/or volatile issues. Buy and hold strategies were clearly outperformed—not in each and every year to be sure, but over the long pull almost certainly. Honeywell, for example, started the 1970–78 period at a price of 135 and ended at a price of 71. Had you simply bought and held, you would have lost 64 points over the nine years, instead of gaining either 117 or 124 points, depending on the combination employed.

IBM started the period of 284 and closed the period at 305. A buy and hold approach would have netted 21 points. By trading via the 10-day, 50-day system, you would have grossed 256 points over the period—a considerable difference, even considering the commissions involved in 57 round trip trades.

Moreover, as we shall see in our forthcoming discussion of capital management, judicious employment of stock options can provide very favorable leverage, which can slant the odds even more in your favor. Moving average systems tend to produce fairly large gains when trades run favorably but small, if fairly frequent, losses when the trades run the wrong way. Those long gains can produce very large percentage profits when trading options because of the leverage stock options provide. Small losses, on the other hand, will result in relatively small losses in your options.

You should, of course, secure far superior results if you operate only in harmony with major market trends, purchasing on buy signals during bull markets (but not selling short) and selling short on sell signals during bear markets (but not buying long). You must, of course, be able to make the necessary determinations, but right now let's return to a short term system, one which is specifically designed to operate in harmony with intermediate stock market trends.

**How to increase
profitability
by employing a
longer term moving
average
to confirm a signal
rendered by
a shorter term
moving average**

Followers of short term moving averages, employing the basic moving average system, are likely to tack on considerable numbers of market points over the years, according to our research. Such systems tend to produce profits that average between three and four times the size of losses when trades prove unprofitable, and to become profitable themselves approximately 40 percent of the time. The net profit accrues not so much from the percentage of accuracy of the signals rendered, but from the fact that profits are allowed to run while losses are taken quickly.

As we have seen, the advantages of such systems for certain vehicles are their mathematical reliability (track record consistent and demonstrable over many years) and the simplicity of conducting trading with them. Their disadvantages lie in the frequency of whipsaws and in the relatively small average profit per transaction.

FIGURE 4–2

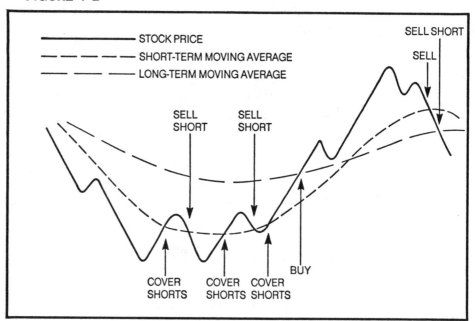

When you employ the confirming moving average system, you sell short when the stock price falls below both the long term and short term moving average, and you buy when the stock price rises above both moving averages; at other times, you maintain a neutral position.

We did subject some of the shorter term moving average systems to certain side conditions to ascertain whether the total gross profitability and/or the rate of profit per average trade could be improved, meeting with some success along the way. Among the modifications we made was a requirement that no short term moving average signal would be acted on unless it were in conformity with a moving average signal rendered by a longer term moving average. See Figure 4–2. We hoped to confirm the theory that short term signals prove more accurate when confirmed by favorable intermediate term trend signals.

To test this hypothesis, we set up the following conditions:

1. Buy signals are rendered when the index or stock price employed crosses above *both* the shorter and longer term moving average employed. If a cross above a shorter term moving average takes place, you do not follow it with a buy action unless and until the signal is confirmed by a crossover above the longer term moving average.
2. Sell signals are rendered when the index or stock price employed crosses below *either* the shorter term or the longer term moving average.
3. If you wished to employ such a system for short selling, you would sell short and remain short only when the stock price or stock market index crossed below *both* the shorter term and intermediate term moving average.

Table 4–4 shows an example of this situation.

TABLE 4–4

Date	Closing price	0.15 Exponential average	0.04 Exponential average	Signal
7/29/70	22.13	22.17	25.61	
7/30	22.50	22.22	25.48	Cover shorts
7/31	22.50	22.27	25.36	
8/03	22.75	22.34	25.26	
8/04	22.63	22.38	25.15	
8/05	22.88	22.46	25.06	
8/06	22.38	22.45	24.96	Sell short
8/07	22.00	22.38	24.84	
8/10	21.13	22.19	24.69	
8/11	19.88	21.83	24.50	
8/12	19.75	21.51	24.31	
8/13	19.38	21.18	24.11	
8/14	19.88	20.98	23.94	
8/17	20.13	20.85	23.79	
8/18	20.38	20.78	23.65	
8/19	20.38	20.71	23.52	
8/20	21.50	20.84	23.44	Cover shorts
8/21	22.88	21.15	23.42	
8/24	24.50	21.66	23.46	Buy long

Purchase Hewlett Packard only when its closing price closes above *both* its 0.15 and 0.04 exponential averages; sell when it crosses beneath either one, and sell short when it crosses beneath both.

Evaluation of the confirmed crossover system

We did find in our research that employment of a second moving average as a confirming trigger improved both the percentage of profitability of short term trading signals and the average profit per trade. The improvements were not highly significant, but they were clear, nonetheless, and could prove meaningful where commission costs and/or frequency of allowable trading are factors.

Some typical comparisons are given in Table 4–5.

TABLE 4–5
Comparison of single crossover system with confirmed crossover systems (NYSE Index; February 1970–January 1978); buy and sell signals only; (no sell short signals)

Basic system, 0.15, exponential average		*0.15 Exponential average, 0.04 exponential confirming*	
Number of trades:	112	Number of trades:	57
Profitable trades:	46	Profitable trades:	24
Unprofitable trades:	66	Unprofitable trades:	33
Percent profitable:	41%	Percent profitable:	42%
Total points gained:	45.67	Total points gained:	31.04
Average percent gain:	0.87%	Average percent gain:	1.1%
Average points per trade:	0.40	Average points per trade:	0.54

You can see that the simple 0.15 exponential average did accumulate more total points during this period than a 0.15 exponential average with confirmation by a 0.04 exponential average required. If frequency of trading is of no concern, then the basic system should serve you very well. If, however, you are attempting to increase your percentage per trade profit, the use of a confirming filter should provide some assistance.

The best of the confirming combinations

Of the combinations tested, the combination of the 0.08 exponential average (roughly a 24-day front weighted moving average) and the 0.04 exponential average produced the best results when applied to the NYSE Index. From 1970 into 1978, this combination produced total gains of 38.83 units on the NYSE Index, involving 55 transactions. Twenty-one of these transactions, or 38 percent, were profitable. The average trade gained 0.71 units, or 1.57 percent per transaction.

If this last figure seems low, keep in mind that the average profitable trade using the 0.08–0.04 combination showed an average percentage gain of 5.25 percent. The average unprofitable trade showed an average loss of only .70 percent. In other words, the average profit came to approximately 7.5 times the size of the average loss. It is *very* difficult to arrive at a system that produces average gains per transaction of above two to three percent. Later on, we will examine such systems.

We did test out the use of moving averages of longer term than 50 days as confirming filters, and found that the use of longer term moving averages added little to profitability. The 50-day or 10-week moving average appears to be of ideal length for service as an intermediate trend indicator. Longer term moving averages appear insufficiently sensitive, too slow to respond to changes in market climate. Many profitable signals are lost en route when lengths such as 100 days and 150 days are employed.

We also found that the 50-day moving average served better as confirmation for the 0.15 exponential average (approximately a 13-day moving average) than the 25-day moving average—too short a term, apparently, to signal intermediate trend reversals.

The shifting moving average system: Another means of improving your profit per trade results

In evaluating and in applying basic moving average systems, you will find that during rising market periods you will very frequently repurchase positions at higher prices than those at which you sold. During intermediate uptrends, the majority of sell signals will prove false, with repurchase signals coming in at higher levels than preceding sell signals perhaps 60 percent of the time. On balance, if frequency of trading is not a concern, you may find it simpler to maintain only one moving average and to follow *all* signals. You never really know which sell signal will be followed by a severe rather than a moderate decline. Although the majority of sell signals will prove false, you are still likely to net more by selling than by not selling.

However, if frequency of trading is of some concern and if you prefer trying to eliminate some of the whipsaws involved in the basic moving average system, you might use the "shifting moving average system." Figure 4–3 shows how it works.

1. You employ *two* moving averages, a shorter term moving average and a longer term moving average.
2. *Buy signals* are rendered whenever the stock price (or market index) crosses from below to above the shorter term moving average.
3. *Sell signals* are rendered when the stock price (or market index) crosses from above to below the shorter term moving average *except* when the sell signal occurs at a price level higher than the preceding sell signal.
4. If your sell signal occurs at *a higher price than the preceding sell signal,* then *you disregard the sell signal unless and until the price or market index crosses below both the shorter term and the longer term moving average.*

By following this procedure, you are attempting to "ride" intermediate uptrends for as long as possible, while still retaining the protection afforded by moving averages as stop loss points. In exchange for reducing the whipsawing generated by the basic system, you are sacrificing some potential timeliness when the market does, indeed, change direction since your longer

FIGURE 4–3

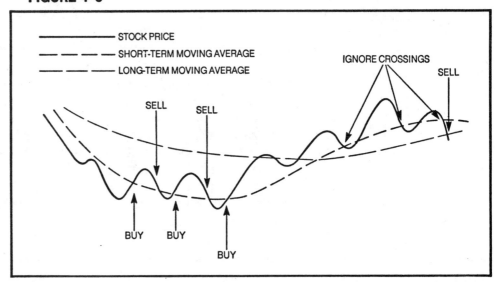

In the shifting moving average system, you shift your sell trigger from the short term moving average to the long term moving average whenever downside penetrations of the shorter term moving average occur at successively higher levels; if a downside penetration of the shorter term moving average occurs at a level below the previous downside penetration, then it is acted on as a sell signal.

term moving average will usually take longer to signal a sell than your shorter term moving average.

Does the tactic produce the desired results? Yes, at least as well as the preceding system and probably better. Whereas the confirming system described previously keeps you out of the market until all signals are in gear (thereby also delaying entry at market bottoms), the shifting moving average system allows you to enter early, although it does tend to delay exit a bit at market tops.

To keep our results comparable, we'll sum up results (in Table 4–6) of employing the 0.15 exponential average as the shorter term trigger, the 0.075 average as the secondary or shifted-to-moving average. We'll keep the NYSE Index as our pricing measure and the period 1970–78.

These results are almost exactly comparable to the results achieved by employing a 0.04 exponential average to confirm signals generated by a 0.15 exponential average. However, there are some significant differences that suggest that the shifting moving average system may prove more viable than confirming systems.

1. The shifting moving average system will trigger more frequent buy signals than the confirming system. This system produced an average of approximately 12 trades per year. The confirming moving average system, employing the 0.15 and the 0.04 exponential averages, produced an average of seven trades per year.

2. Although the frequency of trading was higher in our studies, the average profit per trade using the shifting moving average system was virtually

TABLE 4-6

Number of trades:	105
Profitable trades:	40
Unprofitable trades:	65
Percent profitable:	38.1%
Total points gained:	54.08
Average percent gain:	1.10%
Average points per trade:	.52

Buy when the NYSE Index crosses from below to above its 0.15 exponential average. Sell when the NYSE Index crosses from above to below its 0.15 exponential average; if, however, the sell signal occurs at a level higher than the previous sell signal, then await a crossing from above to below the 0.075 exponential average (Period: 1970–78)

equivalent to the average profit per trade generated via the confirming system. Therefore, total profitability is likely to be higher, at no sacrifice in per transaction profitability. This system appears to be a significant improvement over the basic systems, providing at least an equivalent gross annual point profit within fewer trades—one of the few instances, it seems, in which you actually receive something for nothing. (The average frequency of trading for the 0.15 exponential average alone came to 14.)

We emphasize systems using a 0.15 exponential average, of course, because this length moving average is most suitable, on balance, for the trading of no-load mutual switch funds. Longer term moving averages produce lesser profit, all told, and shorter term moving averages involve more frequent transactions than many funds will allow. In our actual experience trading no-loads over the years, these conclusions have proven valid.

We have two more tricks employing two or more moving averages, which we want to show you. We will reserve them for Chapter 5, following which we will go on to examine other aspects of stock market behavior.

5

How to set price objectives
with multiple moving averages,
plus some additional trading systems

In evaluating the basic multiple moving average crossing system, we found that while signals were generally profitable, particularly for longer term pairings, many signals did arrive later than we liked, since it takes some time for moving averages to reverse direction sufficiently to achieve a re-cross following a previous signal. To some extent this is an advantage: fewer whipsaws occur in such systems. To some extent this is a disadvantage: delays are often encountered that may prove costly.

In addition, signals generated by both the basic moving average system and the basic multiple moving average system tend to occur after a new trend is already well into motion. These signals do not occur very early at market reversal junctures. As a result, if you are buying, there is a fair chance that you will be buying into an already optimistic marketplace, competing with other anxious bidders. If you are selling, you may be selling in competition with other anxious sellers.

There is one trading system which, when applied short term, will frequently provide signals that anticipate other timing signals. The odds are greater that your signals will allow you to enter the stock market somewhat earlier than the typical moving average player and to exit a bit sooner. This will *not* be true in all instances, of course, and you may expect plenty of whipsaws—but the system should serve your purposes very well, particularly if you frequently trade no-load mutuals. Many mutual fund traders employ moving average systems, and many find themselves triggered into and out of mutual funds simultaneously. To repeat a point made earlier, this system will frequently trigger on days other than the typical moving average system, thereby helping you avoid the crowd.

The multiple moving average convergence-divergence trading system

The multiple moving average convergence-divergence trading system (MMACDTS) illustrated in Figure 5–1 employs two moving averages, one of a shorter and one of a longer time span, one usually about twice as long as the other, although variations are possible.

FIGURE 5–1

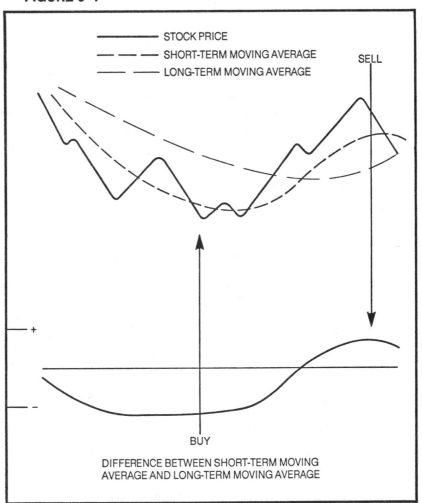

Buy signals in the moving average convergence-divergence system are rendered when the difference in levels between the short term moving average and the long term moving average changes in a positive direction; sell signals are rendered when a negative turn takes place.

1. *Buy signals* are rendered when the distance between the shorter term moving average and the longer term moving average becomes smaller, provided that the shorter is at a lower level than the longer.

If the shorter term moving average is at a higher level than the longer term moving average, then *buy signals* are rendered when the distance between them increases. In other words, a buy signal is rendered whenever the shorter term moving average improves its position relative to the longer term moving average by any degree. No crossing is required, so signals occur much earlier during market reversals.

2. *Sell signals* are rendered when the distance between the two moving averages decreases (if the shorter term moving average is at a higher level than the longer term one) or increases (if the shorter is at a lower level than the longer).

You may simply plot the difference between the short term moving average and the longer term with the formula,

$$\text{Short Term M.A.} - \text{Long Term M.A.}$$

As long as your plot is rising, you will be on a buy signal. When your plot falls, you will be on a sell signal.

The shorter the terms of the moving averages employed in the combination, the greater the frequency of trading. Do keep in mind that, with this system, sell signals could be generated even in the absence of a market decline. Distances between the moving averages could narrow if the market simply flattens out after a rise. Such a configuration would flatten shorter term moving averages while longer term moving averages continue to rise, thereby narrowing the distance and creating a sell signal. You may therefore be afforded opportunity to sell into strength. Conversely, at market bottoms, buy signals may be rendered during base formations as the shorter term moving averages flatten, while longer term moving averages continue to fall. This configuration will allow you to purchase into relative weakness—a major advantage of this system.

Figure 5–2 plots the signal level of the 0.15 exponential − 0.075 exponential combination for the year 1978. Waves of market advances and declines are clearly delineated in such graphs. Notice too that as market movements mature, each successive wave of the oscillator of the MMACDTS lessens in magnitude—an early warning that intermediate advances and declines are coming to an end. Another early warning occurs when the distance between the 0.15 and the 0.075 exponential averages, applied to the NYSE Index, reaches ±1.00 (extreme readings for this indicator).

Results of trading automatically via MMACDTS

We tested a number of combinations of moving averages for this system. Results employing the 0.15 − 0.075 and the 0.08 − 0.04 exponential average combinations are typical of what you might expect from the time spans involved—13 days, 27 days and 49 days, as shown in Table 5–1.

Discussion

This is another system that appears most suitable for the trading of very low-commission vehicles, since the average result per transaction is relatively low. The combination of the 0.08 − 0.04 exponentials produced

FIGURE 5–2
The moving average convergence-divergence pattern
for 1978

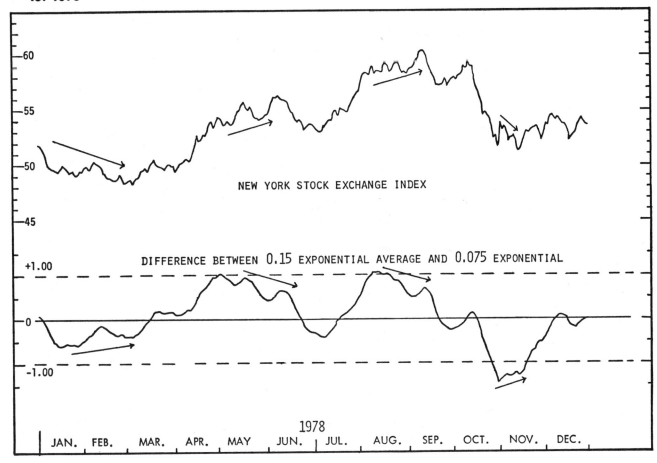

TABLE 5–1
Results of trading the NYSE Index via two combinations
of the MMACDTS, 1970–78

0.15 Exponential − 0.075 exponential		*0.08 Exponential − 0.04 exponential*	
Total number of trades:	152	Total number of trades:	141
Profitable trades:	72	Profitable trades:	55
Unprofitable trades:	80	Unprofitable trades:	86
Total points gained:	55.70	Total points gained:	55.49
Average gain per trade:	.37	Average gain per trade:	.39
Average percent gain:	.61%	Average percent gain:	.90%

somewhat superior results on balance, although a smaller percentage of transactions proved profitable, producing larger gains per transaction than the more sensitive 0.15 − 0.075 combination. The latter configuration, however, did produce a higher percentage of profitable trades than we usually encounter in moving average systems: 46.0 percent. To secure considerably higher percentages, we will have to enter into our more complex systems.

How to compute the market movement required for an advance signal

You will usually find it advantageous to compute the market level at which a signal will be rendered in advance of the close of the stock market each day, so that you can take action on the *day of* instead of the *day after* your signals are rendered. This ability is particularly useful in the trading of no-load mutual switch funds, which will usually give you the day's closing price if you telephone before the close of the stock market. Since trends tend to persist, you will generally get better results by taking action on the days of signals instead of the days after.

You may determine your closing signal levels in advance via the following formulas, if you are employing the above combinations of exponentials:

New signal level =
$$(2 \times 0.15 \text{ exponential average}) - 0.075 \text{ exponential average}$$

New signal level =
$$(2 \times 0.08 \text{ exponential average}) - 0.04 \text{ exponential average}$$

Example. Let's assume that the NYSE Index closes at 50.25, and that we are currently on a buy signal. The 0.15 exponential average stands at 50.08 and the 0.075 exponential average stands at 49.70. What will be the closing of the NYSE Index that will move the two exponentials closer together, thereby generating a sell signal?

$$
\begin{aligned}
\text{New signal level} &= (2 \times 50.08) - 49.70 \\
&= \quad 100.16 \; - 49.70 \\
&= \quad\quad 50.46
\end{aligned}
$$

Notice that *unless* the NYSE Index manages to gain .21 on the next day, a *sell* signal will be rendered. The MMACDTS will frequently signal a sell even on market up days. As we said, this device often helps you exit from the market early, in advance of other traders.

How to use the MMACDTS to predict intermediate market reversals before they become apparent to the crowd

Let's go back now to review Figure 5–2.

The stock market, as measured by the NYSE Index, made a new low for the year 1978 during March. However, *the MMACDTS did not fall to a new low* during that period, even though a short term trading sell was rendered by a brief turndown in the indicator. This divergence—the market falling to a new low while the MMACDTS failed to do so—signaled an imminent end to the intermediate decline that was taking place.

MMACDTS continued to achieve new high readings with the stock market until May, when it peaked. A failure in late May to match peaks in the market averages indicated that the intermediate upturn was near an end. A severe market decline ensued within three weeks.

A similar configuration took place between August 1978 and September, the market making new highs, unconfirmed by new highs in the indicator. The time at which the first divergence took place, during September 1978, would have proven a most propitious period in which to liquidate stocks. The market advance during October failed to carry MMACDTS to anywhere near its August and September highs, and a very serious market decline followed soon after.

The basing area during November and December 1978 is similarly instructive. Notice that MMACDTS rose steadily even as the market vacillated uncertainly within a broad basing area. A strong market advance occurred very soon, during January of 1979.

We will be reviewing the action of similar trading oscillators as we proceed in this book, but this oscillator does provide, by itself, excellent advance warning signals of intermediate market trend reversals. If you are an intermediate rather than a short term trader, you might try this oscillator, buying on the first higher double bottom and selling at the first turndown from a lower double top. Use as measurement points peaks and troughs spaced at least three weeks apart.

How to employ two or more moving averages to determine in advance where stock or stock market is likely to change direction—setting price objectives via crossings of centered moving averages

The following method was first brought to our attention in the excellent book, *The Profit Magic of Stock Transaction Timing* (by J. M. Hurst, Prentice-Hall, 1970).

To use this method, you must take the following continuing steps:

1. You should maintain weekly price charts of the stocks (or the market averages) that you are following.

2. You should also maintain at least two and preferably four straight moving averages of significant length. I suggest the maintenance of 5-week, 10-week, 20-week, and 40-week moving averages, each of which represents the time span of a significant short, intermediate, or longer term market cycle. Market cycles will be discussed in some length later in this book, but for now let's just note that the stock market tends to make minor, intermediate, and long term bottoms at regular time intervals. In other words, if you will study a stock chart, you may notice that you can determine five- to six-week intervals on the chart when the market seems to bottom. Further study will show you the 10-week intervals and the 20-week intervals, market bottom to market bottom. A longer term, weekly based chart should illustrate the 40-week cyclical period.

3. Each week, you should plot the high, low, and close of the market average and/or stock price that you are tracking. In addition, each week, plot your moving averages on the same price scale as the index or stock price— but you *must* make the following modification of usual practice:

Instead of plotting the moving average readings on the same time scale as the market index or stock price, move them back in time one half the length of the time period or cycle covered by the moving average.

For example, you would plot your latest 5-week moving average reading three weeks behind the latest posting of the stock price or market index that went into the computation of the 5-week moving average. This is called "centering" the moving average, or placing it midway in the data from which it is calculated. This is its true statistical placement since a 5-week moving average, centered, properly reflects the week it is placed in, plus the two previous weeks, plus the two following weeks. A 10-week moving average may be centered between the fifth and sixth weeks back. A 20-week moving average is centered backward in time between the tenth and eleventh week; the 40-week moving average is set between the 20th and 21st week back.

Figure 5–3 illustrates the layout involved. You can see the weekly ranges of the NYSE Index and the 5-, 10-, 20-, and 40-week moving averages.

FIGURE 5–3

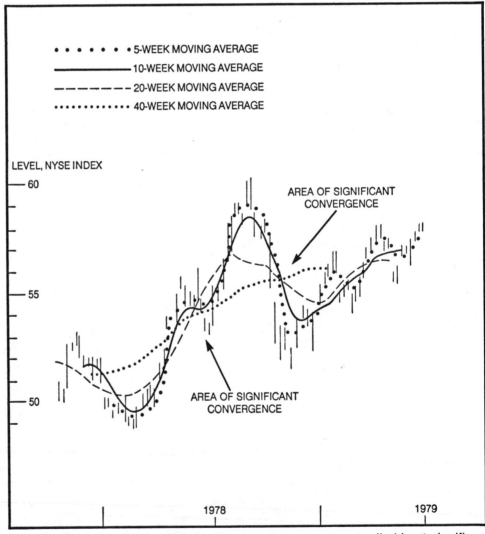

Areas in which several centered moving averages converge usually bisect significant market moves.

How to apply your plots to determine price objectives for the stock market

To determine price objectives for the 20-week market cycle, first determine the area in which the 10-week moving average crosses either above or below the 20-week moving average.

If the market is rising, the crossing will take place from below to above. If the market is falling, the crossing will take place from above to below.

Measure the distance between the point at which the market move in question began and the area at which the crossover takes place. Add that distance to the level of the crossover. The result is your price objective for the move.

Example. The NYSE Index (Figure 5–3) started to rise in early 1978 from a level of approximately 48.00. The 10-week moving average crossed over the 20-week moving average at a level of about 52.00, or four points up from the low area. We add those four points to the crossover point, 52.00, and get a price objective of approximately 56.00. This level was achieved in April and exceeded only slightly during May.

A subsequent crossing at around 56.50 almost perfectly bisected a later market advance during 1978, which carried from approximately 53.00 to just over 60.00.

To determine longer term price objectives, locate the area in which *all* of your moving averages, the 5-, 10-, 20-, and 40-week moving averages, seem to converge. This area will roughly bisect very significant intermediate advances and declines.

Examples. If you will refer to Figure 5–3 once again, you may note that the 5-week, the 10-week, the 20-week and the 40-week centered moving averages all converged in the area located between 54.00 and 55.00 of the NYSE Index. Since the advance that preceded this crossing originated at NYSE Index 48.00, a distance of approximately 6.00 units from the convergence, we could anticipate a final objective of approximately 60.50 (54.50 + 6.00), an objective that was almost exactly attained during September of 1978.

The market decline that ensued from that point resulted in the moving averages once again converging—this time at approximately NYSE Index 55.50. The distance between the start of the move (60.38) and the crossover point (55.50), approximately five points, yielded a downside objective of 50.50. The ultimate bottom came within 1.00 unit of matching this objective.

Further discussion

This method provides excellent results when applied in hindsight. In actual use, you will find that you frequently must extrapolate crossings into the future since the longer term moving averages in particular may not have reached the crossover point by the time that price objectives are reached. Remember, they are plotted with a lag period to current data. The necessity to extrapolate does weaken results of using this system a bit, but you should find that you can almost always secure reasonably close price objectives. At the very least, this system can help you to determine when the market is getting late for buying and late for selling, and can assist you in selling into strength and buying into weakness.

The time required to maintain these graphs yourself is only minutes per week. We have found, in our trading experience, that this has been time well spent.

Changing the lead time in moving averages, watching their change in direction, and some further tactics for trend-following traders

Moving average systems, as we have seen, come into their own during strongly trended market periods, but they run afoul of frequent whipsaws during periods when the stock market fluctuates within narrow trading ranges. In an effort to reduce these whipsaws, many technicians employ various devices and tactics designed to reduce the amount of whipsawing generated by moving averages. Many of these techniques find wide circulation among advisory services—whether or not they actually survive the crucible of computer evaluation. We have already explored a number of these techniques, and will now examine two more of these tactics. Let's see whether your favorite market advisor has really done his homework.

Significance of a moving average changing direction

As we have seen, exponential moving averages must, because of their construction, change direction when they are penetrated by the data used in their construction. This provides one advantage in that you are employing crossovers of such averages as triggering signals, the average will follow in the direction of the action you are taking. In other words, if you buy because an exponential average has been crossed to the upside, the turnup in the exponential average will automatically and rapidly raise your stop-loss point to follow the trade. This stop-loss point will continue to rise for as long as your data—stock price or market average—stays above the exponential average.

50

FIGURE 6-1

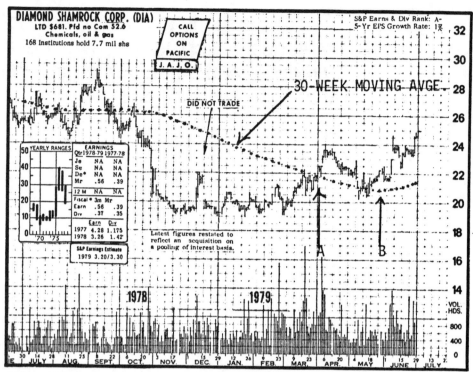

Although the price of Diamond Shamrock penetrated its 30-week moving average in April (A), no buy signal was rendered by the change of direction of moving average system until the moving average itself changed direction (B).

Source: *Trendline Daily Basis Stock Charts*, 345 Hudson Street, New York City, N.Y. 10014.

As a result, you incur less risk on each trade, at least theoretically, and your buy and sell trigger points will tend to activate with greater sensitivity than straight moving averages, which may or may not change direction upon penetration. Exponential averages, as we have seen, are very useful for in-and-out trading where neither commission costs nor frequency of transactions is significant.

Advantages of straight moving averages

Where commission costs and/or frequency of transactions are significant, straight moving averages, which respond less sensitively, may be preferred. Penetrations and repenetrations of straight moving averages are likely to occur somewhat less frequently than penetrations and repenetrations of exponential moving averages encompassing similar time spans.

The change of direction trading system

One of the popular conditions applied to straight moving average penetration systems to reduce the frequency of trading is the condition that for a signal to be rendered the straight moving average must change direction as well as be penetrated. Adding this new condition slows down the trading somewhat.

Given this condition, a short term buy signal might be considered to be generated when a 10-day straight moving average changes direction from down to up. For this to take place, the price level of the data employed (market index or stock price) would have to be higher at the latest reading than at the reading eleven days before—the reading that is dropped in the computation of a 10-day moving average. A longer term buy signal might be considered as generated when a 50-day moving average changes direction from down to up. Sell signals would be considered to have been generated when the direction of these moving averages changes from up to down.

In theory, since many minor penetrations of moving averages may not alter direction of the moving average, many whipsaws will be avoided if a change in direction rather than a penetration of the moving average is the triggering signal. Whether results justify the tactic is the question that we shall be exploring.

Evaluating the change in direction system: A computer study

We evaluated the results of acting on changes in direction of straight moving averages for moving average lengths of from 2–70 days, presuming that buy signals were rendered whenever the moving average in question turned up and that sell signals were rendered whenever the moving average in question turned down. Several representative issues and market averages were considered in the study, which covered the years 1970–78.

Results of employing this system appeared roughly on a par with other moving average systems that we have evaluated, in terms of total performance. However, there were differences in typical performance profiles. In general, change of direction systems underperformed simple penetration systems insofar as short term trading was concerned, but occasionally outperformed penetration systems if somewhat longer term trading patterns were followed. The requirement of a change in direction of a moving average does seem to reduce the frequency of trading to a considerable degree. A 10-week moving average, for example, is likely to change direction only about 2–8 times per year. In that regard, this system does meet one of its basic objectives—the reduction of whipsaws.

Comparing the change of direction system to the penetration system in terms of profit potential

Evaluating the results. It does appear fairly clear, as in Table 6–1, that systems that require a change in the direction of a moving average offer little advantage over trading systems that require simply a penetration of a moving average, although systems based on changes in direction do provide some edge over simple buy and hold strategies if commission costs and taxes are ignored. The simple penetration systems are far superior when shorter term moving averages are employed, less superior when longer term moving averages are involved.

TABLE 6–1
Comparison of trading results of change in direction of moving average system versus simple moving average penetration system (Market index employed— NYSE Index)

Year	Simple moving average penetration			Change in direction system		
	No. of trades	Total gain	Avg. gain per trade	No. of trades	Total gain	Avg. gain per trade
10-day average						
1970	24	+19	.79	27	+ 2	.07
1971	19	+23	1.21	21	+ 8	.38
1972	29	+ 9	.31	20	− 1	− .05
1973	35	+10	.29	42	0	0
1974	35	+13	.37	29	+ 2	.07
1975	35	+10	.29	26	+ 2	.08
1976	39	+ 4	.10	37	− 6	− .16
1977	36	+ 3	.08	23	− 6	− .26
1978	27	+18	.67	28	− 4	− .14
34-day average						
1970	16	+ 9	.56	11	+14	1.27
1971	13	+11	.85	15	+ 4	.27
1972	19	+ 3	.16	11	+ 4	.36
1973	19	+11	.58	16	+ 4	.25
1974	11	+10	.91	17	− 2	− .12
1975	14	+15	1.07	8	+ 8	1.00
1976	23	+ 3	.13	19	+ 3	.16
1977	22	− 3	− .14	15	− 7	− .47
1978	13	+ 8	.62	19	+ 2	.11

We chose the 34-day moving average for comparison because this is the time frame that seems to produce the best results on balance with change of direction systems. Simple penetration systems achieve their best results on an intermediate basis when applied to time spans of from 40–50 days.

Frequency of trading is reduced somewhat by the imposition of a condition requiring that a moving average change direction, but the penalty in terms of performance can be considerable, particularly where shorter term time spans are involved.

Do changes in direction of moving averages carry statistical significance? Yes, we suppose so. But hardly to the degree that their popular press would seem to indicate.

The moving average plotted with a lead time—can some of those false whipsaws really be eliminated by use of this simple technique?

A somewhat different style of attack upon the problem of whipsaws takes place when we attempt to plot moving averages with a lead time over the data that enters into their computation. Figure 6–2 shows how this is done. The moving average computed with the inclusion of the latest data is plotted on a chart a specified number of days or weeks ahead in time of the most recent data. By so doing, you place some additional headroom between the latest entry and the current moving average, hoping, thereby, to reduce the amount of false whipsaws created by simple penetration systems.

Buy signals are generated when the market average or stock price crosses from below to above the moving average plot that appears on the same time line in the plot as the most recent data. Sell signals are rendered via a downside penetration. This means that a past computed moving average becomes the trigger level, not the most recently computed moving average. For example, if we are employing an 8-day moving average with a 1-day lead time, the latest price entry will appear on the same time scale as the moving average computed one day previous, and will have to cross above or below that one day old moving average to render an action signal.

FIGURE 6–2

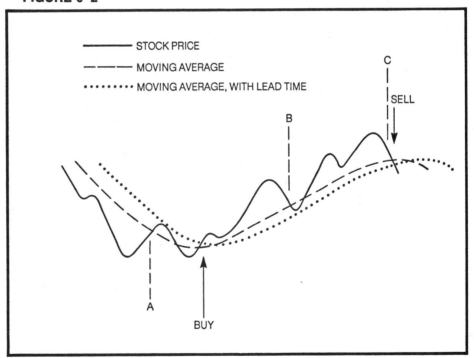

By plotting your moving average ahead with a specified lead time, you can often reduce the amount of whipsaws in your trading. Notice that signals at points A, B, and C, which would have been rendered in the basic moving average system, are not rendered when the moving average is plotted with a lead time.

For purposes of comparison, we will consider the 8-day moving average, basic penetration system versus the 8-day moving average with a 1-day lead time as representative of short term trading systems. For intermediate systems, we will compare the straight 50-day moving average basic penetration system to the 50-day moving average, plotted with a 15-day lead time.

In our efforts to develop improvements over the basic system, we will hope that the lead time does, indeed, reduce whipsaws and the amount of trading with no penalty in loss of total performance. Table 6–2 shows a comparison of performances.

TABLE 6–2
Comparison of basic moving average system results with moving average penetrations of moving averages plotted with various lead times. The market index employed is the NYSE Index

Year	8-day moving average, basic system			8-day system, 1-day lead time		
	No. of trades	Total gain	Avg. gain per trade	No. of trades	Total gain	Avg. gain per trade
1970	24	26	1.08	22	20	.91
1971	25	24	.96	19	19	1.00
1972	27	11	.41	27	9	.33
1973	33	14	.42	33	10	.30
1974	35	22	.63	35	11	.31
1975	43	11	.26	36	7	.19
1976	33	7	.21	37	3	.08
1977	32	7	.22	34	5	.15
1978	34	15	.41	33	15	.45
	50-day moving average, basic system			50-day system, 15-day lead time		
1970	10	12	1.20	6	12	2.00
1971	11	9	.82	9	4	.44
1972	15	6	.40	15	1	.07
1973	12	8	.67	10	7	.70
1974	12	6	.50	8	8	1.00
1975	8	10	1.25	10	9	.90
1976	17	7	.41	17	3	.18
1977	19	− 4	− .21	15	− 6	− .40
1978	13	6	.46	10	8	.80

Analysis of results

The employment of a lead time in the plotting of moving averages does seem to reduce the amount of trading somewhat as compared to the employment of straight moving averages plotted with no lead time, and the employment of a lead time will, in general, serve to reduce your frequency of trading without essentially penalizing your performance *per trade*. You will, however, gain fewer total points than by employing straight moving averages with no lead time. So if frequency of transaction carries relatively little significance, you may prefer to employ straight moving average penetrations (the basic moving average system) or exponential penetrations alone as your triggering signals.

Why we emphasize market signals

Many readers may wonder why we have not included results of trading individual issues rather than simply the NYSE Index in Table 6–2. For one, we believe that few investors will actually track large numbers of stocks on a regular basis, whereas many investors may maintain regular postings of one or a few market indicators. Therefore, throughout this book, we emphasize market signals as opposed to individual stock timing. Second, our research has demonstrated to us—and we will demonstrate to you—that there is a very close correlation between the action of the major stock market averages and the action of individual securities, particularly when you maintain at least five to seven securities in portfolio. As a general rule, you can almost certainly trade a diversified group of issues upon market based signals. Although one or two issues in your portfolio may diverge from the "market", your total portfolio is very likely to run in tandem with market based timing signals. This will be particularly true if you trade in mutual funds.

The moving average/chord trading system

This trading system was developed by the Dunn & Hargitt Market Guide (22 North Second Street, Lafayette, Indiana 47902) and was published in the December 11, 1978 issue of that service.

The moving average/chord trading system is based upon two variables:

1. the length of the moving average period employed
2. the length of the chord you are employing.

We are all, by now, quite familiar with the straight moving average, on which this system is based, and with the construction of straight moving averages. No need to repeat the definitions and procedures at this point in the game.

A *moving average chord* is the segment of a straight line which intersects the moving average curve at two points.

For example, in Figure 6–3, we see a three week chord, which joins moving average readings spaced three weeks apart. A one week chord would join moving average readings spaced one week apart. A four week chord would join moving average readings spaced four weeks apart.

FIGURE 6–3

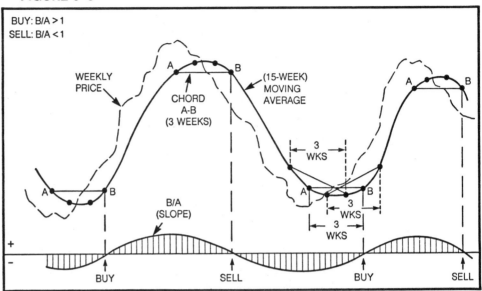

Here is how the moving average/chord system works:

Buy rule: slope of chord across moving average trendline changes from negative to positive.

Sell rule: slope of chord across moving average trendline changes from positive to negative.

Source: *Dunn & Hargitt Market Guide*, 22 North Second Street, Lafayette, Indiana 47902.

The rate of gain for the stock market or for a particular stock may be measured by dividing the most current moving average reading by a reading a chord length previous. For example, you might divide the most recent 5-week moving average reading by the 5-week moving average reading three weeks previously. If the current reading is higher, your result will be greater than one. If the current reading is lower, your result will be less than one. By making a division in this manner each week, you can measure the slope of any advance or decline, ascertaining thereby whether market or stock movement is gaining or losing momentum.

Buy and sell signals via the moving average/chord trading system

Buy signals are rendered whenever the slope of the chord you are employing in conjunction with your selected moving average turns positive. This means the latest posting of the moving average has turned higher than its reading a chord length previous.

Sell signals are rendered when the slope of the chord employed turns negative. Your designated moving average now stands at a lower reading than it did one chord length previous.

Figure 6–3 illustrates buy and sell signals generated via the use of a 15-week moving average, coupled with a 3-week chord.

Results of employing the moving average/chord trading system

Table 6–3 provides a workout of the application of the moving average/ chord trading system to a universe of 219 stocks, 1967–78. The presumption was made that issues were either purchased and sold (Long only) on chord signals or purchased on buy signals and sold short on sell signals (Long & short). The total final dollar value of the portfolio, operating on generated signals, was then compared to the final dollar value, assuming a buy and hold strategy. The percentage returns shown in Table 6–3 reflect the differences between the annualized rate of return achieved via use of the chord method and the hypothetical buy and hold strategy.

For example, had you employed the 5-week moving average/1-week chord combination/long only/system your annualized rate of return would have come out to be 19.45 percent per year better than a buy and hold approach to the 219 stock portfolio. The portfolio's mean annual return for the entire period was 4.06 percent, based on a buy and hold strategy.

TABLE 6–3
Moving average/chord system, 1967–1978

Chord length (weeks)	Long only, moving average period (number of weeks)				Long and short, moving average period (number of weeks)			
	5	10	15	20	5	10	15	20
1	+19.45	+13.30	+51.97(3)	+28.81	−38.66	− 50.98	+13.79(2)	− 12.06
3	+57.88(1)	+15.02	+55.91(2)	+17.98	+11.82(3)	− 49.01	+28.81(1)	− 25.86
5	+30.54	+ 6.15	+23.39	+ 2.46	−31.03	− 57.63	−17.73	− 46.79
10	+ 6.15	+ 1.47	−13.30	− 9.85	−57.63	− 61.33	−64.77	− 72.66
13	+35.96	− 5.41	− 9.11	−24.63	− 7.88	− 61.33	−65.02	− 94.33
15	+23.39	−13.30	−11.33	−18.96	−17.73	− 64.77	−69.95	− 87.68
20	+ 2.46	− 9.85	−18.96	−26.35	−46.79	− 72.66	−87.68	−102.46
25	− 6.89	−23.89	−21.42	−28.57	−63.54	− 93.59	−92.61	+102.21
30	−15.76	−27.58	−27.33	−31.03	−83.25	−104.43	−98.27	−102.40
40	−14.77	− 6.65	+ 0.49	− 3.94	−74.63	− 57.38	−45.56	− 54.43
50	+19.95	+ 4.18	−10.59	−14.28	−16.50	− 36.94	−56.40	− 58.86
60	− 9.35	− 6.15	− 3.69	−12.06	−53.20	− 47.78	−55.91	− 60.09

Data: Weekly stock prices (adjusted for splits) using mid-week daily close on Wednesday.
Period: 6/15/67–10/18/78 (11 years)
Universe: 219 stocks* with listed options as of October, 1978.
* Houston Oil (HOI) was excluded because the stock's mean annual return (1058.29 percent) was 88 standard deviations from portfolio mean annual return (4.06 percent) and was thus classified as an outlier which would badly distort research results.

The values in the table were obtained by investing $1,000 in each stock at the beginning of the period and trading the stock at the close price of each buy and sell signal based on the Moving average/chord system. If the first trade had a loss then there was less to invest on the second trade. Thus, it was directly comparable to a buy/hold strategy. The dollar profit was totalled for the period and expressed as a percent return on an annualized basis. The returns for each stock were totalled and an average portfolio return was calculated. This was divided by the return from a buy/hold system to find a return relative to the market.

Source: *Dunn & Hargitt Market Guide*, 22 North Second Street, Lafayette, Indiana 47902.

The majority of combinations did not produce profit, which is not surprising since this system is very closely related to the change of direction of moving average system described above. Certain combinations of chords and moving averages, however, did theoretically prove profitable and may well be worth your attention, particularly since the frequency of trading via this system is quite moderate.

FIGURE 6-4

5-Week Moving Average/3-Week Chord

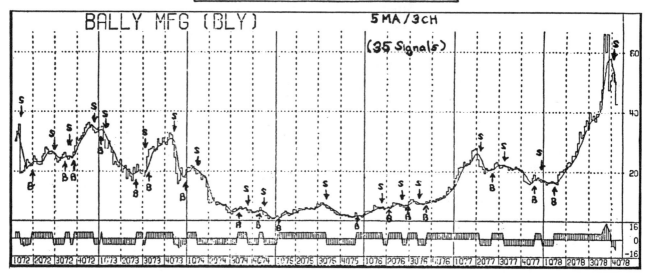

15-Week Moving Average/3-Week Chord

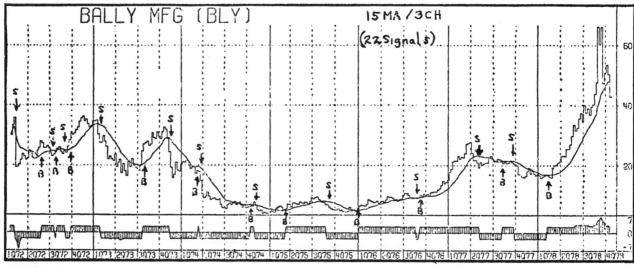

Bally has been an excellent candidate for the moving average chord trading system.

Source: *Dunn & Hargitt Market Guide*, 22 North Second Street, Lafayette, Indiana 47902.

The best chords and the best moving averages to employ in the moving average/chord trading system

The 3-week chord, applied to either a 5-week moving average or a 15-week moving average, produced the best results with this system, followed by the employment of a 1-week chord, applied to a 15-week moving average.

Although the 1-week chord/5-week moving average system worked very well, the 3-week/15-week moving average combination did appear to be suprior, producing at least comparable results on fewer transactions.

Figure 6–4 illustrates the signals generated by these combinations in relationship to Bally Manufacturing. In terms of your total portfolio, you might have anticipated results, on the long side only, would be 57.88 percent better than a buy and hold strategy via the use of the 3-week chord/5-week moving average combination. Nearly identical results (+55.9 percent) were hypothetically achieved using the 3-week chord/15-week moving average combination instead.

In general, a long only approach outperformed the long & short approach with this system. We have found in our own research that short selling signals generally underperformed long signals, given the same trading devices—a result we might expect given the fact a stock can decline by only so much while it may, at least theoretically, rise infinitely. However, we will present trading systems that do provide additional profit when short sales are employed as well as long only positions.

For the moment, however, let's go on to examine another, and very significant, measurement related to the stock market—excessive condition, an ingredient which will come to play a very significant role as we move into more advanced trading systems.

7

How to recognize and measure
market excesses,
and how you can build
trading systems around them

Trend following systems such as the basic moving average system are designed to enter into and to exit from the market as confirmed changes in market trend occur—changes in trend for the most part defined by changes in the direction of the moving average itself or by penetrations of the moving average. In theory, advocates of such systems believe in buying into strength and selling into weakness. Their major strategy lies in securing the "safe" middles of market moves, a profitable enough strategy, presuming that it works.

"Excess swingers" prefer to play the game in a somewhat different manner, gambling on entering into the stock market too soon or exiting too early in the hope of garnering additional points; not simply the safe middle, but virtually entire market swings. In exchange for the additional hoped for reward, excessive condition followers are willing to "guess" when the market "should" turn and to attempt to take positions in advance of the trend-following public.

As we shall see, their guesses may be more than simply guesses, and their gambles may be based, in fact, on some demonstrable qualities of stock market behavior rather than merely on hope and fantasy.

Measuring market excesses: The basic wave theory and approach to market movement and data

The basic wave approach operates under the presumption that the stock market operates and can be measured by waves similar to the typical sine wave (Figure 7–1). In other words, the approach presumes that the various fluctuations of the stock market and of price forecasting data can be plotted in the form of a sine wave, that bottom areas can be defined as the wave reaches bottom and that top areas can be defined as these waves reach peaks. A bottom area—where the wave seems to have no further room on the downside—is considered an *oversold* area; the market, overly-extended on the downside, is likely to rise. Peaks in these sine waves—hopefully at predictable levels somewhere above a center line—mark overbought areas, areas in which the market has become overly extended during a rise and due to turn down.

Given the premise that extreme readings of these waves are predictable and somewhat immutable, the excess trader awaits such extreme readings and then operates, somewhat out of phase with the general public. Although various problems (and resultant solutions) do arise with such systems, the basic premise appears, actually, to be fairly sound—provided that proper attention and tactics are applied to exceptional cases.

Before we go further into tactics, strategies and representative measurements of market excessive condition, let's first examine one major premise: that virtually all stock market data can be measured and plotted in the form of a basic wave.

Examples of the basic wave theory in action. Figures 7–2, 7–3 and 7–4 illustrate bar charts of stocks within their trading channels. Figure 7–2 is a chart of a neutral stock, with the centerline of the channel marked in. You can see the close similarity of the pattern to Figure 7–1, representing the sine wave or basic wave. Given such a stock, you simply buy as the wave nears bottom and sell as the wave nears a top.

FIGURE 7–1

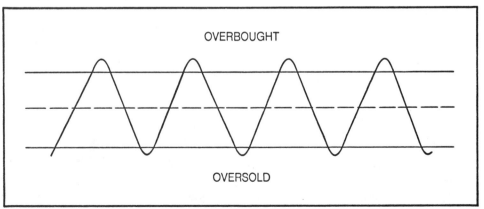

OVERBOUGHT

OVERSOLD

The classic sine wave simply oscillates at regular intervals between overbought and oversold territory.

FIGURE 7–2

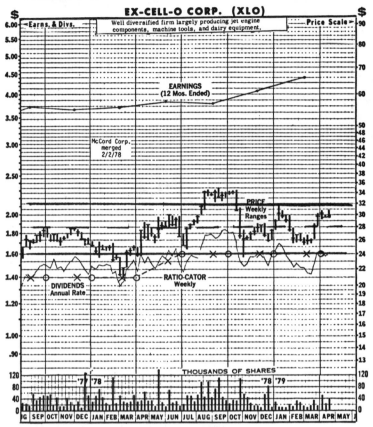

The price movements of Ex-Cello traced out a rough, neutral sine wave around the center-channel line.

Source: *Securities Research Company*, 208 Newbury Street, Boston, Mass. 02116.

Figure 7–3 is also a bar chart, but this time of a rising stock—the configuration of the wave tilts a bit. However, the basic premise remains intact in that the price action of the stock vacillates around the center area—the dotted line or centerline of the channel. Only the slope of the centerline distinguishes the wave of Figure 7–3 from the waves of Figures 7–1 and 7–2. Figure 7–4 illustrates the same principle, applied this time to an issue in a downtrend.

The basic wave in action:
How to employ moving average excesses to catch excellent short term trading moves

We did not have to go very far to select two excellent examples of the basic wave in action, no further in fact than one page selected more or less at random from the *Trendline* chart book.

First, let's examine the chart of International Paper. We have marked off the line which denotes the 150-day moving average of the stock. Although this line fluctuates upwards and downwards in a rather even oscillation during the 1978–79 period shown on the chart, we may employ the moving average line as though it were the centerline of our basic wave oscillator.

FIGURE 7–3

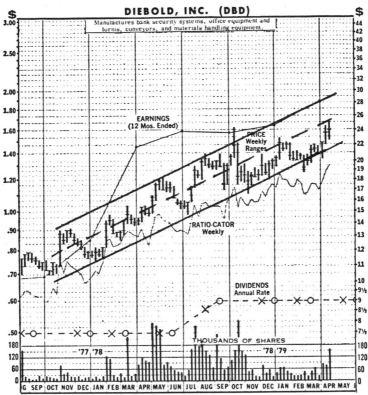

Diebold's price oscillated around a rising neutral line—the pattern of price movement forming a rising sine wave.

Source: *Securities Research Company*, 208 Newbury Street, Boston, Mass. 02116.

FIGURE 7–4

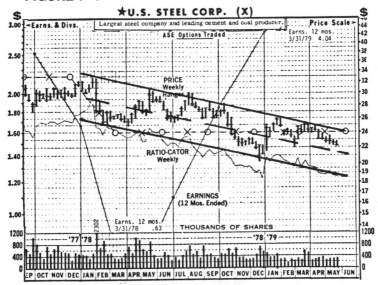

The price of U.S. Steel formed an irregular descending sine wave around a center-channel line.

Source: *Securities Research Company*, 208 Newbury Street, Boston, Mass. 02116.

FIGURE 7–5

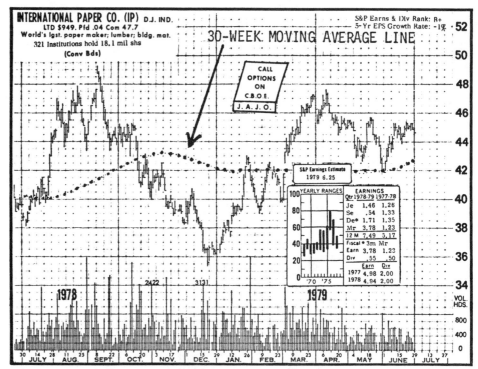

International Paper has been a good buy when its price falls by six points below its 30-week moving average and a good sale when its price rises by six points above its 30-week moving average.

Source: *Trendline Daily Basis Stock Charts*, 345 Hudson Street, New York City, N.Y. 10014.

With International Paper in a broad trading range over this period of time, you can see that the issue lay in good buying position whenever it drifted to approximately six points below its moving average and that the issue lay in a good selling position whenever it rose to a level approximately six points above its 150-day moving average. International Paper, during 1978–early 1979, would have, indeed, proven to be an excellent candidate for excess condition traders. You might have, had you chosen, plotted the price of the issue each day with a graph beneath, plotting the differential between the stock prices and the 150-day moving average.

One further item worthy of note: the oscillator you would have so constructed would *not* rise and fall from extreme reading to extreme reading. Very frequently, it would have reversed direction mid-way in its oscillating channel, appearing like Figure 7–7.

This form of configuration is actually more usual than the ideal pattern of the sine waves which reflect the trading oscillators we employ. Extreme signal readings occur with relative infrequency, which does mean that either 1) you will miss opportunities from time to time; for example, the market rise that took place in International Paper during July and August 1978, or 2) you will have to employ some means of determining when your trading oscillator is unlikely to reach an extreme before reversals in price take place. We have

FIGURE 7–6

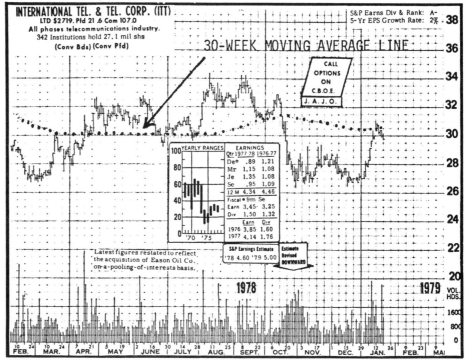

During 1978 International Telephone reversed direction whenever its price deviated from its 30-week moving average by four points.

Source: *Trendline Daily Basis Stock Charts,* 345 Hudson Street, New York City, N.Y. 10014.

devised a number of such methods, utilizing time and momentum measurement, all of which will become considerations in our Time-Trend-Momentum Trading System.

You might observe, incidentally, that International Paper, a choice basic wave trader during this period, would have proven a disaster for moving

FIGURE 7–7

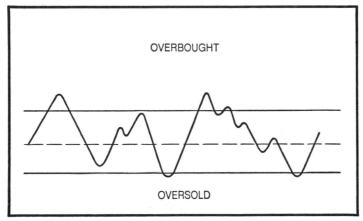

The typical profile of sine waves as they usually appear in the real life stock market.

average traders, particularly any who employed the 150-day moving average as their cross-over point. A practice of buying and selling IP on moving average crossings would have netted less than nil profit because crossovers of the moving average all took place in the same price vicinity.

We may conclude the following: *Stocks that lie within trading ranges are very poor candidates for moving average systems, but are excellent candidates for oscillator trading.* As we shall very shortly see, *Strongly trended stocks are excellent candidates for moving average traders but poor candidates for oscillator traders.* The Time-Trend-Momentum trading system bridges the gap when a trading range stock breaks out and when a breakout stock reverts to a trading range swinger. But again, more regarding that later on.

Another example of a trading range oscillator candidate. International Telephone, another trading range issue, shown in Figure 7–6, could also have been traded very nicely during 1978–79, with purchases and/or sales made at the appropriate ±4.00 point deviations from the 150-day moving average. In employing such systems, you await the ideal conditions in which to act. You do not take action at midpoints. Good signals will generally occur from between 3–6 times per year.

Your strategy in employing the moving average excessive trading system

Your strategy in applying such systems is relatively simple, and you might, in fact, want to check for excesses before ever taking any stock position—buying into oversold areas (stock well below its moving average) and selling, hopefully, into overbought areas (stock well above its moving average). You may employ either the 150-day moving average shown in the above charts or you may opt to rely on a 50-day moving average instead, which will move somewhat more rapidly in line with stock price movement. Some traders may prefer to employ very short term moving averages such as a 10-day moving average for this purpose, but we do suggest the somewhat longer term moving averages for true intermediate term trading.

It is necessary, of course, to back-check the history of your portfolio candidates before applying the moving average excessive system. More volatile issues will habitually swing to further extremes than less volatile issues, even within similar price ranges. In general, heavily capitalized institutional grade issues will prove more regular in their movements than thinly traded issues with small floats.

An excellent, quick posting excessive signal for timing the general stock market

Trendline Daily Basis Stock Charts publishes each week a short range trading oscillator, which we show in Figure 7–8, combined with a chart of the major market averages. This oscillator is essentially similar to an oscillator you can create by maintaining a 10-day moving average of the daily differences between the number of advancing issues on the New York Stock Exchange and the number of declining issues. Each unit on the *Trendline* scale is equivalent to approximately 50 units. For example, a +3.00 reading on the

FIGURE 7–8

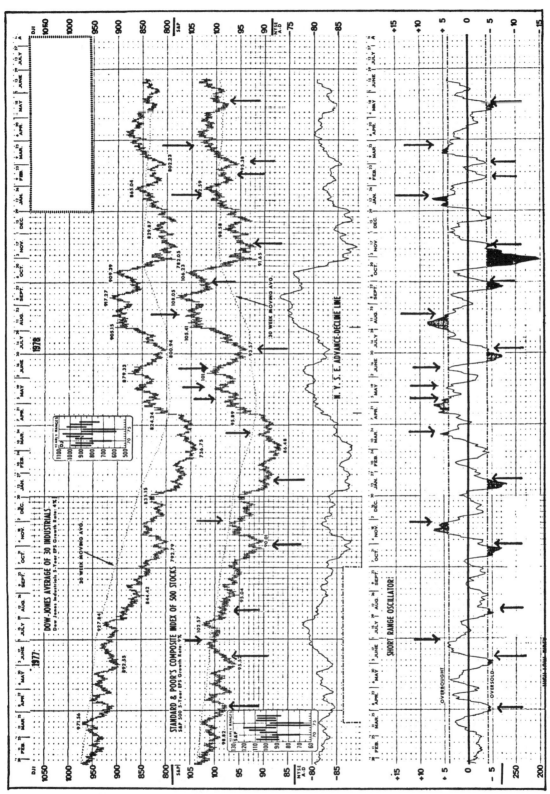

The signals generated by the overbought-oversold index. Rising arrows denote buy signals; falling arrows denote sell signals.

Source: *Trendline Daily Basis Stock Charts*, 345 Hudson Street, New York City, N.Y. 10014.

Trendline scale would be equivalent to an average 10-day advance-decline differential of +150. A −5.00 reading is equivalent to an average 10-day advance-decline differential of −250. Readings in the ±4.00 area may be considered as overbought (+4.00) or oversold (−4.00).

The oscillator demonstrates the typical form of the sine wave, as we actually tend to see this form of wave in practice. I have marked off buy and sell areas, which might be based on this single indicator alone. *Buy signals* are rendered when this indicator falls to below the oversold line then emerges to above the oversold line. *Sell signals* are rendered when this indicator rises to above the overbrought line then falls to below the overbought line.

Tracking the advance-decline overbought-oversold indicator through two full market years—excellent results from a single indicator

We have marked off the buy areas on the chart with rising vertical arrows and the sell areas with descending vertical arrows. You can see the excellent correlation between signals rendered by this indicator and movement in the market averages.

This trading system, however, in and of itself, is NOT perfect. Not all buy signals are followed by market advances of sufficient extent to produce profit, and many sell signals occur prematurely. The Time-Trend-Momentum system, which employs a similar oscillator, provides more refined signals for entering and exiting from the marketplace. The basic sine wave, overbought-oversold system, employed in its simple form, however, can point to areas in which the market has already risen sufficiently to provide greater risk to buyers and already fallen sufficiently to provide greater risk to short sellers.

The basic overbought-oversold oscillator provided excellent buy signals in early June 1977, November 1977, February 1978, December 1978, and February 1979. Excellent sell signals were rendered during November 1977, May 1978, August 1978, January 1979, and March 1979—all shown, again, with declining arrows.

How to maintain this simple and useful indicator

To maintain the overbought-oversold advance-decline oscillator, you follow what amounts to a very simple procedure.

1. Each day, secure from your daily financial newspaper the number of issues that rise and the number that fall on the NYSE.
2. Subtract the number of issues that fall each day on the NYSE from the number that rise. Your result will be the net for that day. For example, if 800 issues rise and 500 fall, your net reading for the day is +300. If 500 issues rise and 800 fall, your net reading for the day is −300.
3. Maintain a 10-day moving total of the daily net readings. You may divide by ten to create a 10-day moving average, if you prefer, or you may employ a 10-day moving total of advances minus declines as your oscillator. If you opt for the latter procedure, then a reading of +2,000 represents an overbought condition and a reading of −2,000 represents an oversold condition.

4. *Keep in mind that the achievement of an overbought or oversold condition in and of itself is no guarantee the market will turn. Await some sign that the wave has peaked, before taking action on the short side, or that the wave has troughed, before taking action on the long side.* Very extreme conditions of overbrought areas sometimes occur during strong bull markets, and some extreme and long-lasting oversold conditions sometimes occur during bear markets. The Time-Trend-Momentum trading system makes full allowance for these contingencies.

A further sampling of useful sine wave indicators. We've taken the time to discuss the advance-decline overbought-oversold trading oscillator in some detail just to familiarize readers with the basic concepts involved in trading by rules of excesses.

In our experience the following indicators have often proven useful in supporting market timing decisions.

The *Trendline* percentage of issues above and below their moving averages	*Trendline* publishes, in each issue, the percentage of issues within its coverage that lie above their 30-week moving averages. A 5-week moving average is maintained of the weekly postings to smooth the data. This chart is shown in Figure 7–9. You can see the stock market usually lies in a buy area when this percentage declines up to the 30 percent area or below then starts to turn up. The market usually lies in a general sell area when the percentage of issues above their 30-week moving averages rises to above 70 percent and then starts to turn down. Double top and double bottom formation in overbought and oversold areas are particularly significant. I have marked sell areas with descending arrows and buy areas with rising arrows.

There were few significant market rallies over the years covered in Figure 7–9, that is, truly significant advances as opposed to simple trading rallies. These occurred in early 1975, early 1976, early 1978, and early 1979. In each case, a low was made in the *Trendline* indicator deep in oversold territory. A double bottom formation was then completed within approximately three months, the second trough higher than the first. Turn-ups in the indicator from the second, higher bottom signalled the onset of strong market moves.

Double top formations high in overbought areas provided excellent warning of serious impending intermediate declines during mid-1975 and mid-1978. I have marked off the major buy areas on Figure 7–9.

Even if you do not subscribe to *Trendline* but do subscribe to another chart service which provides moving average data, you can create your own oscillator by maintaining a sample of from 25–50 issues in respect to their 30-week moving averages. A sample of such size will very closely approximate the total marketplace in its action.

A shorter term indication of market excess may be secured via use of an indicator that plots the percentage of issues that lie above their 10-week moving averages. You may assume the market is overbought when such an indicator rises to 70 percent, with definite caution indicated as the indicator turns down. You may assume the market is oversold when readings fall to

FIGURE 7–9

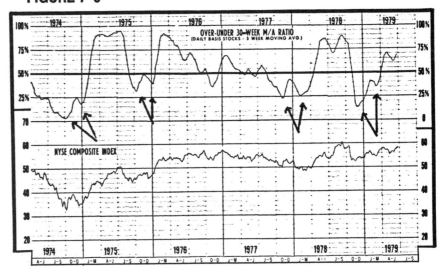

Trendline's indicator, the percentage of stocks that lie above their 30-week moving average, is an excellent supporting market indicator. Buy signals occur when readings fall to 30 percent or less and a double bottom formation develops. The market is generally at a top when the indicator turns down from overbought territory.

Source: *Trendline Daily Basis Stock Charts*, 345 Hudson Street, New York City, N.Y. 10014.

below 30 percent. A series of higher highs in this indicator within the oversold region usually indicates that the market is ready to turn up.

We did subject both these indicators to computer analysis to ascertain whether simple and effective buy and sell signals could be developed from their data alone. Unfortunately, we found this could not be accomplished. During very strong market periods, prices often rise even after these indicators begin to decline, and during very weak markets oversold conditions persist for very long periods of time. During the majority of market climates, however, the parameters discussed above should prove very useful.

Specialist short sales

Just as an example of how typical market indicators appear when plotted along a neutral axis as a sine wave, we have reproduced a chart of the *NYSE Specialist Short Sale Ratio*, which measures the amount of short sales put out each week by specialists as a percentage of all short sales put out each week on the New York Stock Exchange. This data is released weekly by the exchanges and is published weekly in such media as *Barron's* and *The Wall Street Journal*.

This indicator approaches its overbought range when specialist short sales reach 55 percent, based on recent readings in this indicator. It approaches its oversold levels when specialist short sales fall to approximately 35 percent. Experience has shown that it generally pays to buy stock when readings of below 35 percent are encountered, and to consider selling when readings of 55 percent are encountered.

FIGURE 7–10

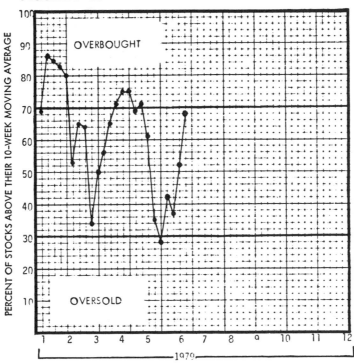

Termination of upmoves are signaled when the percentage rises above 70 percent, 80 percent, or 90 percent, depending on the strength of the upmove in progress; termination of downmoves are signaled when the percentage drops below 30 percent, 20 percent, or 10 percent, depending on the strength of the down-move in progress. The optimum period for establishing long positions is when the percentage is below the 30 percent level and the chart shows a series of higher bottoms; the optimum period for taking profits is when the percentage is above the 70 percent level and the chart shows a series of lower tops.

Source: *Investors Intelligence*, Two East Avenue, Larchmont, N.Y.

Some further examples of excesses

1. The stock market may be considered excessive when approximately 13 million shares trade during the first hour. Avoid placing long orders into buying panics.
2. The Dow Industrial Average is almost certainly excessive on a long term basis when it deviates from its 30-week moving average by more than 100–130 points.
3. If a stock advances by more than 20 percent within two weeks, you can almost certainly anticipate a consolidation, at the least.
4. If more than 1,000 issues decline for three consecutive days on the New York Stock Exchange, you can generally anticipate a price recovery, particularly if volume is high.
5. If 500 issues reach either new high prices or new low prices on the New York Stock Exchange within a given week, expect an imminent market reversal.

FIGURE 7–11

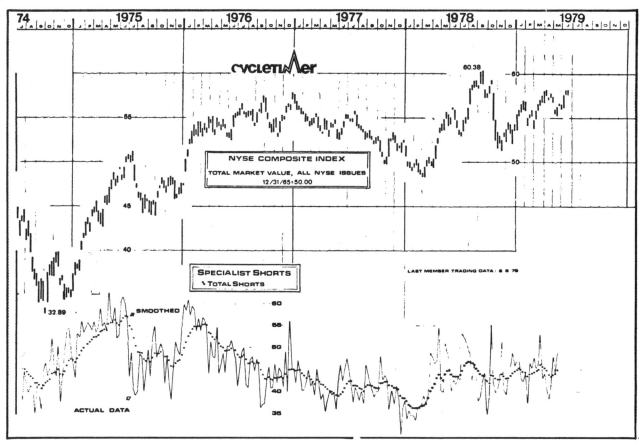

Specialist short sales peak near market tops and drop to low areas near market bottoms.

Source: *Cycletimer*, 861 Sixth Avenue, #808, San Diego, Calif. 92101.

**One major problem
in employing
the basic excessive
trading system,
and a promise of a
solution
to this problem**

We have, up to this point, been examining the use of excesses in the stock market from a more or less ideal position—making the assumption that the sine waves generated by plotting data above and below a neutral axis will, indeed, reverse direction at the proper boundaries. For the most part, your excessive waves will, in fact, behave properly, reversing direction more or less on schedule, thereby providing excellent buy and sell junctures for trading swings.

Unfortunately, the picture does not always remain that clear. For example, let's consider the chart of Cyprus Mines, Figure 7–12. The stock behaved very properly from May into November 1978, falling whenever it reached a level two points above its 30-week moving average and rising from levels that stood two points below the issue's 30-week moving average. Taken as a whole, Cyprus demonstrated typical behavior for a stock fluctuating within a well defined trading range.

The picture suddenly altered in January of 1979 when the issue exploded

FIGURE 7–12

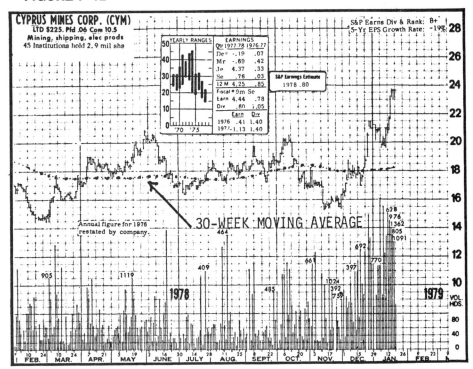

A trading range stock that suddenly exploded on the upside.

Source: *Trendline Daily Basis Stock Charts*, 345 Hudson Street, New York City, N.Y. 10014

from this range. The first sign the pattern was shifting emerged when the issue quickly rose to a level nearly four points above its 30-week moving average. The ability of the stock to generate such strong upside momentum indicated an impending shift from a trading range price fluctuation to the emergence of a strong trend perhaps about to take place. The issue then continued a steady rise—a rise that would have benefitted moving average traders, but which would have proven very troublesome to excessive swing traders; the issue remaining excessive for many weeks thereafter.

This is the sort of pattern that can confound traders who employ excessive swings alone for trading, just as issues that trade within confined boundaries tend to confound moving average players.

The trick, as you have probably deduced by now, is to know when to shift from an excessive trading system to a moving average or trend following trading system. Had you been alerted by the force of Cyprus' initial thrust in January 1979, you might have made that switch, thereby riding the stock to its March top.

There are certain indications, which can be measured mathematically, that point to those few occasions when you should switch from an excessive oscillator system to a trend following system. We shall, however, have to await some later chapters for those indications.

In the meantime, let's move into the first of our more sophisticated trading systems, one that combines moving average trend following devices with excessive swing oscillators.

8

The 10-week moving average swing system—A trading system for intermediate to long term market traders

Would you be interested in a trading system that would have produced the following results for the period 1966–79?

58.6 percent of trades on the long side were theoretically profitable. Only 41.4 percent of trades on the long side would have proven unprofitable (results based on the NYSE Index).

The average profitable trade on the long side would have gained 10.2 percent. The average unprofitable trade would have lost only 3.6 percent.

73.9 percent of trades on the short side would have proven profitable. Only 26.1 percent of trades would have proven unprofitable.

The average gain per profitable short side trade came to 6.5 percent. The average loss came to only 1.4 percent.

There were 52 trades—including both long trades and short trades—between June 1966 and February 1979, so you would average only about four trades per year, qualifying this system as a true intermediate market trading system.

These results were the results you would have hypothetically achieved had you applied the 10-week moving average swing system to the NYSE Index, 1966–79. We think they are excellent, and even if you decide not to employ the full system in its entirety, there are almost certainly some aspects of the rules employed which you will find useful in your current market operations, whatever the method of trading you employ.

And now, on to examine this effective and useful trading system itself.

The basic concepts underlying the 10-week moving average swing system

The trading rules underlying the 10-week moving average swing system have been derived from combining our research in moving averages with our research within the areas of excessive swing, market time cycles and momentum, and with our experience over the years with the actual behavior of stock prices. In other words, this trading system has been derived partially from computer research and partially from actual experience—when all is finally said and done, the basic crucible of any stock market technique. A certain amount of "retrofitting" did enter into the creation of the system. However, we believe the trading rules involved are logical and will remain essentially valid in the future.

The rules are codified fully and may be applied on a fully automatic basis. You may, however, from time to time, based on your own experience and common sense, make slight modifications in the parameters to suit market conditions. Our theoretical results are based on the codified trading rules. The system, itself, requires only a few minutes per day for posting. This is a market timing system and the presumption is made you will trade either mutual funds or a diversified portfolio of stocks based on market timing signals. Our research indicates that either procedure will produce results very comparable to results achieved by measuring the market averages on which the system is based. If you opt for vehicles more volatile than the market averages, your results should surpass the results achieved by the market averages themselves, all else (such as relative stock performance) being equal.

The ingredients of the 10-week moving average swing system

To maintain the data required to operate via the 10-week moving average swing system, you must plot the following tabulations on the following bases:

1. Each week, compute the 10-week moving average of the NYSE Index.
2. Each week, compute a 0.20 exponential average of the difference between the closing level of the NYSE Index and its 10-week moving average. The difference in level between the weekly close of the NYSE Index and the 10-week moving average of the Index is our trading oscillator.
3. Each *day,* measure the difference in level between that day's closing price of the NYSE Index and the 10-week moving average that you computed at the end of the previous week. This presumes that the last closing price of the NYSE Index is employed each week for computation of the 10-week moving average. This difference is plotted on a graph weekly, but maintained daily on your worksheet.
4. Once each week, plot the closing level of the NYSE Index for that week on your working graph.

Your daily worksheet will look like this:

1979 date	A Closing level, NYSE Index	B Latest computed 10-week M.A.	C Difference, A − B	.20 exponential average of C, computed weekly
4/2	56.73	55.88*	+ .85	+ .62
4/3	57.55		+1.67	
4/4	57.71		+1.83	
4/5	58.06		+2.18	
4/6	58.04	55.99	+2.05	+ .91
4/9	57.88		+1.89	
4/10 ...	58.18		+2.19	
4/11 ...	57.67		+1.68	
4/12 ...	57.53	56.16	+1.37	+1.00
4/13 ...	Holiday		Holiday	
4/16 ...	57.05		+ .89	
4/17 ...	57.05		+ .89	

* From week ending 3/30.

Do notice that the 10-week moving average, computed following the close of the last trading day each week, usually Friday, will be employed for comparison readings (Column C) each week on Friday, and from Monday through Thursday of the following week. This sometimes results in high variances between the Thursday and Friday readings, since the moving average base as well as the closing level of the NYSE Index will change between Thursday and Friday. If Friday is a holiday, then the Thursday close is used as the weekly close data for computation of the 10-week moving average.

You may, if you prefer, employ a 50-day moving average, updated daily, in lieu of a 10-week moving average, updated weekly. We are quite certain that you will secure similar results, although we did not formally test out this assumption.

Figures 8–1, 8–2, and 8–3 show the weekly closes of the NYSE Index, our trading oscillator, which represents the week-ending differences between the close of the index and its 10-week moving average (Column C in the worksheet), and the 0.20 exponential average of these differences (dotted lines on the bottom scale of the graph).

Drawn also are the excessive swing areas for this indicator. The areas including ±2.00 represent normal excessive swing levels. The areas including ±4.00 represent extreme swing areas—areas which, as we shall see, carry special significance.

Trading rules for the 10-week moving average swing system

Buy rules

Code 1. You may take long positions according to Code 1 signals, immediately following any week the trading indicator (bottom scale of chart, Column C on worksheet) falls below "0" then etches out a double bottom

FIGURE 8–1
**Action signals generated by the 10-week moving
average swing system method, 1966–69**

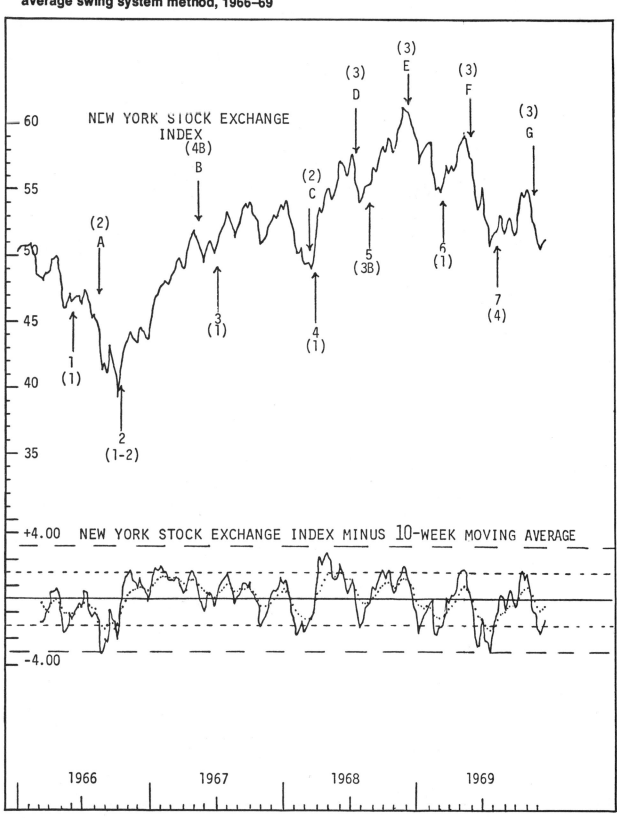

FIGURE 8–2
Action signals generated by the 10-week moving average swing system, 1970–73

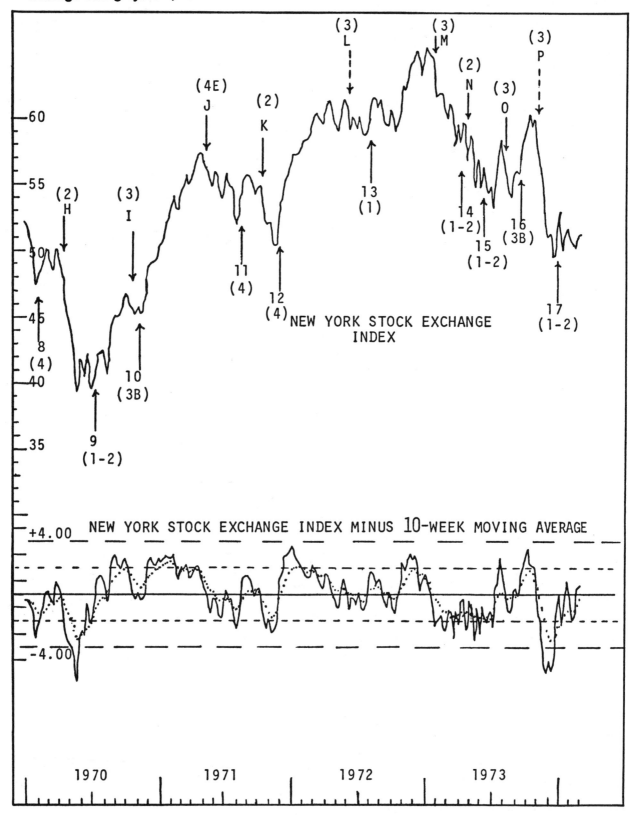

FIGURE 8-3
Action signals generated by the 10-week moving
average swing system, 1974-79

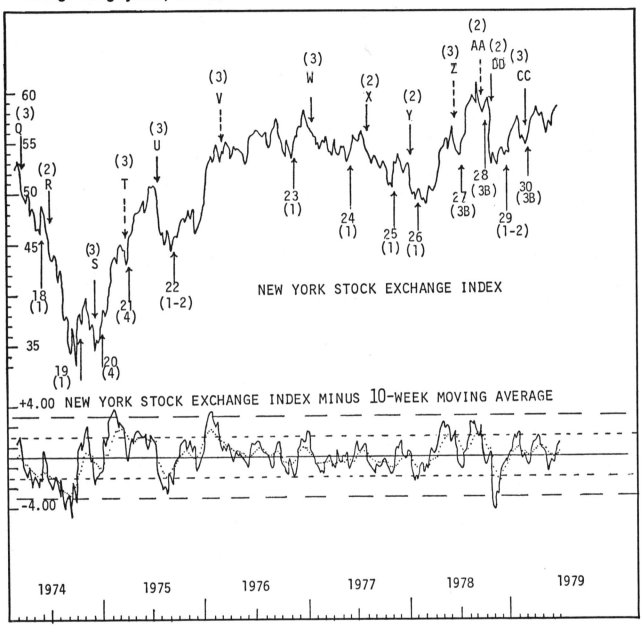

formation upon turning up, *providing that the indicator does not reach a low of −3.00 during the decline.*

A double bottom is defined as two spikes, the second higher than or virtually identical in level to the first, and, in any case, no lower than .20 in level than the first. These spikes should be spaced at least three weeks apart in time.

Code 2. Code 2 signals are employed following those occasions when the trading oscillator falls to below −3.00 on its most recent downswing.

Following the decline to −3.00, and a turnup in the indicator, you must wait at least *four weeks,* measured from the lowest low of the indicator, and must see thereafter a clearly rising double bottom formation in the indicator, a double bottom in which the second spike down does *not* reach a lower level than the first. If the second spike reaches a lower level than the first, you apply the four-week waiting period and rising double bottom test to that spike. Should a third spike reach a lower level still, you would apply the waiting and testing rule to that spike.

For an example of this rule, refer to Figure 8–1, on the left, the period between August and October 1966. The indicator dipped to below −4.00 during August of 1966, before turning up. A four-week wait was therefore required before long positions could be assumed. In October, the indicator once again fell to below −3.00, to −3.03. However, since this reading was clearly above the −4.06 reading rendered on August 26, a buy signal was generated on October 14, 1966 when the indicator rose from −3.03 to −.76.

You can see on Figure 8–1 the clearly defined rising double bottom formation traced out between August and October 1966. The buy signal in October proved excellent, occurring only one week after the actual lows of the 1966 bear market.

Code 3a. If you have previously sold because of a downside penetration of the 10-week moving average (described under selling rules), you may repurchase on any day that 10-week moving average is repenetrated to the upside, providing that the previous sell signal developed following the indicator's rise above and descent below the +2.00 level.

Code 3b. You repurchase immediately following any sell signal on any day that the NYSE Index rises to a level 1.00 above its immediately preceding highs.

Code 4. If the indicator falls to below −2.00 (but not as far as −3.00), you may repurchase, even in the absence of a double bottom formation, if the indicator rises back upwards through "0", which means the market index has risen through its 10-week moving average.

In all cases, place a stop loss point 1.00 unit below the lows set on the most recent downswing in the NYSE Index.

Sell rules

Code 1. Shorter term traders may sell (and even, if nimble, sell short) on any day the trading oscillator falls from above +2.00 to below +2.00. In reviewing Figures 8–1, 8–2 and 8–3, you will see that, following such occurrences, the market rarely rises to any degree—almost always falling thereafter, fairly quickly, to a level below your selling level.

However, such signals do produce smaller profits, on average, than less sensitive signals, and we recommend this practice only to very aggressive traders, willing to step back into the market quickly upon any market reversal to the upside.

You may employ this rule, in any event, as a cautionary rule—avoiding purchases when the market has risen to the +2.00 area (sign of excessive, overbought condition) and employing initial repenetrations of the +2.00 line to weed out weaker holdings.

In calculating our trading results, we did *not* include any Code 1 sell signals.

Code 2. Sell, if, shortly following a buy, the lows registered by the market on the preceding second spike down or on the preceding downswing are violated by 1.00 on the NYSE Index. This is your stop loss protection against serious market decline.

If you are selling short, or have just sold, employ a level 1.00 above the most recent market highs as your stop-loss point if you are short selling or as your re-entry point if you have simply sold. This is your protection against taking serious loss on short sales or against missing strong market recovery moves, following sell signals.

Code 3.   If the trading oscillator reaches +3.00 during a market rise, indicating particularly strong momentum to the market advance, do *not* sell until the market index falls to below its 10-week moving average. Hold positions until this takes place. *Do not sell short on a downside penetration of a 10-week moving average which immediately follows on the market's achieving a +3.00 reading,* with the following exceptions:

a.   If the market has, within the previous six months, achieved a +3.00 reading, and there has been an intervening sell signal, you can sell short on the next market sell signal even if the oscillator has reached +3.00. Do notice, that some intervening sell signal must follow upon the first occasion the market reaches the +3.00 level within a six month period before you can sell short following such a reading.

For an example, refer to Figure 3, 1978. The oscillator reached the +3.00 area during two clearly defined periods. However, a sell signal did separate these periods and the two peaks above +3.00 were spaced within a six month span of time. Therefore, a sell short signal could be observed following the sell signal of October 19.

b.   You may sell short (and admittedly, this does involve a bit of subjectivity) if, after reaching a level of +3.00, the oscillator falls to below "0" without even one weekly "uptick" in the indicator between its maximum reading and the point at which it falls below "0." This pattern occurs very rarely—almost always following strong bear market rallies. Refer to October–November 1973 for an example.

Code 4.   You should sell and sell short on *4a,* a violation of a previous low point in the .20 exponential average of the trading oscillator or *4b,* the third successive penetration to the downside of the +2.00 level of the trading oscillator. Short sales should be initiated following this penetration even if the trading oscillator has recently reached the +3.00 area.

For an example, refer to Figure 8–2, the period January–April 1971. The oscillator, during February, managed to reach +3.00 (exactly), which would have forestalled short selling had the market index immediately fallen to below its 10-week moving average. This did not, however, take place. A series of three penetrations upwards through then downwards through the

+2.00 level developed. The third of such a series should always be acted on, action consisting of both a sell and a short sell action.

How typical stock market behavior explains the effectiveness of the trading rules of the 10-week moving average swing system

We can see that the 10-week moving average swing system does involve both some judgment and some care in posting and interpreting the signals involved. It is, in fact, something more than a simple moving average crossing system or a simple excessive swing trading system: it combines both elements into a total trading system making use of the virtues of each, while avoiding the majority of pitfalls of both.

It may help in the application of this system if you understand the logical bases of the rules involved.

Buy rules, explanations

Code 1. The double bottom formation in stock trading oscillators is generally an excellent buy formation. The formations of rising double bottoms show that downside momentum has been decreasing. By requiring that the double bottom take place below the "0" level, we are increasing the odds you will be buying into an area of market weakness rather than strength.

By requiring a period of three weeks between spike bottoms, we are making use of the 3-week market cycle, described in Chapter 10, which will become an integral element in our Time-Trend-Momentum Trading System.

Code 2. As we have observed, excessive market conditions provide excellent signals at their turning points *except when they become very excessive*. Very excessive market momentum conditions—such as conditions which exist when the market falls below its 10-week moving average by as much as 3.00 units—almost always imply that the market move in force is very powerful, too powerful to reverse rapidly. Some further market declines following readings in the trading oscillator of −3.00 almost always take place, particularly in the absence of a rising double bottom in the indicator, a pattern which indicates diminishing momentum to market declines taking place.

Empirically, our research has indicated to us that a period of three to six weeks is usually required following the maximum downside readings of very excessive oversold conditions before the market will be ready to embark on a new advance. Therefore, the Code 2 buy signal was instituted, a signal which builds in a time delay to allow for a slowdown in downside momentum before purchases can be made.

Code 2 rule signals come into play rarely, generally during the final phases of bear market selling climaxes. However, this rule can prevent many serious losses since the temptation to purchase prematurely during final bear market phases can be great. During such periods, the stock market provides oversold readings, stocks appear cheap, and periods of sharp decline may become interspersed with sharp daily bear market advances. The presence of oversold conditions—compounded by investment advisors who do not fully understand that oversold means "Buy!" only when oversold does not become too oversold—lures many investors into premature purchases, purchases made before bear markets have fully run their course. The purchase delay implicit in the Code 2 trading rules should reduce your own premature purchases.

You may refer to the bear market bottoms of 1966, 1970, 1974, and 1978. Review the positions of the trading oscillator just weeks before the final lows were reached and draw your own conclusions.

Code 3. The 10-week moving average is one of the stronger of the moving averages for trading. We have, therefore, employed it as the moving average trigger for re-entry into the market following sell signals.

Do notice how the trading system is constructed. We attempt to institute at least a portion of our purchases and sales some distance away from the 10-week moving average, at points of excessive swing, either overbought or oversold. The use of excessive condition in this manner often provides a "jump" on the typical moving average crossing system. However, once a strong trend is in motion, we use the moving average for protection and as a trend following action trigger.

Code 4. Self-explanatory. We hope that our buy signals will be triggered in market low areas, but lest we miss a strong market move, we can fall back on the basic moving average crossing system.

Sell signals

Code 1. Here, we are relying strictly upon the basic rules of excessive swing. Given the likelihood that a ±2.00 deviation from a 10-week moving average represents an excessive swing for the NYSE Index, we are employing as a sell signal some sign that a reversal is taking place. The majority of such sells will prove at least temporarily profitable. However, by trading short term, you assume a greater risk of missing some really fine market moves. We advise most longer term investors to ignore Code 1 signals. Shorter term traders should employ the *Time-Trend-Momentum Trading System* as an alternative.

Code 2. Self-explanatory. The majority of buy signals made while the market lies deeply within oversold territory will produce profit *eventually*, but for the purposes of preservation of capital, some stop-loss protection should be maintained.

The violation of a previous reaction low does constitute a sell and sell short signal in and of itself. Our research into market reversal systems (Chapter 9) indicates that it will, on balance, pay to sell short upon violations of previous low points.

Code 3. This is another time delay rule, designed to keep investors in the market until strong uptrends lose momentum and clearly show signs of coming to an end.

The *Code 2 buy rule* is designed to keep you out of the market during periods of strong downside market momentum, building in a time delay until downside momentum ebbs and "good" market bottoms are completed. The *Code 3 sell rule* is designed to accomplish the same end, but this time on the

84

sell side, allowing you to remain in the stock market until advances are fully spent.

The stock market rarely achieves sufficient momentum to carry the price level of the NYSE Index to a point +3.00 units above its 10-week moving average. Such readings are generally seen only at the onsets of either fresh bull markets or at the onsets of particularly strong intermediate advances. The attainment of a +3.00 reading is our signal to convert an excessive swing signal into a trend following signal. In other words, if momentum of sufficient strength develops, this indicates the stock market is likely to continue to rise. We hope to stay with that rise for as long as possible.

If oversold readings frequently confound the trader during strong market downtrends, overbought readings (such as +3.00 on this indicator) frequently lure the unwary into prematurely bearish market positions. Short sales may be put out prematurely, or sales may be made simply because the market appears overbought. Code 3 prevents premature selling as well as premature short selling.

Readers may wonder why, if we employ the 10-week moving average for selling following a reading of +3.00 on the indicator, we do not await a 10-week moving average crossing following a reading of −3.00 before taking long positions in the stock market. The answer lies in the typical differences shown between stock market behavior at market bottoms and stock market behavior at market tops. At market bottoms, prices often reverse very sharply—in the form of a spike, perhaps a double spike. If we await a crossing through a 10-week moving average at such junctures we will frequently lose a goodly portion of subsequent market advances. Therefore, our aim is to act quickly, right near the bottom.

At market tops, conversely, prices tend to roll over gradually, a tendency which allows the 10-week moving average time to "catch up" to prices. Fewer points are usually lost in the trend reversal process.

Why you should almost never sell short following a Code 3 sell signal

We refer you once again to Figures 8–1, 8–2 and 8–3. Notice how rarely market declines continue for any length of time following the first sell signals, which in themselves follow the indicator's ability to reach +3.00. Very strong upside momentum rarely gives way immediately to serious market decline. In fact, tax minded investors can probably profitably ignore the first sell signals following +3.00 readings altogether in hopes of achieving long term capital gains.

Readings in the trading oscillator of as high as +3.00 have been recorded during 1968, 1970, 1971, 1973, 1975, 1976, and 1978—almost always during periods of very strong market advance. Historically, the odds are simply very strong that any short sales put out on such occasions will be doomed, if not to loss, than to minimal profit at best. We suggest the awaiting of higher percentage opportunities to play the short side, all the more so since short selling, as a rule, provides poorer risk-reward ratios than the purchasing of stocks.

If readings of +3.00 indicate such powerful market strength, then why do we allow short selling upon the attainment of the second of two such readings within a six month period? Here, too, we have opted to follow empirical experience. We suggest once again that readers peruse Figures 8–1, 8–2 and 8–3. You may observe that strong market advances, even during bull markets, tend to wear themselves out following two major upwaves. Although entire bull markets may consist of three large waves up, these waves generally will be interrupted by at least one very significant market decline.

Refer, for example, to the early 1975 period. The trading indicator we employ rose very sharply as the 1974 bear market came to an end, reaching a level of +4.76 in February, 1975—a very strong reading, implying considerable latent strength in the stock market. The sell signal in April (based on a downside penetration of the 10-week moving average) proved short lived, the market rapidly resuming its advance, which carried into July. However, by the time a secondary peak was achieved, the advance had just about exhausted itself—stock prices were ready for the strong decline that took place into August 1975.

A similar situation developed during 1978. You can see the paired succession of +3.00 readings that took place during the spring and late summer of 1978. The second reading during this period also exhausted the market's upside potential. If you track the Trendline Barometer of Issues That Lie Above Their 30-week Moving Averages, cited in the last chapter, you may note the double peaks in that indicator etched during both 1975 and 1978. On both occasions, the market lay in a vulnerable position following its continuation of the first legs up via the second subsequent waves.

Code 4. The Code 4 selling rules have been created to meet those market situations in which prices roll over, but do not quickly fall below their 10-week moving averages. The Code 4 rules provide an early jump on moving average signals under conditions which favor a rapid decline in stock prices. Do notice that downside penetrations of the 10-week moving average do not constitute sell signals in and of themselves. Attainment first of an overbought condition is a pre-requisite. This trading system is designed to reduce the number of moving average whipsaws which take place within neutral market areas.

Code 4 states that you should sell and sell short upon the third successive penetration down through the +2.00 oscillator line even if the 10-week moving average has not been previously violated, and even if a +3.00 reading has been recently attained. Intermediate market movements, as well as primary trend movements, frequently consist of three clearly defined waves, a concept derived from the well-known Elliott Wave Theory. The succession of three penetrations down through the +2.00 line both occupies time—time required to work through the implications of market strength created by the initial powerful +3.00 readings (presuming they have occurred)—and also usually represents the three waves, which are all we can anticipate in any market move. Therefore, the third of such successive penetrations is likely to conclude a third intermediate rising wave of stock prices and is likely to initiate more serious declines to follow.

We employ the .20 exponential of the trading oscillator as a measurement of the trend of momentum in the absence of other clearly defined signals. Use of this exponential average will occur rarely—other signals usually precede a downtrend in this indicator—but we employ *Code 4b* as a back-up to other signal systems.

Tracking the 10-week moving average swing system over the years: A case history of an excellent intermediate trading system

We have marked on Figures 8–1, 8–2 and 8–3 the areas within which all trading signals—long, sell, and sell short—would have hypothetically developed during the period 1966–1978. Each buy signal is marked with a rising arrow, accompanied by a number, designating the number of the signal, and a code, designating the code of the rule which created the signal. Each sell signal is marked with a falling arrow, a designating number, and a code number. Sell signals which are not sell short signals are marked with a dashed, rather than a completely formed, arrow. The majority of sell signals are also sell short signals.

Table 8–1 shows the dates, codes, and results of all buy signals hypothetically rendered between 1966 and the conclusion of 1978. You can match the numbers and codes on Table 8–1 to the numbers and codes which appear on Figures 8–1, 8–2 and 8–3. Table 8–2 shows the results, dates and codes of all short sales which would have taken place during the period, 1966-conclusion of 1978. These can also be matched to the numbers which appear on Figures 8–1, 8–2 and 8–3.

Again, observe that crossings of the 10-week moving averages do not constitute buy and sell signals unless specific prior conditions exist. Frequent whipsaws are therefore eliminated, and capital is protected by use of stop-loss orders placed at 1.00 unit below previous low points in the NYSE Index.

Results of trading via the 10-week moving average swing system

Summaries of trading results appear at the bottoms of Tables 8–1 and 8–2. Had you employed the 10-week moving average swing system from 1966 through 1978, you would have 1) participated in all significant market advances that took place during that period of time, 2) avoided, if long, any of the severe market declines that took place during the period and/or, 3) participated fully on the short side during all severe market declines.

The high percentage of success achieved via the sell signals generated by this system is particularly worthy of note—the majority of investors probably finding it much more difficult to determine favorable selling areas than favorable buying areas. Even if you do not employ this trading system in its entirety, you should certainly make use of the sell signals generated via the system's selling rules. They certainly appear to carry particular effectiveness.

In assessing the usefulness of this system for you, we suggest you keep in mind the following:

1. Both the buy signals and the sell short signals appear to produce profit a clear majority of the time.

TABLE 8–1
Results of buy signals employing the 10-week moving average swing system, 1966–79, presuming that purchases of the NYSE Index were made on buy signals and held until sell signals were received

Buy signals				Sell signals					
Date buy	Signal number	Action code	Price level, NYSE index	Date sell	Signal number	Action code	Price level, NYSE index	Point change	Percent change
6/10/66	1	1	46.78	8/1/66	A	2	44.60	−2.18	−4.7%
10/14	2	1–2	41.21	5/9/67	B	4B	51.40	+10.19	+24.7%
7/7/67	3	1	50.91	3/4/68	C	2	48.86	−2.05	−4.0
3/8/68	4	1	49.43	7/22	D	3	55.81	+ 6.38	+12.9
9/4	5	3B	56.00	12/23	E	3	59.67	+ 3.67	+ 6.6
3/7/69	6	1	55.33	6/2/69	F	3	57.58	+ 2.25	+ 4.1
8/22	7	4	53.11	11/20	G	3	53.04	− .07	−0.1
2/27/70	8	4	50.10	4/16/70	H	2	47.44	−2.66	−5.3
7/2	9	1–2	39.64	10/30	I	3	45.28	+ 5.64	+14.2
11/2	10	3B	45.44	4/20/71	J	4B	57.03	+11.59	+25.5
8/20/71	11	4	54.38	10/20	K	2	52.85	−1.53	−2.8
12/1	12	4	52.73	4/25/72	L	3	59.75	+ 7.02	+13.3
7/7/72	13	1	60.15	1/22/73	M	3	64.18	+ 4.03	+ 6.7
5/4/73	14	1–2	58.77	5/14	N	2	56.20	−2.57	−4.4
6/29/73	15	1–2	54.84	8/13	O	3	55.23	+ .39	− .7
9/19	16	3B	56.90	11/2	P	3	57.61	+ .71	+ 1.2
1/16/74	17	1–2	51.16	3/28/74	Q	3	50.63	− .53	−1.0
5/24	18	1	46.59	7/1	R	2	44.90	−1.69	−3.6
10/11	19	4	37.39	11/19	S	3	36.19	−1.20	−3.2
1/2/75	20	4	37.06	4/4/75	T	3	42.98	+ 5.92	+16.0
4/9	21	4	43.88	7/22	U	3	49.12	+ 5.24	+11.9
9/19	22	1–2	45.53	1/9/76	V	3	53.41	+ 7.88	+17.3
11/19/76	23	1	54.61	1/12/77	W	3	55.95	+ 1.34	+ 2.5
3/4/77	24	1	54.98	5/26	X	2	53.06	−1.92	−3.5
11/11	25	1	52.70	1/9/78	Y	2	50.05	−2.65	−5.0
2/3/78	26	1	49.72	6/20	Z	3	54.22	+ 4.50	+ 9.1
7/14	27	3B	54.82	9/19	AA	3	57.84	+ 3.02	+ 5.5
10/9	28	3B	58.90	10/19	BB	2	55.71	−3.19	−5.4
12/22	29	1–2	53.77	2/7/79	CC	3	54.47	+ .70	+ 1.3

The above results are based upon hypothetical research; no actual trading took place through use of this system for the majority of the period shown. Commission costs, dividends, and taxes are not included in the above tabulations.

Summary of results of trades reflected in table 8–1

Number of profitable trades: 17

Number of unprofitable trades: 12

Average number of points gained per profitable trade: +4.73

Average number of points lost per unprofitable trade: −1.85

Average percentage gain per profitable trade: 10.2%

Average percentage loss per unprofitable trade: −3.6%

Total net points gained (1966–79): +58.23

Results of buy and hold, NYSE index (1966–79): +7.69

TABLE 8–2
**Results of short sale signals employing the 10-week
moving average swing system, 1966–79, presuming
that short sales of the NYSE Index were made on short
sale signals and held until cover short sale signals
were received**

Sell short signals				Cover short signals					
Date short sale	Signal number	Action code	Price level, NYSE index	Date cover	Signal number	Action code	Price level, NYSE index	Point change	Percent change
8/1/66	A	2	44.60	10/14/66	2	1–2	41.21	+3.39	+ 8.2%
5/9/67	B	4B	51.40	7/7/67	3	1	50.91	+ .49	+ 1.0
3/4/68	C	2	48.86	3/8/68	4	1	49.43	− .57	−1.2
7/22	D	3	55.81	9/4	5	3B	56.00	− .19	− .3
12/23	E	3	59.67	3/7/69	6	1	55.33	+4.34	+ 7.8
6/2/69	F	3	57.58	8/22	7	4	53.11	+4.47	+ 8.4
11/20	G	3	53.04	2/27/70	8	4	50.10	+2.94	+ 5.9
4/16/70	H	2	47.44	7/2	9	1–2	39.64	+7.80	+19.7
10/30	I	3	45.28	11/2	10	3B	45.44	− .16	− .4
4/20/71	J	4B	57.03	8/20/71	11	4	54.38	+2.65	+ 4.9
10/20	K	2	52.85	12/1	12	4	52.73	+ .12	+ .2
1/22/73	M	3	64.18	5/4/73	14	1–2	58.77	+5.41	+ 9.2
5/14	N	2	56.20	6/29	15	1–2	54.84	+1.36	+ 2.5
8/13	O	3	55.23	9/19	16	3B	56.90	−1.67	−2.9
3/28/74	Q	3	50.63	5/24/74	18	1	46.59	+4.04	+ 8.7
7/1	R	2	44.90	10/11	19	4	37.39	+7.51	+20.1
11/19	S	3	36.19	1/2/75	20	4	37.06	− .87	−2.3
7/22/75	U	3	49.12	9/19	22	1–2	45.53	+3.59	+ 7.9
1/12/77	W	3	55.95	3/4/77	24	1	54.98	+ .97	+ 1.8
5/26/77	X	2	53.06	11/11	25	1	52.70	+ .36	+ .7
1/9/78	Y	2	50.05	2/3/78	26	1	49.72	+ .33	+ .7
10/17	BB	2	55.71	12/22	29	1–2	53.77	+1.94	+ 3.6
2/7/79	CC	3B	54.47	2/12/79	30	3B	55.04	− .57	−1.0

The above results are based on hypothetical research. No actual trading took place via this system for most of the period involved. Commission costs, dividends, and taxes are not included in the above tabulations.

Summary of results of trades reflected in table 8–2
    Number of profitable short sales: 17
    Number of unprofitable short sales: 6
    Average number of points gained per profitable short sale: +3.04
    Average number of points lost per unprofitable short sale: −0.67
    Average percentage gain per profitable trade: +6.5%
    Average percentage loss per unprofitable trade: −1.4%

2. The average gain per buy signal, measured in terms of market average (the New York Stock Exchange Index), is nearly three times the size of the average loss.
3. The average gain per sell short signal (measured in terms of the New York Stock Exchange Index) is nearly five times the size of the average loss. Selling and selling short via these signals does appear to be a relatively low risk maneuver.

Assessing the bottom line: What can you anticipate in the way of a rate of return by using the 10-week moving average swing system?

Figure 8–4 shows the results hypothetically achieved had you traded "shares of the New York Stock Exchange Index" in accord with the signals represented in Tables 8–1 and 8–2. The middle scale shows the results of a buy on buy signal and sell on sell signal strategy. We have presumed that proceeds from sales were retained in cash between sell and buy signals, but have not included any computation of interest derived from such cash. Nor have we included the effects of commission costs, dividend payouts or taxes. You can obviously not trade "shares of the New York Stock Exchange Index" but you can trade their virtual equivalent, no-load mutual funds, or a well-diversified stock portfolio. We wish to emphasize that results are purely hypothetical and that no guarantees can be made for future performance of this or any other system presented in this book.

Based on the signals listed, a $10,000 investment into the New York Stock Exchange reinvested fully upon every buy signal would have grown between February 1970 and February 1979 to $22,631.91. This amounts to a compounded annualized rate of return of 9.42 percent. This may not sound like much to become excited about, but keep in mind that dividend payouts and income from cash positions are not included. During the period of time for which these tabulations are made, the New York Stock Exchange Index rose from 50.10 to 54.47—an annualized rate of gain of only 0.94 percent, just about one-tenth the rate of gain you could have achieved had you traded on signals generated by the 10-week moving average swing system.

Try going both ways for really good returns

Had you followed all signals generated by the 10-week moving average swing system, buying on buy signals, selling on sell signals and selling short on sell short signals—employing all available capital at each transaction— theoretically you would have seen your $10,000 grow between 1970 and 1979 to $46,005.81. This amounts to an annualized rate of return of 18.3 percent, nearly eighteen times the growth of the New York Stock Exchange Index over the same period!

Taken all told, the results certainly do seem to be worth the few minutes required each day to post the data—or would you prefer to rely upon emotion, guesswork or perhaps the advice of your friendly investment adviser instead?

FIGURE 8–4

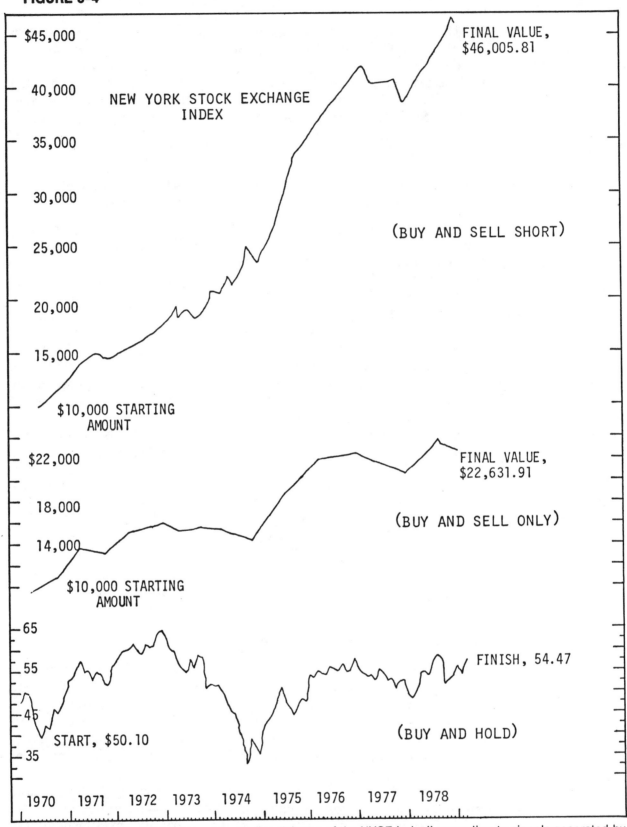

Hypothetical rates of return achieved by trading "shares of the NYSE Index" according to signals generated by the 10-week moving average swing system, 1970–1979. (All results are hypothetical; no actual trading took place by use of this system for the period shown.)

Applying the 10-week moving average swing system market signals to a portfolio of popular trading stocks

We have mentioned previously we have been emphasizing market timing signals as opposed to stock timing signals because by operating via market generated signals, you have to 1) maintain only one or a few indicators on a regular basis, and 2) you should find a very close correlation between your general market timing signals and the results you may expect to receive if you trade a diversified portfolio of common stocks based upon such signals. So far, we have accepted this statement on faith. The time has now come to weigh some hard evidence relating to the matter.

Table 8–3 reflects the results of trading a selected group of issues on the basis of buy and sell signals generated by the 10-week moving average swing system—signals which appear in Table 8–1. The presumption has been made that stocks were purchased on the days market buy signals were rendered, and sold at their closing prices on the days of market sell signals. No adjustments have been made for commission and dividend factors.

TABLE 8–3
Results of trading a portfolio of selected stocks, long side only, based on market signals generated by the 10-week moving average swing system, 1970–1978

Issue	Number of profitable trades	Number of unprofitable trades	Average point gain, profitable trade	Average point loss, unprofitable trade	Average percent change per trade
Schlumberger	13	9	+ 5.03	− 2.33	+ 6.8%
Minnesota Mining	12	10	5.98	3.31	+ 3.8%
Atlantic Richfield	11	9	5.10	3.24	+ 5.4
Raytheon	10	12	5.18	3.24	+10.7
Digital Equipment	11	9	6.92	2.79	+10.6
Teledyne	12	10	9.14	2.74	+16.8
Avon	11	11	8.18	6.02	+ 3.3
Burroughs	12	10	10.28	4.98	+ 4.7
Halliburton	13	9	5.55	3.98	+ 7.0
Honeywell	11	11	10.30	8.03	+ 5.1
Boeing	13	8	3.78	1.59	+12.6
Corning Glass	13	9	13.08	9.05	+ 8.8
Hewlett Packard	14	8	11.89	6.31	+ 9.6
DuPont	15	7	11.30	6.12	+ 4.7
IBM	11	11	29.56	10.94	+ 4.6
Texas Instruments	13	9	11.09	6.55	+ 6.7
American Broadcasting	12	9	3.50	1.99	+ 9.8
Aetna Life and Cas.	12	8	3.83	2.47	+ 6.3
Averages	12.2	9.4	+ 8.9	− 4.8	+ 7.7

Trades which resulted in no change are excluded from first four columns but included in final column. Results are hypothetical and do not include effects of commissions, dividends, and taxes.

Table 8–4 reflects the results of trading this group of stocks on sell short signals, selling short at the closing price when market sell short signals were rendered and covering at the closing daily price when market cover short signals were received. The stocks selected were chosen more or less at random as representative of the "glamour" group most likely to track well with the market averages. No other selection criteria were applied; results of trading in this manner did not lead to the inclusion or exclusion of any issue.

Results on the buy side conformed very nicely to market buy signals, although, in general, individual stocks showed greater percentage movement per signal than did the market average we employed by itself. You can see that the majority of buy signals proved profitable, that the average gain was nearly double the size of the average loss, and that the average trade produced a gain of 7.7 percent—considerably higher than the average change in the New York Stock Exchange Index itself, measured on a per transaction

TABLE 8–4
Results of selling short a selected portfolio of stocks on market short sale signals generated by the 10-week moving average swing system, 1970–1978

Issue	Number of profitable short sales	Number of unprofitable short sales	Average number of points gained, profitable trades	Average number of points lost, unprofitable trades	Average percentage change per trade, all short sales
Schlumberger	7	9	+ 2.04	−4.08	−3.6%
Minnesota Mining	7	9	7.27	1.97	+3.3
Atlantic Richfield	7	8	2.32	2.60	−0.7
Raytheon	9	7	1.29	0.44	+3.8
Digital Equipment	6	9	5.26	2.61	+1.8
Teledyne	9	7	2.55	1.90	+5.5
Avon	10	5	5.46	3.53	+4.2
Burroughs	8	7	10.57	4.05	+3.8
Halliburton	10	6	3.10	3.10	+1.0
Honeywell	7	9	17.1	3.54	+6.2
Boeing	11	4	1.28	4.55	+4.8
Corning Glass	11	5	11.64	4.86	+8.3
Hewlett Packard	7	9	11.43	2.73	+4.7
Dupont	12	4	7.46	3.19	+3.0
IBM	9	7	24.12	7.76	+4.0
Texas Instruments	10	6	9.32	7.91	+3.5
ABC	9	6	2.05	1.78	+3.2
Aetna Life & Casualty	8	7	3.44	2.53	+2.4
Averages	8.7	6.9	+ 7.1	+3.1	+3.3%

Trades which resulted in no change are excluded from first four columns but included in final column. Results are hypothetical; no actual trading took place via this system for most of the period shown.

basis. Although results did vary, stock by stock, no issue showed an average loss when traded according to market signals generated by the 10-week moving average swing system.

Results on the short sale side produced similar configurations, although changes, on average, were of a lower magnitude than price changes generated by buy signals. This difference could, of course, be anticipated. Stocks generally provide greater upside than downside potential and trading systems on the long side generally prove more profitable than trading systems on the short side.

Sixteen of the eighteen issues sampled produced an average profit per short sale. The worst performers on the short side—Atlantic Richfield and Schlumberger—are both issues which lay in long term uptrends between 1970 and 1979. Only Schlumberger showed serious losses when traded short against market sell short signals. There did seem to be greater variations among the performances of the components of this portfolio on the short side than on the long side, but as a group, these issues performed well on both sides when traded by market signals. We do suggest that you emphasize weak issues when selling short and stronger issues when buying long.

Compounding your capital by trading individual stocks

IBM and Honeywell are two issues which, in our research, tracked well with a variety of trading systems—including the 10-week moving average swing system and the Time-Trend-Momentum Trading System, which we shall discuss in Chapters 12 and 13. Honeywell is the more volatile of the two issues, and provides greater price change per market swing. We would anticipate the most favorable returns from such issues, issues which swing broadly in price and which conform in their action to major market averages.

Figure 8–5 reflects the rates of return you would have hypothetically secured had you traded IBM on market signals generated by the 10-week moving average swing system. The middle scale on the chart shows the results of acting on buy and sell signals only. The upper scale reflects action on buy, sell and sell short signals. Full employment of capital is presumed for all signals. The lower scale shows the price movement of IBM itself. No adjustments have been made for commissions, dividends and taxes.

IBM rose in price during the period (February 1970–February 1979) from a price of 272 to a price of 298, an annualized rate of gain of only 1.01 percent per year. A $10,000 investment, made in February and compounded at each trade on the long side, would have theoretically grown during this same period to $23,353.16—a compounded annualized rate of return of 9.79 percent, almost exactly equivalent to the results we achieved by compounding the New York Stock Exchange Index on the same basis. A $10,000 investment in IBM, compounded on both buy and sell short signals, and traded via the market signals generated by the 10-week moving average swing system, would have grown to $41,481.77—a compounded annualized rate of return of 16.96 percent, nearly seventeen times the rate of return achieved via a buy and hold approach to the issue over the same period of time.

Honeywell (Figure 8–6) provides even more dramatic results. The issue

FIGURE 8–5

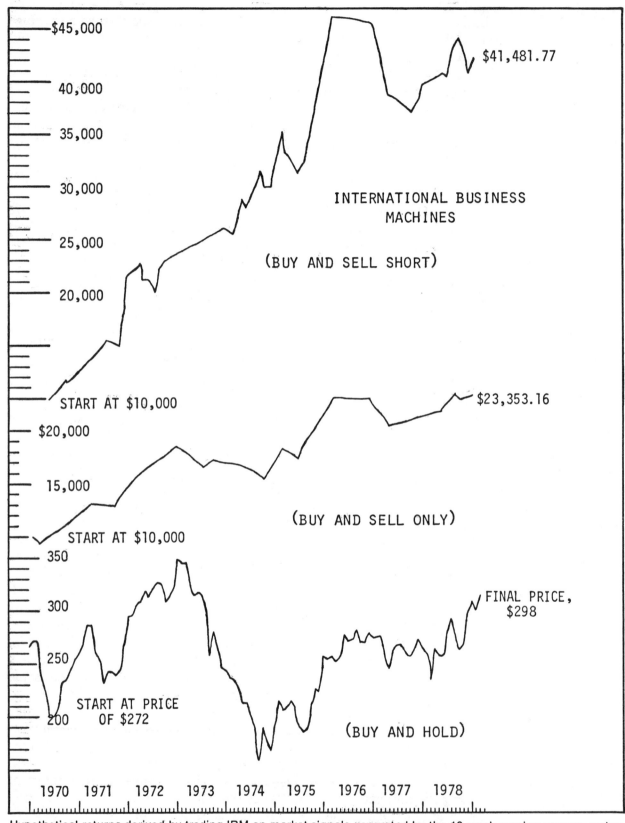

Hypothetical returns derived by trading IBM on market signals generated by the 10-week moving average swing system, 1970–1979. (Results are hypothetical; no actual trading took place via this method during the period shown.)

FIGURE 8–6

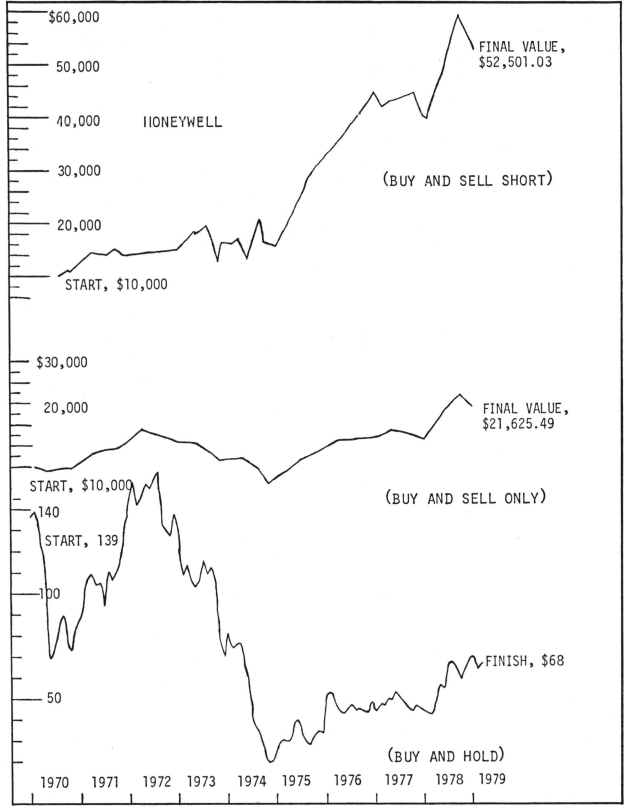

Hypothetical results achieved by trading Honeywell via market signals generated by the 10-week moving average swing system, 1970–1979. (Results are hypothetical; no actual trading took place via this method for the period shown.)

declined between 1970 and 1979 from a price of 139 to a price of 68—a rate of loss of 7.53 percent per year. Buy and sell signal trading would have seen $10,000 grow to $21,625.49, a compounded annualized rate of return of 8.87 percent. The spread between buy and hold and buy and sell on the trading system would have amounted to a difference of 16.4 percent per year.

Had you employed signals fully, buying on buys, selling on sells, and selling short on market sell short signals generated by the 10-week moving average swing system, you may well have seen your original $10,000 investment in Honeywell parlayed to $52,501.03—a compounded annualized rate of return of 20.04 percent. We have not, of course, adjusted for commissions, dividend costs or taxes. But nor have we considered the potential that both Honeywell and IBM offer for the use of listed put and call options in lieu of the underlying common. Such options provide great risk and must be considered highly speculative, but also provide additional profit opportunity because of the leverage possibilities involved in their use. The judicious employment of listed options does offer the potential of greatly magnifying profits which can be derived from profitable trading systems.

We hope you have found the 10-week moving average swing system of more than passing interest. Let's return now, once again, to somewhat lighter fare—a survey of market channel and other reversal trading systems.

9

Tracking market junctures
and catching market turns
with the channel reversal
and filter trading systems

Having explored a reasonably complex trading system, with diverse buying, selling and selling short rules of operation, let's move along now to some very basic systems: the channel reverse and filter systems. These systems, in and of themselves, may not necessarily prove particularly profitable, at least not particularly more so than the moving average systems we have been exploring, but they do have their own particular merits and will form an integral part of the Time-Trend-Momentum Trading System, which does happen to be a rather powerful trading system.

Moreover, the channel reverse systems may prove useful for the trader who simply refuses or does not have the time to perform even the minimal calculations required of our basic and more complex trading systems. These systems require virtually no calculations whatsoever, yet they provide short-term trading signals that are very powerful as short-term trading systems go, and intermediate trading signals that in many ways surpass trading systems based on moving averages.

The channel reversal trading system

Stocks do have a tendency to rise and fall within trading channels, channels that can more or less be created on stock charts by connecting significant high points and significant low points during price fluctuation. Channels can be drawn to reflect short term moves of the stock market, intermediate term moves and primary movements. In general, the broader the time span encompassed within the channel, the wider the channel and the broader the price fluctuations that lie within.

A short term channel, spanning a period of approximately three weeks, might carry within its band price fluctuations of perhaps 40 points on the Dow Industrial Average. An intermediate term trading channel might carry within its boundaries price fluctuations of approximately 60–100 points. Figure 9–1 illustrates a short term trading channel. Figure 9–2 illustrates an intermediate term trading channel, which includes, within its boundaries, several shorter term channels as well.

FIGURE 9–1
The short term trading channel of AMP Incorporated

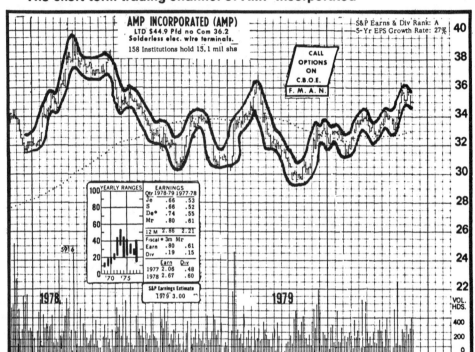

Source: *Trendline Daily Basis Stock Charts,* 345 Hudson Street, New York City, N.Y. 10014.

Channel reverse systems carry the following basic assumptions:

1. Once a channel reversal has taken place, the market can be expected to move sufficiently in the direction of the reversal to produce profit prior to a subsequent reversal.
2. Significant reversal junctures can be determined by either 1) the amount of price movement the market or a stock has made from a previous extreme peak or trough reading or 2) the number of previous trading days either surpassed in recent action or fallen beneath in recent action.

Channel reversal systems based on a degree of price movement are often referred to as "filter systems," and have received wide discussion in market literature. Readers are referred to *The stock market—theories and evidence,* by Lorie and Hamilton, Dow Jones-Irwin, 1973 (© 1973 by Richard D. Irwin, Inc.) and to *Filtered waves—Basic theory,* by Arthur A. Merrill, Analysis

FIGURE 9–2
The intermediate trading channel of Dresser

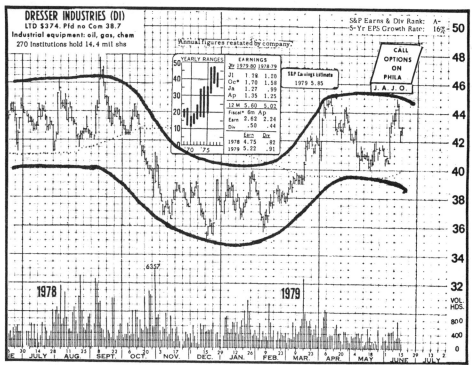

Source: *Trendline Daily Basis Stock Charts*, 345 Hudson Street, New York City, N.Y. 10014.

Press, Box 228, Chappaqua, New York, 10514, 1977. The former work takes the position that reversal systems are of little use to investors. Merrill, on the other hand, studies a five percent filter system carefully, and comes to the conclusion it can, indeed, be a powerful market tool. (In the five percent filter system, you buy whenever the market has risen by five percent from its latest low point. You sell whenever the market has declined by five percent from its most recent high point.)

Apparently, the usefulness of such systems remains a debatable point among theoreticians. To some degree, the issue rests on the amount of assumed transaction costs. Lorie and Hamilton, for example, concede that a five percent filter system will produce profit in excess of a naive buy and hold strategy—presuming that commission costs are excluded from any calculations. Given that assumption, such systems may well prove viable for the trading of no-load mutual funds and/or for stocks and stock options at those brokerage houses which offer deep commission discounts. There is no doubt that payment of full, listed stock commissions will heavily penalize any trading system.

Calendar channel reverse trading

We did not study reversal systems which employ a certain price reversal for the triggering of buy and sell signals via computer, although one of the authors (Appel) has successfully employed a .35 reversal factor of the NYSE Index for rapid short term trading. (You buy when the NYSE Index rises by .35 from a low; you sell when it falls by .35 from a high. Various combinations may be employed. For example, during strongly uptrended markets, you may await a downside move of greater amounts for selling. Readers are invited to experiment themselves.)

Channel reversal systems were investigated which require a penetration of a specified amount of previous days' pricing for signals to be triggered. The rules of such systems may be quickly summarized.

Rules for application of the calendar channel reverse trading system

1. Select the time frame for your reversal system. Short term traders will employ a reversal period of three to five days. Intermediate term traders will employ a reversal period of four to six weeks.
2. A *buy signal* is rendered whenever the stock (or stock market average) rises above the highest price level attained within the specified reversal period. A *sell signal* is rendered whenever the stock (stock market) falls below the lowest low point achieved during the specified reversal period.
3. In the case of individual stocks, best results are achieved via the employment of intra-day figures, and by acting intra-day, if necessary, via the employment of stop-loss and previously entered limit orders left with your broker. In the case of market averages (particularly the Dow Industrial Average), best results will be achieved if you employ closing penetrations of the highest and lowest closing averages for the periods employed. See Figures 9–3 and 9–4.

As a short term stock trader, you may opt to purchase and sell IBM whenever short term signals are rendered, and employ a four day time frame for your operations. You will purchase IBM whenever its price rises above the highest price reached by the stock at any time within the previous four trading sessions. You will sell (and, perhaps, sell short) whenever the price of IBM falls intra-day to below the lowest low reached by the stock over the previous four trading days.

As a mutual fund trader, you will take a long position in a mutual fund whenever the NYSE Index closes at a level which surpasses the highest closing level of the previous four trading days. You will sell when the NYSE Index falls to a level below the lowest close of the previous four trading days.

If you are an intermediate trader, you will lengthen the time periods involved to periods of four to six weeks. In other words, you will purchase IBM and cover short sales only if the issue rises to above its highest level, attained intra-day, over the previous 20–30 trading days, depending upon the exact period you select. You will sell your long positions and put out short sales when IBM falls to below its lowest level of the previous four to six weeks.

Analysis of hypothetical results

In assessing the results of this trading system, we presumed that only one transaction would be made each day in a stock, although the possibility does

FIGURE 9–3

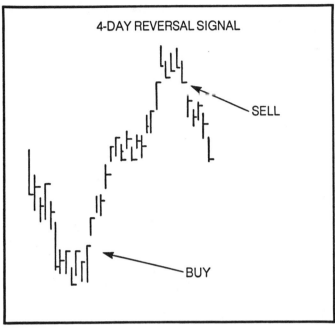

4-DAY REVERSAL SIGNAL

SELL

BUY

In the 4-day reversal system you buy on a close that exceeds each of the four previous closings. You sell on a close that falls below all of the four previous closes.

exist that particularly wide intra-day fluctuations could carry it first above and then below the previous four day price range. Market average results were computed at the closing levels of the market average employed. For the purposes of this study, the NYSE Index was employed, although actual trading experience has revealed that other market indices such as the advance-decline line and the Dow Industrial Average can be employed as alternatives.

We are presuming, of course, that transactions can be made at the exact signal levels—a questionable assumption in practice since it may be impossible to actually transact at those levels in a rapidly moving market. In assessing the suitability of this system for yourself, we suggest that you assume that actual transactions will take place at least ¼ point range away from the signal levels for stocks in either direction.

Results of trading automatically by the channel reversal method

Some surprisingly favorable results were obtained, employing the short term signals for the market averages and by employing somewhat longer term signals to higher priced, individual stocks. Let's examine some of the best of the time frames involved.

The channel reverse system and the market averages

Table 9–1 applies the channel reverse system to the NYSE Index. We are presuming in this case that a signal is rendered whenever the NYSE Index

FIGURE 9–4

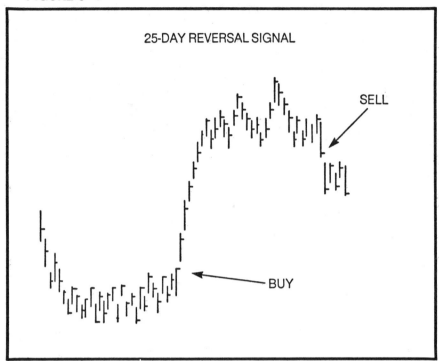

In the 25-day channel reversal system, you buy on a new 25-day high; you sell on a new 25-day low.

closes either above or below its highest or lowest closing level for the number of days specified in the table. If you choose to apply this method to individual stocks, you must use intra-day penetrations for satisfactory results. However, useful results may be achieved via the market averages as "market signals" if closing levels are employed.

Analysis of results

As an automatic, short term trading system, the four-day reversal system appears clearly superior to the short term basic moving average systems, including the straight moving average systems, the weighted moving average systems and the exponential systems.

In terms of total points gained, the four-day reversal system produced greater profits than the 10-day exponential average in six of the eight years from 1970–1977. The percentage of profitable trades runs higher by use of the 4-day reversal system as well, although risk per transaction also runs a bit higher, because the stop-loss point is originally set usually at a greater distance from the entry point than in the moving average systems.

Although the average gain of .47 remains below what we would need to trade full commission vehicles profitably, this does equal a comparable change in the Dow Industrial Average of approximately 7 points, well above what we were able to secure from moving average methods which involved comparable frequency of trading.

TABLE 9–1
The NYSE Index and the best of the channel reverse signal periods

Year	4-day reversal period			25-day reversal period		
	Total points gained (lost)	Number of trades	Average per trade	Total points gained (lost)	Number of trades	Average per trade
1970......	25	26	.96	7	5	1.40
1971......	24	25	.96	10	5	2.00
1972......	14	31	.45	1	7	.14
1973......	17	35	.49	8	6	1.25
1974......	21	34	.62	4	7	.57
1975......	10	36	.28	2	7	.22
1976......	2	41	.05	0	8	.00
1977......	7	34	.21	− 6	8	−1.25
1978*.....	16	28	.57	13	5	2.60
	136	290	.47	39	58	.67

* Through November 17, 1978.

Profitability	Number profitable	Number unprofitable
4-day reversal	148	142
25-day reversal	25	33

The simplicity of the system provides a further advantage. No computations of moving averages are required; you simply buy if the market closes above any level achieved at the close of the previous four days and you sell if the market falls to below its lowest reading of the previous four days.

The 25-day reversal rule

The 25-day reversal period performed credibly as well, gaining an average of .67 on the NYSE Index per transaction, or approximately ten points on the Dow, if we were to make an approximate conversion of 15 Dow points to 1.00 on the NYSE Index. The total gain of 39 points, therefore, would be roughly equivalent to a total gain in the Dow during this period of 585 Dow points, over 58 transactions, a rate of gain per transaction larger than our most favorable results employing straight moving average systems.

Why are these time spans most successful?

We are not including herein tables of the entire breakdowns of various time spans which may be employed in the reversal system, but we did secure such tables in our research work. Some slight increase in total points gained may be achieved by use of a 2-day reversal period, but at a considerable increase in the number of transactions. The 4-day period seems to reflect the turning juncture of a 15–18 day market cycle which marks short term market swings. If you have a copy of *The Wall Street Journal* handy, turn to the chart of the Dow Industrial Average on the next to the last page. Once alerted, you should be able to clearly identify this 15–18 day cycle—15–18 days tending to elapse from short term market bottom to short term market bottom. Once this is identified, you should have little trouble seeing the significance of days in which the market rises to above its previous four day high and/or falls to below its previous four day low.

The 25-day reversal period appears to reflect the 5–6 week cycle of the stock market. The market tends to create short term bottoms at 5–6 week intervals as well as at 15–18 day intervals. The 5–6 week bottoms do carry some greater significance.

Because of the 5–6 week cycle, market trading ranges tend to be bounded by tops spaced at approximate five to six week intervals and by bottoms spaced at approximate five to six week intervals. During bull markets, these five to six week tops will tend to show a rising pattern, and each bottom will occur at a higher level than the previous bottom. Should a five to six week low fall below a previous five to six week low, triggering a sell signal on the 25-day reverse system, a reversal in intermediate trend at least is probably being signalled as well.

An upside penetration, above the previous high achieved over the past 25 days, is not likely to occur unless a previous downtrend is also in the process of reversal. Again, the 5–6 week cycle seems to come into play here. Figure 9–5 shows the 25-day reversal pattern with the market's 5–6 week cycle.

Trading stocks and stock options with the channel reverse system: 205 points gained on Honeywell long and short over less than nine years

Although the channel reverse system does have some more or less obvious drawbacks, it has been able to produce some pretty nifty gains with certain stocks, at least, if certain intermediate term channels are employed. As usual, shorter term channels tack on greater numbers of points, but at an insufficient rate per transaction to cover commission costs.

Table 9–2 illustrates the intermediate system with Honeywell and IBM for the period, 1970–78. IBM is not likely to perform as well in the future because, split 4:1 during 1979, it is not as likely to show the price swings which make automatic trading systems profitable. However, I suspect that issues such as Honeywell, Digital and Teledyne will perform quite well. In assessing the following results, keep in mind again, that many issues can be traded via stock options which greatly magnify the leverage and potential profits from automatic trading systems. For example, if we can secure an average profit of four points per transaction on a $90 stock, that 4.4 percent average gain per transaction may convert into an average gain of 20–30 percent per transaction if a put or a call option is employed as a trading vehicle instead of the underlying common.

FIGURE 9–5

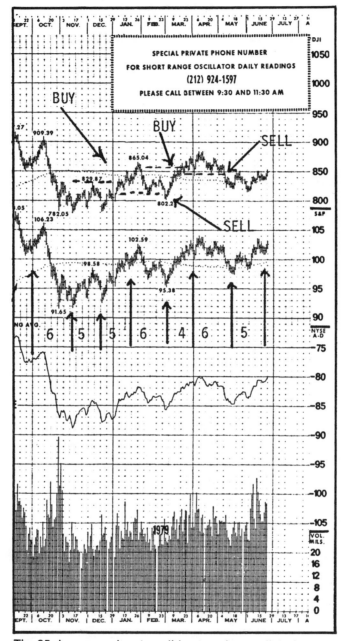

The 25-day reversal system did not work as well during early 1979 as it has during other periods. You can see the 5–6 week trading cycle.

Source: *Trendline Daily Basis Stock Charts*, 345 Hudson Street, New York City, N.Y. 10014.

Significant caveat

We did apply this trading system to a number of issues providing both listed puts and listed calls, in the hopes of finding a broad roster of option available issues from which investors could choose to trade. Issues sampled and tested included American Broadcasting, Amerada Hess, Aetna, and Allis

TABLE 9–2
Some representative results of trading stocks via the channel reversal system

Year	Honeywell (29 days)			IBM (30 days)		
	Total points gained (lost)	Number of trades	Average per trade	Total points gained (lost)	Number of trades	Average per trade
1970	52	5	10.40	70	3	23.33
1971	38	5	7.60	38	7	5.43
1972	19	7	2.70	3	7	.43
1973	35	6	5.83	64	4	16.00
1974	9	7	1.29	− 21	7	− 3.00
1975	12	9	1.33	49	6	8.17
1976	17	8	2.13	28	7	4.00
1977	1	6	.17	12	7	1.71
1978	22	5	4.40	35	6	5.83
	205	58	3.53	278	54	5.15

Notes: The use of a 29-day reversal period proved best for Honeywell. A 30-day period proved best for IBM. Of the 58 transactions hypothetically recorded in Honeywell, 29 would have been profitable and 29 unprofitable. Of the 54 transactions hypothetically recorded in IBM, 29 would have been profitable and 25 unprofitable. Commission costs excluded in all cases.

Chalmers. Although this group of stocks did tend to post gains per year in the aggregate based on reversal periods of 28–30 days, none of these issues produced a sufficient gain per transaction to warrant the use of this system.

Although Honeywell is, historically, a volatile issue, IBM is not, though it has, in the past, been high-priced. We believe that the majority of automatic trading systems, applied to individual stocks, will perform best with high priced vehicles which tend to swing broadly in price.

Some further observations: How the channel reversal system can help your market timing even if you do not apply it literally

The channel reversal system, particularly when channel periods of from 25–30 days are employed, tends to produce larger gains and losses than many other systems. The system will usually hold you on the right side of the market during all protracted market moves with fewer whipsaws than moving average systems, but you do incur greater risk per transaction because of the distance of your stop-loss points from your original entry points.

You will frequently find, in using this system, that an issue may rise above one five-week trading range only to pause and then reverse its immediate direction. We did not computerize and formally evaluate the decision making, but you will almost certainly secure improved results if you do not buy and/or sell short immediately upon a penetration of a 25–30 day high. Instead, take the penetration of the trading period as a sign of strength (or weakness, if the penetration is downwards) and try to take action on a reversal in the direction opposite the penetration.

For example, let's suppose that Honeywell has a 30-day trading range of from 60–75. The stock reaches 76, which would be a buy signal. Following such signals, you will often see a pullback, sometimes to a point very close to the lows of the previous trading range; in this case, perhaps optimally to 61–62. Initiate your long positions immediately upon the first turn-up in the stock following such a retracement. Follow the breakout immediately only if very large volume accompanies the breakout and the price spread of the stock on breakout day is broad.

As a general rule, you may buy immediately if the issue seems to be reversing an intermediate downtrend, and if it has been lying within a pronounced basing area for several weeks. If the issue is already in an uptrend, you should await the pullback following the breakout.

Figure 9–6 illustrates an ideal buy point following a breakout above a channel. Figure 9–7 illustrates the sort of chart pattern which should be acted upon on the short side instantly.

FIGURE 9–6

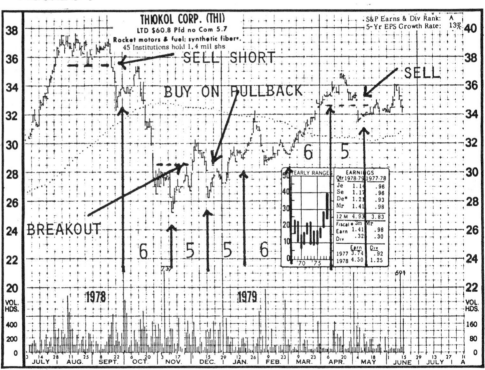

Thiokol was an excellent trader on the 25-day channel reversal system during late 1978 and early 1979. You can see the regular 5–6 week trading cycle.

Source: *Trendline Daily Basis Stock Charts*, 345 Hudson Street, New York City, N.Y. 10014

If you do act immediately upon a breakout, or if the stock in question has risen above the channel by an amount equal to the depth of the channel, you might consider taking profits immediately rather than awaiting a reverse signal. Do not reverse your position, however, until a signal is rendered.

For example, let's suppose again that Honeywell has been trading in a

FIGURE 9-7

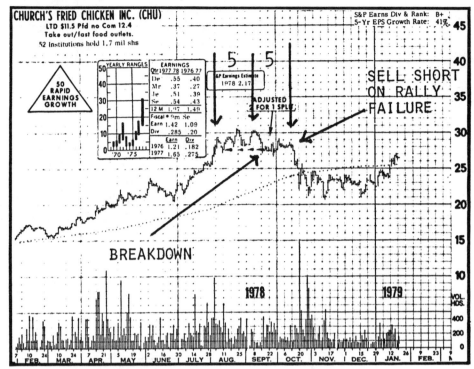

The ideal short sale candidate! Stock has had a long rise, but then makes a 25-day low. Subsequent retracement fails to make a new high within 25 days. Notice the 5-week cycle at tops.

Source: *Trendline Daily Basis Stock Charts*, 345 Hudson Street, New York City, N.Y. 10014.

range of from 60–75. You have purchased on a pullback, following a penetration above 75 to 76. The issue then rises to 90, 15 points above the channel high of 75. Since the depth of the channel previously established (75–60) was also 15 points, you may take your profits at 90, give or take, rather than await a reversal signal. Stocks frequently retrace approximately 50 percent of price movements. Honeywell, in rising from 60 (the previous channel bottom) to 90, would have gained 30 points. Since a retracement of between 10–15 points would be likely in any case, you are likely to find that a selling price near 90 represents at least a near term optimal selling juncture. Even if you wish to retain your position in the security, you should find yourself with opportunity to repurchase at at least somewhat lower price levels.

This strategy will often help you to nail down rapid trading profits before they do evaporate, but you do risk losing some very powerful gains from time to time in issues that do not retrace previous gains. On balance, you will probably find that it pays to sell (or to buy) on a doubling of a channel width, but do remain nimble if you wish to reinstitute your positions following such actions.

Summing up the channel reversal system

This trading system does appear to provide some promise if high priced, volatile issues are traded, but it does have its drawbacks. *The major advan-*

tages: relatively few transactions and whipsaws in the intermediate versions, few calculations required, excellent results trading the market averages short term. *Major disadvantages:* According to our research, many issues will not track reliably with short term market fluctuations. You should trade either mutual funds or a well-diversified group of volatile issues. Stop-loss points are placed relatively far from initial purchase prices, which reduces whipsaws but increases risk per transaction.

Calendar channel reverse systems may be successfully applied to the trading of commodities as well as to stocks. If you do happen to prefer hogs to Honeywell, we suggest that you write to Merrill Lynch for their July 1978 *Commodity Research Report,* "Channels and Crossovers," which is based on results derived from one of the author's (Hitschler) trading model computer programs.

Market momentum—
How to use the velocity of market
movement to predict turning points
in advance of actual price change

Market momentum
defined

In referring to market momentum, we are actually referring to the velocity of stock and market price movement—not the price level of stocks but the rate at which prices are actually changing.

For example, were IBM to close today at 315 and had it closed six days ago at 310, we might say that the current rate of change for IBM stands at +5.00 per five day period. If IBM were to close tomorrow at 320 and had it closed six days prior to that close at 312, then we might say that IBM's 5-day rate of change had increased to +8.00.

Rate of change measurements always include two variables: price differential between two points of time measured in regular fixed intervals (in the above example, five days), and a specified time interval. You may elect to measure rates of change over relatively short periods of time such as five to ten days or over longer periods of time such as six months to one or more years. If you are measuring rates of change over shorter periods of time, you are measuring market momentum for minor market swings. If you are measuring momentum over longer periods of time, you are measuring momentum in relationship to intermediate or major market trends.

Example. The following is a sequence of prices for Honeywell during the month of April 1979.

Day and date	Price, Honeywell	5-day rate of change	12-day rate of change
1. 4/ 5	69.38		
2. 4/ 6	69.50		
3. 4/ 9	68.75	(67.13–69.38)	
4. 4/10	69.50		
5. 4/11	66.88		
6. 4/12	67.13	−2.25	
7. 4/16	67.50	−2.00	(67.88–69.38)
8. 4/17	68.50	− .25	
9. 4/18	69.50	0	
10. 4/19	68.38	+1.50	
11. 4/20	67.63	+ .50	
12. 4/23	68.00	+ .50	
13. 4/24	67.88	− .62	−1.50

The example, above, should serve to illustrate the method we employ for computing rate of change measurements. *Reminder:* Only actual trading days are employed for daily based computations; holidays and weekends are ignored. If you are computing longer term rates of change, you might wish to make your comparisons on a weekly or monthly basis rather than on a daily basis. For periods of twenty-five days or less, however, we do suggest you post your differentials daily in order to maintain smoother oscillator readings. To smooth your rate of change trend lines even further, if you are graphing your data—which we do recommend—we suggest a .20 exponential average be maintained of the daily readings.

The significance of momentum in predicting market reversals and in predicting how far a move in motion is likely to carry

Imagine a baseball hit by a batter, perhaps a long and deep fly ball. At first, the ball will leave the bat at a certain rising trajectory, rising rapidly. As the forces of gravity and wind resistance slow the drive, the rise in the ball will slow, although the ball will continue to rise for a while before arching over. An experienced outfielder can frequently discern from the slope of the ball's rise just how far and for how long the drive will carry. The falling of the ball to earth is initially signalled by the slowdown in its rate of rise—the ball will lose upside velocity before actually starting on its downwards path.

Figure 10–1 illustrates this concept in relationship to stock market prices. Presuming that the wave shown in Figure 10–1 represents the price movement of a particular stock, we can see that the issue moves from a point of low upwards momentum to an area of increasing momentum (gaining more per unit of time) then to an area of decreasing momentum, the area just prior to a price reversal. In Figure 10–1, momentum decreases from +14 to +7 then gradually turns negative as the price reversal gains downside momentum. *Notice that upside momentum shows a decrease in advance of a turndown in the wave, which signifies the stock price.*

FIGURE 10–1

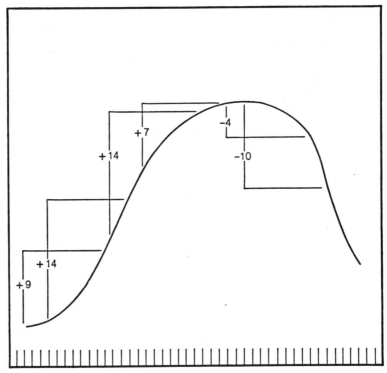

As the wave begins to peak, the momentum, measured by the difference between the last reading and the reading 10 units back, begins to diminish. It turns increasingly negative as the decline accelerates.

This decrease in upside momentum (near the ends of market advances) and of downside momentum (near the conclusion of market declines) provides excellent advance warning of impending market price reversals, a warning which very often allows investors familiar with those tools to sell into strength and to buy into weakness—before market turns actually take place. We will examine some specific indicators shortly.

We mentioned above that rate of change measurements can also provide indications how far market moves and/or stock movements are likely to carry. To understand the concepts involved, let's return to that baseball. Experienced baseball fans are often able to tell—almost as soon as the ball leaves the bat—whether the drive will carry deeply or whether the ball hit will stop far short of reaching the stands. The sound of the ball striking the bat provides one clue, but, unfortunately, stock bids on the tape make no noise. The initial velocity of the drive provides another clue; and here the stock market does provide a useful analogy. *The stronger the initial momentum of any market move, the further that move is likely to carry.* We will explore specific indicators as we go along, but for the moment, let's just state that the stronger the initial momentum of any market move, the further the market is likely to carry in the direction of that move, even after momentum begins to slacken. This concept is very important, and will form an integral aspect of the Time-Trend-Momentum Trading System.

Some quick and useful measurers of market movement

The 5-day rate of change and its smoothing exponential average

Many market technicians employ a 5-day rate of change to measure the momentum of very short term market swings. The procedure for computing the 5-day rate of change was illustrated above. We suggest that, in addition to plotting the 5-day rate of change itself, you plot a .40 exponential average of that rate of change. Figure 10–2 illustrates a 5-day rate of change of the NYSE Index and its .40 exponential average, both plotted on the same time axis as the NYSE Index itself.

FIGURE 10–2

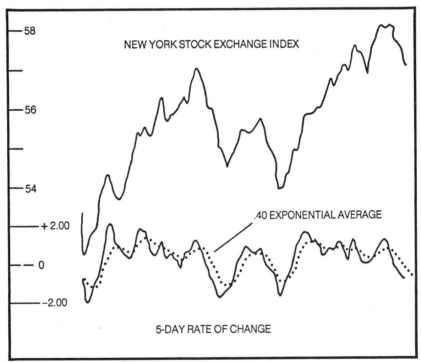

The market often changes direction, at least temporarily, when the 5-day rate of change oscillator reaches the areas of ±2.00.

If you study Figure 10–2, you may make the following observations:

1. The 5-day rate of change of the NYSE Index rarely exceeds ±2.00. A reading greater than +2.00 generally indicates an excessive condition; prices will almost always either consolidate or quickly turn down. Readings below −2.00 are generally followed by market advances.
2. A turndown of the 5-day rate of change line from above to below its .40 exponential average is almost always followed by a short term market decline. A turnup of the 5-day rate of change line from below to above its .40 exponential average is almost always rapidly followed by a short term market upturn.
3. The stronger the initial impulse of the 5-day rate of change line, the

further the carry is likely to be of market movement over the next few weeks in the direction of that impulse.

This is a very sensitive, very short term market indicator, too sensitive to generate valid buy and sell signals on its own. This indicator may, however, be employed to "fine tune" your market purchases and sales. If you are planning to buy, you will usually secure better prices if you await an oversold (−2.00) level in the indicator. If you are planning to sell, sell into strength, just as the indicator starts to roll over from a peak in overbought territory.

The 12-day rate of change indicator and its smoothing exponential average

The 12-day rate of change indicator is an excellent trading oscillator, since its fluctuations frequently run in tune to a 5–6 week trading cycle often reflected in market price action. We will discuss this further in the next chapter, but for the moment let's just note that stock prices often tend to make low points at five to six week intervals, and that successful intermediate term trading can be based on this 5–6 week market cycle, measured from low to low. Since from 25–30 trading days are encompassed within this cycle, we can assume that in a neutral market, the market will rise for approximately 12–15 days then decline for 12–15 days. A 12-day rate of change oscillator will serve to catch these reversals very well indeed.

Figure 10–3 shows the price action of Honeywell during the year 1978, plotted along with Honeywell's 12-day rate of change and 25-day rate of change oscillators. The former reflects the 5–6 week trading cycle of the issue; the latter reflects the 10-week trading cycle. The dotted lines on the oscillator scales represent the .20 exponential averages of the 12-day and 25-day rate of change oscillators. Let's examine Figure 3, a very instructive chart.

1. The range of the 12-day trading oscillator generally ran during this period from between +5.00 and −5.00, give or take. The issue may have been considered as overbought whenever it had gained more than five points over a twelve day period and may have been considered oversold whenever it had lost more than five points over a twelve day period. At least minor price retracements usually took place as overbought and oversold levels in the 12-day rate of change oscillator were approached. The .20 exponential average of the daily readings provided smoother and more accurate readings than the daily postings themselves.

2. The first attainment of a +5.00 or −5.00 reading in the oscillator—if the oscillator then changes direction—often marks the half-way to two-thirds way points in the total advance we can expect of the stock.

Oscillator readings tend to bottom simultaneously with prices at low points, but even here, lowest readings in the oscillator tend to lead upside reversals by periods of one to three weeks. The 12-day rate of change oscillator provided excellent warning of Honeywell's price reversals throughout the year, by changing direction in advance of price trend changes. We have marked off some of these bottom areas on Figure 10–3.

FIGURE 10–3
Honeywell and its 12-day and 25-day rates of change, 1978

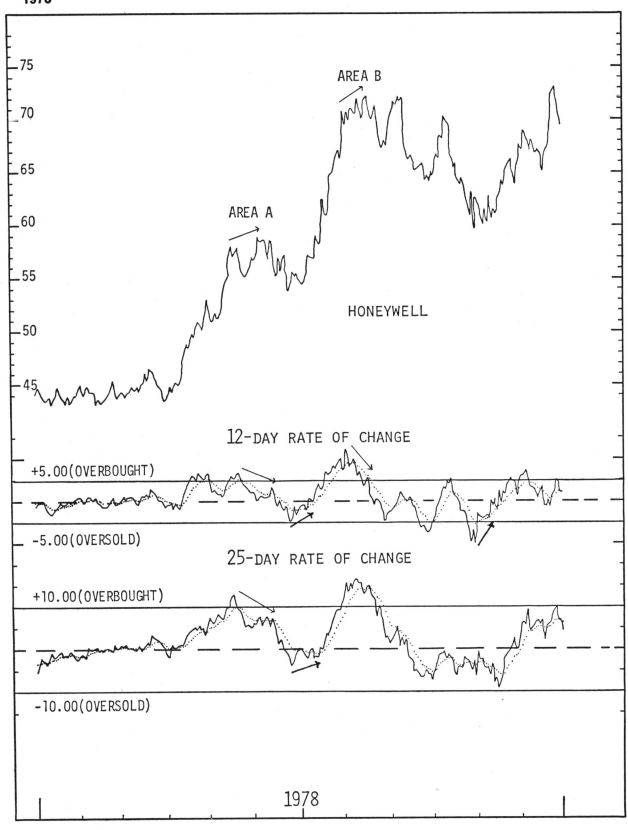

3.   Examine the intermediate tops that took place in Honeywell during May 1978 (Area A on the chart) and during August and September (Area B on the chart). *Each of the intermediate tops was preceded by a clear slackening of upside momentum in the 12-day and 25-day rate of change oscillators.* Again, the smoothed .20 average line presents the picture more clearly than the unsmoothed data. The 12-day oscillator tends to provide superior advance warning to the 25-day oscillator, particularly at market bottoms.

We mentioned before that ±5.00 readings tended to indicate overbought and oversold readings in the 12-day rate of change oscillator. Given that observation, should you have sold during July and early August as the oscillator crossed +5.00. No! The .20 exponential average of the oscillator did not turn down at all; its own upwards momentum remained intact until the top actually formed. Remember what we said during our discussion of excesses in general: *Very excessive readings in the one direction or the other indicate unusual strength. The presence of very strong excessive readings indicates that you should "ride" a move rather than reverse direction.* The ability of the 12-day rate of change oscillator to reach a +10.00 reading in August indicated that you need have been in no rush to sell. The issue did not start to decline seriously for some weeks thereafter.

Applying the 12-day rate of change indicator to a portfolio of stocks: How to tell when any stock is ready to be bought and/or ready to be sold

Figures 10–4 and 10–5 show two more issues, DuPont and Atlantic Richfield, plotted with their 12-day and 25-day rate of change indicators.

In comparing these charts to Figure 10–3, it immediately becomes apparent that whereas Honeywell's 12-day rate of change becomes excessive in the ±5.00 region, DuPont's 12-day rate of change did not become excessive until it achieved readings of beyond ±10.00 units from "0." DuPont has since split, which will result in a reduction of these parameters. Atlantic Richfield, on the other hand, an issue which trades in the same price range as Honeywell, rarely produces readings in its 12-day rate of change oscillator in excess of ±3.00.

Differences in parameters of this indicator, issue by issue, result, of course, from variations in the volatility of the stocks in question as well as from variations in price. Honeywell is more volatile than the majority of issues traded on the New York Stock Exchange. Atlantic Richfield is less volatile than the typical issue. DuPont had been a higher priced issue so we would normally anticipate broader price swings in that issue.

If you are applying this form of indicator to stocks, issue by issue, we suggest you maintain a pricing history on a daily basis of each issue you are tracking, posting your 12-day and 25-day rate of indicators daily. After a period of time encompassing one or two intermediate market cycles, you should have some idea of the range in which each stock's oscillator fluctuates. As a general rule, for an issue priced in the $50 range, you may consider the issue overly extended in the one direction or the other when its price has changed by more than 10 percent over any 12-day period.

A change in price of more than 15 percent over a 12-day period represents rather extreme momentum for an issue in the $50 range, and should be con-

FIGURE 10–4
**DuPont and its 12-day and 25-day rates of change,
1978**

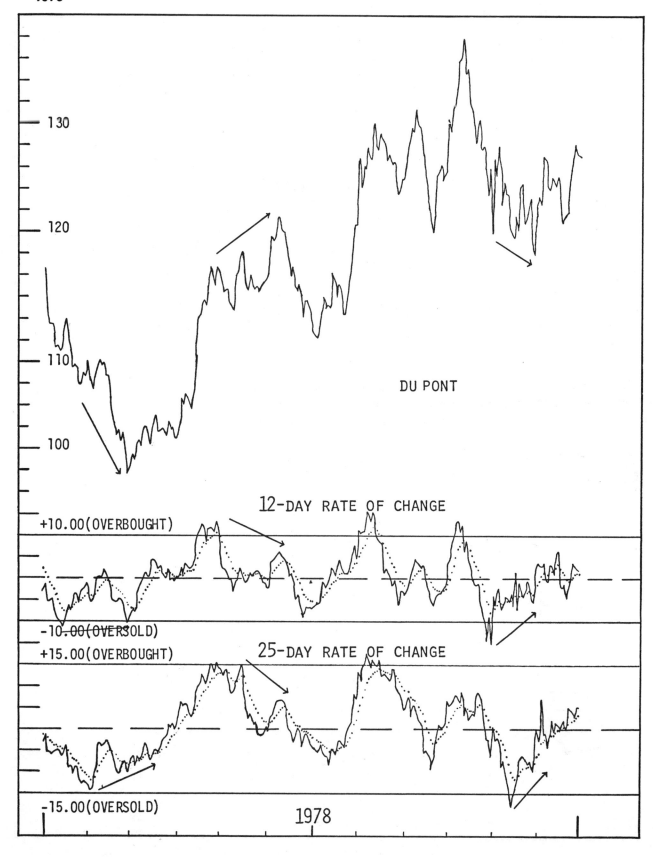

FIGURE 10–5
Atlantic Richfield and its 12-day and 25-day rates of change

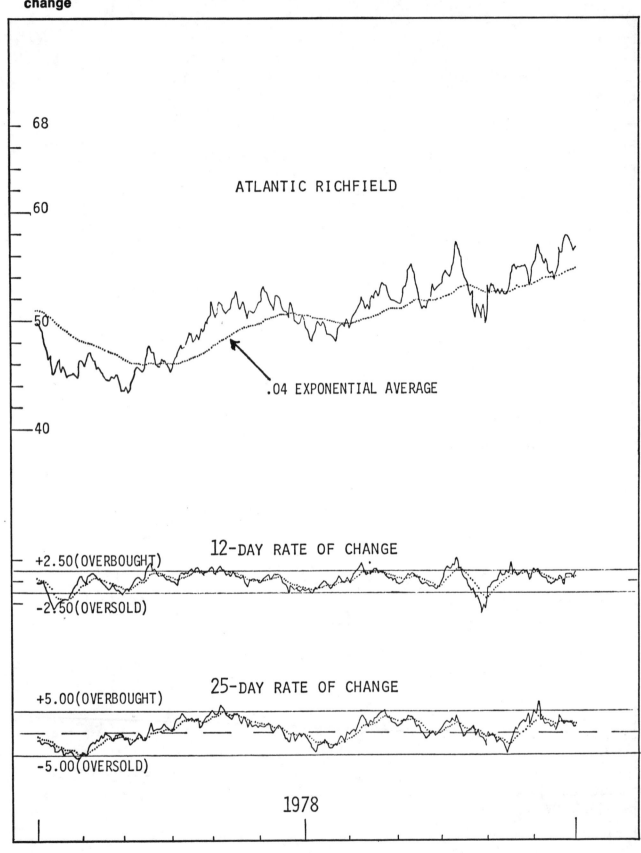

sidered as a sign of either extreme strength or weakness, depending on the direction of momentum.

Higher priced issues will demonstrate somewhat lesser percentage changes. Lower priced issues will demonstrate somewhat greater percentage changes. For example, a change of 20 percent in price for an issue priced in the $20–25 range over a 12-day period is not unusual. Such a variation in price would fall within normal overbought-oversold regions.

As a general rule, for active trading you should probably emphasize higher priced issues with heavy capitalization. Such issues are somewhat less prone to violent price fluctuation relative to their price and will trace more predictably with the market averages and with their own trading oscillators. If, however, you are trading via some other form of trading system, you may opt for low-priced issues, but these will not be as suitable for the methods we are describing herein.

How to compare stock volatilities

You may find it useful, in establishing your oscillator parameters prior to developing a long price history of your issues, to secure a reading of the volatility of issues in which you plan to trade. For example, let's suppose you have established the parameters for an issue such as Honeywell, but are now considering the posting of an issue such as Atlantic Richfield. You might adopt the following procedure.

Establish a volatility rating for Honeywell, based on the formula:

$$\text{Volatility} = 2 \times \frac{(\text{Year's high} - \text{Year's low})}{(\text{Year's high} + \text{Year's low})}$$

For the year 1978, the volatility of Honeywell would be computed as follows:

$$\text{Volatility} = 2 \times \frac{(72 - 42)}{(72 + 42)} = \frac{60}{114} = .53.$$

By comparison, the volatility of Atlantic Richfield would show the following computation:

$$\text{Volatility} = 2 \times \frac{(60 - 48)}{(60 + 48)} = \frac{24}{108} = .22.$$

Using the ratios of volatilities to compute oscillator scales

The ratio of the volatility of Honeywell to the volatility of Atlantic Richfield, .53 : 22, corresponded during 1978 very closely to the ratio of their respective overbought-oversold parameter limits. Whereas Honeywell became overbought and oversold during 1978 at parameters of ±5.00, Atlantic Richfield became overbought and oversold at parameters of ±2.50 for its 12-day rate of change oscillator. You may want to review Figures 10–3 and 10–5 and make your own comparisons.

If you have determined the overbought-oversold parameters for any stock within a given price range, you can probably approximate overbought-oversold levels for other issues within that price range by simply establishing ratios based upon the relative ratios of their annual volatility ratings, as we did above between Honeywell and Atlantic Richfield.

How the 12-day rate of change provides excellent market timing signals

Figure 10–6 illustrates the 12-day rate of change and the 25-day rate of change oscillators, applied this time to the NYSE Index. Readings of ±2.00 represent excessive conditions, a reading of +2.00 signifies and overbought condition, and a reading of −2.00 represents an oversold condition. You may notice, in studying the chart, that readings of +4.00 were approached twice during 1978 and that a reading of −6.00 was surpassed once on the downside.

1978 was a year of extremes for the stock market, a year which saw sharp price movements both upwards (between March and August) and downwards (during October). Further study of the chart will reveal that as per the rules concerning excesses, very excessive readings in plus territory *were followed by further market advances,* and that the very excessive reading in negative territory *was followed by several weeks of base building* prior to any meaningful market advance.

We can take the following as general rules in our use of the 12-day rate of change for predicting market movement:

1. If the 12-day rate of change turns down in the area of from +1.50 to +2.00 without rising any higher, expect only an average size market advance—an advance carrying for no more than four to five percent.
2. If the 12-day rate of change turns down from below +1.00, expect only a minor market advance.
3. If, however, the 12-day rate of change reaches the +3.00 to +4.00 area before turning down, anticipate a stronger than average market gain. If excesses of greater than +4.00 are achieved, the market move in question will probably carry for periods which can be measured in months rather than in weeks.
4. If the 12-day rate of change turns up from levels not exceeding −2.00 on the downside, the market will probably rally quickly and the decline in motion will prove relatively brief.
5. If the indicator reaches −3.00 or lower, further declines may be expected or a period of base building required at the least prior to the start of any significant market advance.

The .20 exponential average of the daily readings may prove a more reliable measure of this indicator than the daily readings alone. You can see, in Figure 10–6, how the .20 exponential average smooths the data and provides excellent momentum readings.

Do not forget to look for divergences!

Market tops and market bottoms are frequently signalled in advance as this indicator traces out positive and negative divergent patterns when the

FIGURE 10–6
The NYSE Index and its 12-day and 25-day rates of change

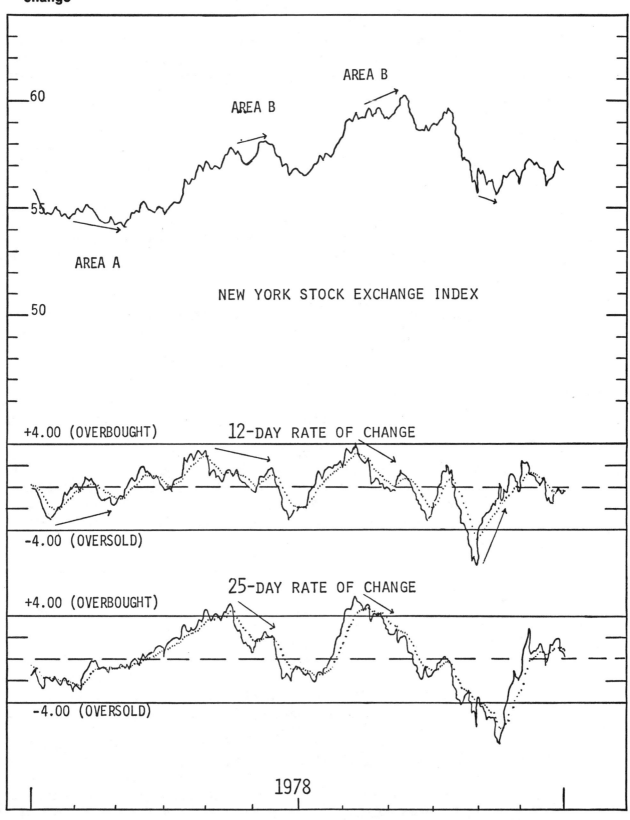

pattern of the 12-day rate of change line is compared to the pattern of the New York Stock Exchange Index itself.

1. A *positive divergence* takes place when the indicator takes on a pattern of rising lows while the New York Stock Exchange Index falls to new lows. Such a pattern developed during January and February 1978, just prior to the strong spring advance that year. The period is marked on Figure 10–6 as "Area A."

2. A *negative divergence* takes place when the 12-day rate of change indicator traces out a series of declining tops as the stock market averages rise to new highs. This pattern developed during May and August 1978 (Areas B), both of which occasions were followed by sharp market declines.

Patterns of momentum divergences are frequently very significant and form an integral part of the Time-Trend-Momentum Trading System, along with codified rules regarding the use of the 12-day rate of change oscillator, described above.

How to adjust your trading oscillators in tune with major market trends

The parameters of almost all trading oscillators will shift in accordance with the phase of the primary trend of the stock market.

1. During early stages of bull markets, anticipate high readings in the overbought area. The stock market will rarely become strongly oversold, and you should be prepared to make purchases as trading oscillators approach neutral levels. During early bull market periods the 12-day rate of change oscillator will rarely fall below −2.00.

2. During the middle stages of bull markets, a general decrease in market volatility will take place. For examples, we refer readers to the market charts of 1972 and 1976 which appear in subsequent chapters. Extreme overbought and/or oversold readings are unusual during these middle stages.

3. During the early phases of bear markets, strongly overbought readings occur very infrequently; oversold conditions become more common, and deeper levels of oversold territory are reached.

   During these periods, you should await very oversold conditions before buying, but you should be prepared to sell quickly as moderate levels in the overbought zones are reached.

4. During the final stages of bear markets, periods in which selling climaxes often appear, very deeply oversold readings are most likely to occur. For examples, we refer readers to charts of the 1970 and 1974 years which appear in subsequent chapters and to Figure 10–6, October 1978, which saw a classic selling climax.

Although the stock market will often advance sharply for a number of sessions during initial rallies following very extreme oversold conditions, you can almost always count on the market retesting its lows and requiring several weeks for basing and testing before being able to embark on a strong market advance. This point has been made before, but we believe it is well worth the restatement. *You do not have to worry about missing the boat if you do not buy into the very lows of bear markets.* You will almost certainly receive second (and perhaps even third) chances, opportunities which involve considerably less risk. For example, review the period during late 1978 which followed the selling climax of October. November and December provided numerous opportunities to reenter the market on the long side at low prices, by which time positive divergences had set in in terms of the 12-day rate of change and the 25-day rate of change indicators. By late December, you could buy with much greater confidence that the downwards thrust of the October decline had been fully spent.

History has shown that the patterns traced out during late 1978 are more the rule than the exception. Similar patterns have existed at virtually every significant intermediate and major bottom of the past decade, and even longer. For example, the bottoms of 1966, 1970, 1971, late 1973, 1974, mid-1975, and early 1978 were all marked by positive momentum divergences prior to the onset of market advances. During all these periods, a wait following the oscillator's initial thrust into deep oversold territory would have produced safer buying opportunities, if not the absolute low in market prices.

In short, while it would certainly be desirable in theory to be a buyer at the very lows of market prices, in practice it almost always pays to wait for definite evidence that downside momentum has slackened. This evidence is provided by a rise in your momentum curves, which should trace out a series of at least two rising low points. Again, the use of the .20 exponential smoothing constant of the daily readings should clarify your position.

Turn-ups from less severe oversold conditions may, again, be followed immediately. And, once again, we suggest that the −2.00 to −3.00 area be considered the lowest area to which the oscillator can fall if you are considering immediate repurchase on a turn-up in the 12-day rate of change.

Some further suggestions regarding the use of the .20 exponential average of the 12-day rate of change

Let's look once again at Figure 10–6, and at Figure 10–3, 10–4 and 10–5. Examine the .20 exponential average lines of the 12-day and 25-day rate of change trading oscillators. You may notice that excellent early sell signals are rendered when, following a period of advance, the .20 exponential lines gradually roll over and turn down. You may also notice that excellent buy signals are rendered when, following a period of decline, the .20 exponential lines roll upwards and start to rise. Simple penetrations of these .20 lines by daily readings are *not,* in and of themselves, sufficient to trigger buy and sell signals. You should look for clear changes in trend, changes which may not always be clear, but which, when they are clear, provide very clear and reliable market action signals.

Fluctuations of the .20 exponential line within trading ranges are not significant. Following long market declines, and during basing periods, movements upwards and downwards of the 12-day rate of change indicator do take place. Similarly, at market tops, brief changes in direction frequently occur as the indicator rolls over. We are looking for basic changes in direction following clearly defined and trended moves in the one direction or the other. It is these changes in direction that carry significance and that indicate a basic change in the direction of intermediate market trend.

It is time now to move along to another major component of the Time-Trend-Momentum Trading System—time. And time for us to examine a major technical market tool, time cycles, and how time cycles can help you predict just when a market trading juncture is likely to take place.

11

Using your calendar to anticipate
market junctures days, weeks,
months, and sometimes even years
in advance: time cycles
and how to use them

This book has, up to now, emphasized the tracking of market trends and the anticipation of trend reversal junctures through the employment of excessive measures of market deviation and measures of excessive momentum. We have alluded to the use of time and time cycles for the determination of *when*, in terms of calendar time, such reversals are likely to take place. The time has now come to pursue the matter in greater depth.

Time cycles:
A definition

Careful study of the movement of stock prices reveals that stock prices tend to fluctuate at rather regular intervals, measured in terms of calendar time. If you will review a number of stock charts, you may be able to discern such regular periods of time which separate market bottom areas. Less significant market bottoms are spaced more closely together in time. More significant market bottoms tend to be spaced at greater intervals, the one from the other.

The regular periods that intervene between market bottom and market bottom are referred to as the time cycles of the stock market. Although periods between market tops are frequently fairly regular, the lengths of time cycles are measured between troughs—the low points of the cycle.

Smaller cycles comprise each market cycle, which is, in turn, a part of a larger market cycle. For example, intermediate market cycles often average approximately 20 weeks in length; the time span between significant intermediate low points averages approximately 20 weeks. Although this 20-week cycle usually stands as the dominant intermediate market cycle, it, in itself, is comprised of two 10-week cycles, three 6-week market cycles and, perhaps, approximately six 3-week market cycles. In other words, within the broader market sweeps that appear to take place at twenty week intervals, you will find lesser market bottoms that occur at ten week intervals of time, at six week intervals of time and at three week intervals of time. Each 10-week cycle is comprised, in itself, of three 3-week cycles.

Figure 11–1 illustrates the configuration of three market cycles of progressive length. The amplitude or height of fluctuations based on the shorter time cycle is less, on average, for shorter cycles than for longer cycles. There are periods when all cycles appear to be moving in the same direction. When this occurs, cycles are said to *coalesce* or to be in confluence. There are periods when the shorter and longer cycles seem to oppose each other. When this occurs, we refer to the cycles as *lying in opposition* to each other.

FIGURE 11–1

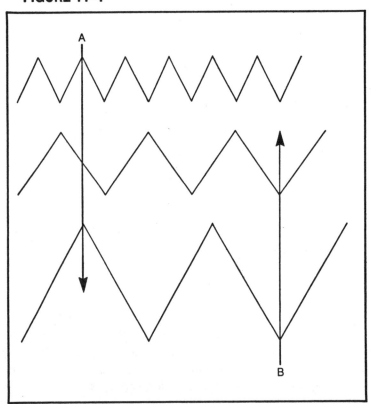

A typical configuration of short, intermediate, and longer term cycles. The market would be cyclically weakest at Point A, where all cycles are heading down. Point B would be an area of major strength—all cycles turning up simultaneously.

Example. Figure 11–2 illustrates the intermediate cycles of the stock market. We have marked in the 6-week, 9–10-week, and 20-week cyclical low points for the period shown on the chart. If you study the chart carefully, you may notice that *the strongest market advances* appear to take place when all of the significant intermediate cycles coalesce—when a number of significant

FIGURE 11–2
The intermediate term cycles of the stock market

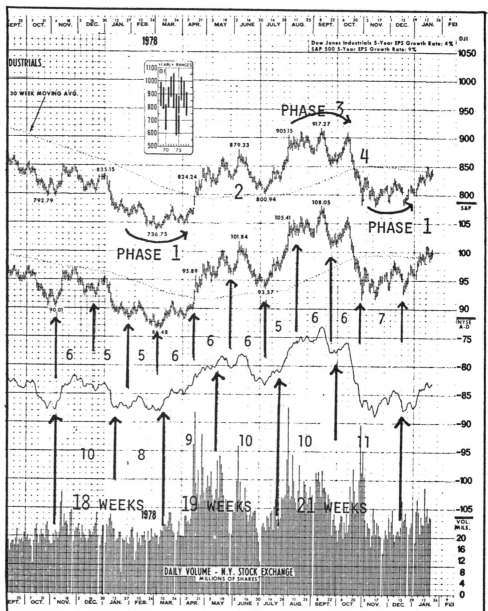

Source: *Trendline Daily Basis Stock Charts*, 345 Hudson Street, New York City, N.Y. 10014.

cyclical periods seem to come to an end simultaneously. You may also notice that the low points of shorter cycles become more clearly delineated as the longer 20-week cycle approaches its mid-way or neutral point.

Coalescence is very significant, particularly for the longer term trader. You are much more likely to catch a significant market upmove if you take long positions at points where both shorter term and longer term cycles are due to reach low points simultaneously.

Figure 11–3 reflects the major term 4-year market cycle. Bear market

FIGURE 11–3
The major term 4-year cycle of the stock market

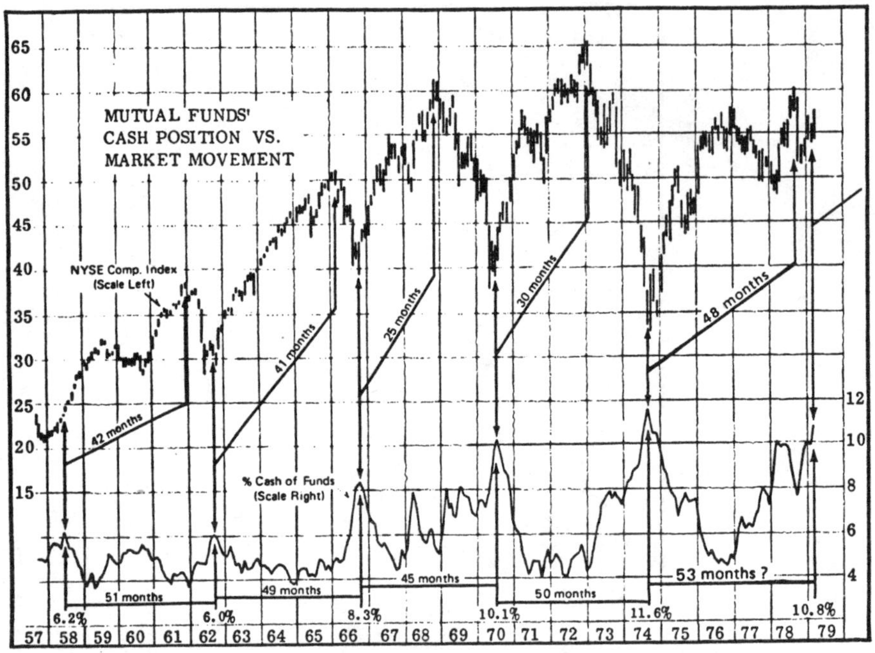

Source: *Growth Fund Guide*, Growth Fund Research Building, Yreka, California 96097.

bottoms tend to occur spaced approximately 48–52 months apart (1962, 1966, 1970, 1974, 1978). The strongest of market rallies generally occur as both the major term and intermediate term market cycles coalesce. Such configurations occurred during early 1975, for example.

How to determine where market cycles lie

The simplest way of determining the location of market cycles is to simply study a daily based (or weekly based, for longer cycles) chart of the stock market as a whole or of individual issues. Generally speaking, most issues tend to reach bottom areas and top areas, on an intermediate basis, more or less simultaneously. However, since each stock does have its own cyclical phases and pattern, you may wish to study individual charts for verification that the issue in question does track cyclically with the broader market.

Your first step will be to locate some clearly defined low points which correspond to the cyclical periods shown in Figure 11–2—the 6-week period, the 9–10-week period, and the 20–24-week period. Once you have established at least one pair of low points which relate to the cycles in question, you should be able to project and to locate other related points. If you maintain some of the momentum oscillators we have described in this book, you will find that these oscillators frequently reveal cyclical configurations more clearly than the movement of stock prices in and of themselves. You will find, for example, that rate of change indicators, particularly the 12-day rate of change indicator, often bottom at 5–6 week intervals, reflecting the

5–6 week trading cycle. More significant low points, again, may be spaced at intervals of 9–10 and approximately 20 weeks.

Longer term market cycles may be readily determined, again, through similar study of weekly based stock charts. Very long term market cycles may be determined via study of monthly based stock charts.

The amplitudes and periods of typical market cycles

We have already mentioned a number of the significant intermediate and short term market cycles you may discern from study of stock charts. The following is a fuller list of significant and consistent market cycles, and the range of stock market movement that usually accompanies such cycles. For example, since the amplitude of the 15–18 day market cycle is approximately forty points, you may assume that market fluctuations based upon the 15–18 day market cycle will *average* approximately forty points from the low of the swing to the high point.

Short term market cycles

6–8 day: amplitude, approximately 20 Dow points.
15–18 day: amplitude, approximately 40 Dow points.

Intermediate term market cycles

5–6 week: amplitude, 50–80 Dow points.
9–10 week: amplitude, 50–80 Dow points.
20–24 week: amplitude, 90–110 Dow points.
9 month: amplitude, 100–150 Dow points.

Long term market cycles

4-year cycle: amplitude, entire bull market swing, ranging up to 500 points.

The shortest cycle which provides sufficient movement for profitable in-and-out trading is the 5–6 week trading cycle. The 15–18 day and 6–8 day trading cycles may be employed for fine tuning your market purchases and sales or for the trading of no-commission vehicles such as no-load mutual funds. Longer term investors, of course, will emphasize longer term cycles such as the 4-year cycle.

Phases of time cycles

Each time cycle may be divided into four phases, according to the market action we may anticipate.

Phase 1. The cycle has reached bottom and is just starting to turn up. Prices will have ended their decline but will have not yet started to rise. Purchases should be made.

Phase 2. Prices will rise with accelerated rates of change. This is the most productive period for long purchases. Call options should be written by covered call writers as Phase 2 comes to an end.

FIGURE 11–4
The phases of a cyclical time cycle

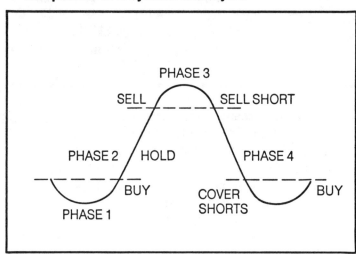

Phase 3. The cycle is topping out and starting to turn down. Prices will rise slightly at the beginning of this phase, will peak during the middle of the phase, and will turn down as Phase 3 comes to an end. Selling and short selling should take place during this phase.

Phase 4. The cycle accelerates on the downside. Short positions should be held until Phase 4 blends into Phase 1, the start of a new cycle.

How the stages of various cycles can help you to plan your trading strategies.

Generally speaking, shorter term market cycles will be dominated or over-shadowed by longer term market cycles providing that the longer term market cycles lie in either Phase 2 or Phase 4. In other words, during the early months of fresh bull markets, while the 4-year market cycle stands in Phase 2, sharply rising, it will not usually pay to trade according to the shorter term 5–6 week and 9–10 week trading cycles. The upwards thrust of the 4-year and the 20-week market cycles will simply overcome the downwards pull exerted as shorter term cycles turn down.

During the crash phases of bear markets, when the 4-year cycle lies in Phase 4, purchases made because of bottoms in the 5–6 week and 9–10 week trading cycles are unlikely to show great profit, particularly if the 20-week cycle is down-trended as well. Your best strategy, if you do track short term cycles, may be to move out of shorts into cash as short term cycles turn up, but not to invest long. Longer term investors may even be able to retain short positions during Phase 4 of the major term cycle.

Similarly, short term market cycles may often be disregarded providing that the 20-week cycle lies in either Phase 2 or Phase 4, and particularly so if the 20-week cycle is moving in confluence with longer term market cycles.

You are likely to find, however, that as longer term cycles move into

Phases 1 and 3, more neutral phases, they exert relatively little influence over short term market behavior. During such periods, when long term cycles are neutral—approximately mid-way into the four year period between bear market bottoms—the market becomes dominated by shorter term intermediate cycles, the 9–10 week market cycle and the 5–6 week market cycle. Within a relatively flat major trend, prices fluctuate upwards and downwards with clear regularity, within relatively narrow trading ranges. You can discern this pattern as the market moved from Phase 4 (October 1978) into Phase 1 (November–December, 1978). In recent years, Phase 3 periods developed during the latter portion of 1976, during the final two-thirds of 1972, and during almost all of 1977. Dynamic Phase 2 advances took place during 1975, early 1976, and during the April–August period of 1978. Severe Phase 4 declines developed during 1974 and late in 1978 as the 4-year 1974–1978 period drew to a close.

We have marked off the phases of the 1978 major trend on Figure 11–2. You might turn back to the chart for review.

The strategy to follow

When major term cycles lie in Phase 1 and/or early in Phase 2, you may purchase stock and/or stock options, holding them for significant gain. As Phase 2 comes to an end, plan to write covered calls against stockholdings, establish neutral option spreads, and/or place protective stops under your long positions.

As major cycles move into Phase 3, plan on emphasizing short term market trading. Weaker holdings should be eliminated. Short selling should not take place until Phase 3 draws to a close, at which point short sales may be placed into peaks of shorter term cyclical upmoves. Short term cyclical patterns will become very clear.

When major cycles move into Phase 4, you should retain short positions, covering as Phase 4 moves along into Phase 1. Short term cycles will have little influence until Phase 4—usually a phase of panic selling—comes to an end.

Mathematically based option hedges such as straddle writing, ratio writing of multiple options against stockholdings, and unbalanced spreads are best reserved for periods such as Phase 3 of the major trend—periods when cyclical forces are liable to lead to a more or less neutral market.

Some further tips and operating rules for profiting through time cycles

1. When the stock market is strong, prices will tend to rally prior to anticipated cyclical lows. When the stock market is weak, prices will tend to rally a bit later than you would expect. For example, let's presume you have isolated the 9–10 week trading cycle, and anticipate the week this cycle will turn up. A strong market is likely to begin to rise a few days before your anticipated due date. It seems almost as though investors have become impatient to buy. In a weak market, prices may not start to turn up until late in the tenth week. It appears as though investors are in no hurry to buy.

2. If prices do not rally within one week of an anticipated short to intermediate cyclical low (based, perhaps, on the 5–6 week cycle), you can expect some fairly severe and immediate market weakness. A market that can only flatten out rather than rise when cyclical lows fall due is likely to be a weak stock market.

Conversely, should prices fail to fall as a cyclical top approaches, the market showing only a flattening or a diminution in its rate of gain, you can usually anticipate a strong stock market in the immediate future.

3. During strong market periods, the majority of time comprising a cyclical period will be spent with prices rising. A neutral market will probably show periods of decline equalling periods of advance over any given market cycle. During weak markets, stocks will spend greater periods of time falling than rising.

The 10-week cycle is a very useful cycle to employ for such measurements. During strong market periods, prices are likely to rise for from 6–7 weeks, prior to declining for 3–4 weeks. It is very unusual for the stock market to show a rising trend for longer than 6–7 weeks prior to at least a short term decline. In a neutral market, the 10-week period will show five rising weeks and five falling weeks. During bear markets, the market may rise for 3–4 weeks of each 10-week cycle then decline for 6–7 weeks.

Should one 10-week cycle show 6–7 weeks of rising prices, you can usually anticipate the subsequent 10-week cycle will show no more than five weeks of rising prices subsequent to price declines. The first segment, which showed such strength, probably comprised the early portion of a rising 20-week cycle. The second segment is likely to take place as the longer 20-week cycle enters into Phase 3, and will therefore become impeded by a declining 20-week cycle.

The highest price levels of any 10-week cycle are almost certain to occur by the sixth or seventh week of that cycle. Do not make purchases—except very early during bull markets—following the fourth or fifth week of any 10-week market cycle.

4. Again, the strongest market gains are achieved when several long term, intermediate term, and short term market cycles coalesce—bottoms occurring simultaneously. The most severe market declines tend to occur when cyclical high points of various cycles occur simultaneously.

Using time cycles in conjunction with stock chart formations to predict the outcome of consolidation formations

We have placed relatively little emphasis in this book on chart formations—certain patterns of price movement that appear on stock charts which are purported to have predictive value. It is difficult to measure the performance of patterns by computer. However, many market technicians do attach considerable credence to chart formations, particularly to such supposedly reliable formations as the "head and shoulders" top and the "head and shoulders" bottom formations.

Figure 11–5 and 11–6 show how time cycles can often assist you in predicting the outcome of head and shoulder formations, not all of which result in penetrations of the necklines.

FIGURE 11-5

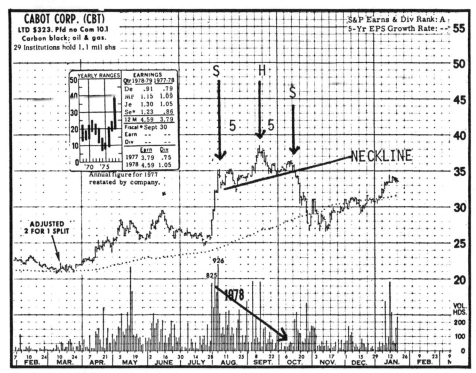

Cyclical analysis provided advance warning of a breakdown through the neckline. This is a classical head and shoulders top formation. Volume diminished as the formation progressed.

Source: *Trendline Daily Basis Stock Charts*, 345 Hudson Street, New York City, N.Y. 10014.

During the formation of intermediate tops, you will often find that intermediate cyclical periods separate the two shoulders of the head and shoulder formation. The head exists as a peak mid-way into the cyclical period. Since you know when prices are due to fall, via your cyclical analysis, the presence of a "shoulder" near an anticipated cyclical peak often provides advance warning of an impending price collapse.

The reverse often develops at market bottoms, where the right shoulder develops at a point where cyclical analysis indicates the market is due to turn up. Figure 11–6 illustrates this concept. Given the potential of this bullish formation, cyclical confirmation provides good reason to take positive action *before* the market starts to rise from the right shoulder through the neckline.

Using the 5–6 week trading cycle to anticipate longer intermediate moves before they develop

We have observed earlier in this book, in our discussion of channel reversal systems, that a market break below the lows of a previous 25–30 day period is likely to result in further market decline. We have also observed that a market rise through the highest high of the previous 25–30 days is likely to be followed through by higher prices.

FIGURE 11–6

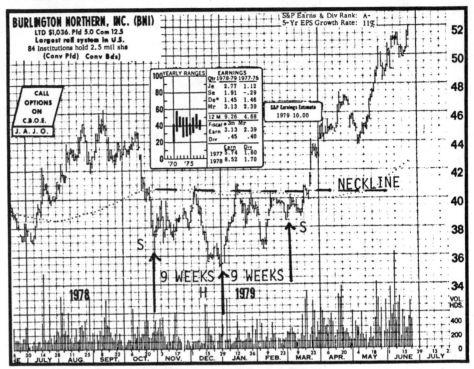

Cyclical analysis could have helped you foretell the breakout in Burlington Northern.

Source: *Trendline Daily Basis Stock Charts*, 345 Hudson Street, New York City, N.Y. 10014.

Figure 11–7 shows some of the applications of these observations to the market period, 1977–1979. We have marked off periods where *stocks failed to make a new high within a 5–6 week period of time*. The failure of stocks to make a new high within 25–30 days, particularly following a previous period of market advance, is almost always a forerunner of serious intermediate decline.

If, following such a failure, the market falls to new 5–6-week lows, you can almost always sell short successfully upon the next market rally, particularly if that rally once again falls short (usually on low volume) of surpassing the previous 5–6 week highs. The period just prior to the October 1978 market plunge was an excellent example of this sort of pattern.

Conversely, *should the market first rally to a new 5–6 week high* following a period of decline, and should the market then fail to make a new 5–6 week low (the test usually on low volume), you can almost certainly buy heavily upon the first market upturn. The period between March and April 1978 is an excellent case in point. After reaching a low point early in March, the market rose for a few weeks, declined, failing to establish a new 5–6 week low (a sign of trend reversal), and subsequently embarked on a very powerful advance.

FIGURE 11-7

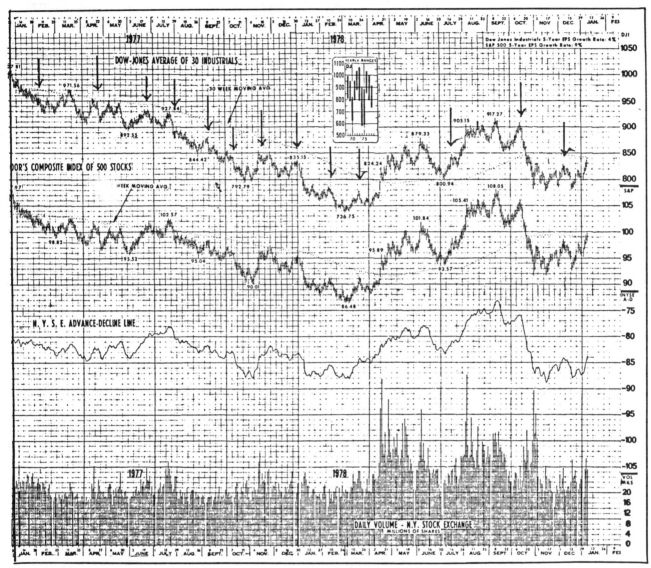

Almost all occasions when the market failed to surpass a previous high within 5–6 weeks were followed by subsequent market declines. You see how useful the 5–6 week trading cycle can be in this regard.

Source: *Trendline Daily Basis Stock Charts*, 345 Hudson Street, New York City, N.Y. 10014.

The 5–6 week buy-sell rules

The following trading rules, implicit in previous paragraphs, are here restated since they will form an integral part of our *Time-Trend-Momentum Trading System.*

1. A *buy signal* is rendered when, after a period of price decline, the market surpasses the highest levels achieved over the previous 25 trading sessions.

For maximum safety, however, await some retest of the lows prior to taking positions. Your best buying opportunity will occur approximately 5–6 weeks from the previous market lows, if prices have failed to fall below that low point.

2. A *sell signal* is rendered when, after a period of price advance, the market falls below the lowest low achieved over the previous 25 trading sessions.

For maximum safety, however, await some retest of the previous highs before selling short. Your best short selling opportunities are likely to occur approximately 5–6 weeks from the previous high areas if prices of that period remain unsurpassed. Place stop loss orders no more than a few points above those previous highs.

3. A *sign that a trend reversal is likely to occur* takes place when, in a rising market, no new highs are achieved within 25 trading sessions or in a falling market if no new lows in prices are recorded for 25 trading sessions. (We have chosen 25 days as a compromise figure; a range of from 23–30 days may actually be more accurate.)

We have now covered all the ingredients—*Time, Trend, and Momentum*—that are employed in our *Time-Trend-Momentum Trading System*. Let's move along at this juncture to Chapter 12, and into a discussion of the *Time-Trend-Momentum Trading System* itself.

The Time-Trend-Momentum
Trading System:
A system for the active,
aggressive intermediate stock trader

During the preceding eleven chapters, we have covered the following
ground:

1. We have learned how to measure stock market trends through the use of
   moving averages, and we have explored the benefits and limitations of
   trading systems based on moving averages.
2. We have explored significant market reversal trading systems and have
   isolated measures of channel reversal that appear, in themselves, to produce trading profit.
3. We have learned to recognize excessive conditions in the stock market
   and to determine which measures of excessive condition are likely to
   result in significant junctures for the stock market.
4. The use of the calendar in determining when to take action has been
   evaluated.

The time has now come to apply a bit of synergism, the combining of all of
these elements into one cohesive trading system that produces greater profit
in total than any of its components can produce alone. The system in question, of course, is the *Time-Trend-Momentum Trading System*.

The basic concept underlying the Time-Trend-Momentum Trading System

The trading system itself is actually relatively uncomplicated, although at times signals may prove open to some subjectivity. As we proceed, you will see what we mean, and you will also see that, whereas interpretation of signals may vary from trader to trader by a day or so, any gross variations in judgment are unlikely if you simply follow the codified rules we will be laying out.

The *Time-Trend-Momentum Trading System* relies mainly on the determination of excessive market conditions, measured by the 12-day rate of change of the NYSE Index. The majority of buy signals are rendered by turn-ups from excessively oversold conditions, and the majority of sell signals by top divergence signals, such as those we discussed in Chapter 7 and Chapter 10.

However, on those occasions when market momentum becomes very strong—strong enough to indicate that a continuation in trend is likely to occur—the system automatically changes from an excessive swing system to a trend following system. As we have seen, moving average systems come into their own during strongly trended markets. The Time-Trend-Momentum Trading System automatically shows you when a trading range market is likely to revert to a strongly trended market.

The calendar is used to identify significant market junctures and to prepare you for their appearance.

Finally, a system of stop-loss points is built in for those occasions when signals prove false, to limit loss and/or to make certain you do not miss any significant market advance or decline.

The system itself requires just a few minutes each day for its application. You need no particular mathematical skills; if you have followed us this far, you already know all the techniques you will require. Although you may apply the technique, stock by stock, market-based signals, as you shall see, are quite reliable and sufficient in themselves for trading a portfolio of securities. In short, although this trading system is by no means perfect, we believe you will find it a highly effective and ultimately very profitable trading tool.

The rules of operation of the Time-Trend-Momentum Trading System: Buy rules

Buy Rule 1A

A 12-day rate of change oscillator of the NYSE Index is maintained on a daily basis. This indicator will reflect the five- to six-week trading cycle in its oscillations, usually rising for the first two to three weeks of the cycle, then declining for the remainder of the cycle. The five- to six-week trading cycle is the shortest that can be employed profitably for commission vehicles, and we consider it the most suitable cycle for active, aggressive traders.

You BUY when the 12-day rate of change indicator turns up from the second trough of a flat or rising double bottom formation, provided that that double bottom occurs in the area between −2.00 and −3.00, oversold areas. An example is shown in Figure 12–1.

FIGURE 12–1

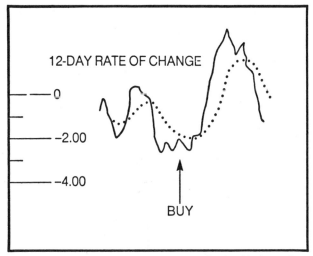

An example of the double bottom, Code 1A, buy signal. This example took place in May 1974, buy signal Number 17.

The double bottom in question may require only a few days for completion. We are not looking for a broad double bottom, only for some evidence that downside momentum has peaked.

As an alternative, if a double bottom formation does not take place, you BUY if the 12-day rate of change oscillator has fallen to the area between −2.00 and −3.00 and then starts to turn up, rising by at least an increment of 1.00 from its low point. An example is shown in Figure 12–2. In other words, presuming that a low point of −2.50 has been reached, you would buy, even without evidence of a double bottom, if the indicator rises to −1.50.

Rationales

Generally speaking, the area in question, −2.00 to −3.00, usually represents the ideal oversold area in which to take stock positions. Such readings occur only about two to four times per year on average, and except for serious bear markets or very severe intermediate declines, represent the junctures from which the stock market usually initiates at least trading advances.

However, since oversold conditions in themselves do not provide signals (the market may indeed continue to decline), we have built in a filter—either the double bottom or a given rise requirement—to reflect actual turning points in this oscillator.

Buy rule 1B

You may BUY, even when the oscillator has not reached the −2.00 area, if the 12-day rate of change shows a clearly defined pattern of rising bottoms, low points of which are spaced at three- to six-week intervals.

FIGURE 12–2

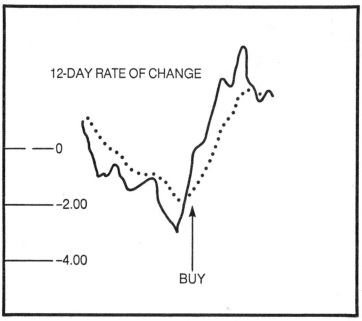

An example of a code 1A buy signal, triggered when the 12-day rate of change oscillator rises by 1.00 unit from its low point; this pattern developed in July 1970, buy signal Number 1.

The recognition of low points becomes greatly facilitated if you maintain a 0.20 exponential posting, graphed, of the 12-day rate of change oscillator. This smoothed rate of change graph often very readily points to the rising bottom formations in question, as it turns up from clearly defined rising low points.

Rationales

During periods of considerable underlying strength, the stock market may not retreat to oversold areas following a decline; the market may simply be too strong to sell off very sharply. Such conditions often exist as the market settles into broad bottoming formations—for example, as the right shoulders of inverse head and shoulder formations are created. As the market bottom progresses from the head to the right shoulder, rate of change indicators will trace out a series of ascending bottoms, none of which may fall to as low as −2.00. This series of ascending bottoms, reflecting diminishing downside momentum, reflects mounting accumulation and provides excellent buy indications.

As we have seen in our cyclical studies, the market is subject to two significant shorter term cycles: the three-week trading cycle and the five- to six-week trading cycle. Double bottoms of the type we are seeking tend to occur either on the three-week cycle or on the five- to six-week cycle, with low points spaced approximately three weeks or roughly five to six weeks apart. Such lows, confirmed by cyclical factors, generally prove highly significant.

Figure 12–3 illustrates the pattern in question. Notice how the 0.20 exponential average of the 12-day rate of change indicator highlights the rise in the double bottom formation, smoothing out the more jagged daily readings.

FIGURE 12–3

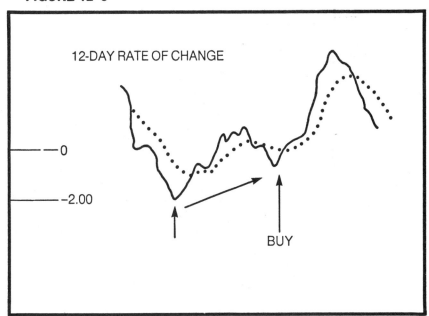

A Code 1B buy occurs when the 12-day rate of change oscillator traces out a clearly rising double bottom formation, the low points of which are spaced three to six weeks apart (the above buy pattern developed during November 1970).

Buy Rule 2

BUY even in the absence of other signals, if the market rises above its highest closing price achieved during the previous 25 days of trading (Figure 12–4). If you have previously sold short, cover all short sales.

Rationales

This is *not* among the more reliable of the buy rules, but it is included to prevent your missing a truly significant breakout and/or suffering grievous loss should you have sold short on a sell signal that backfires.

Computer study of channel reversal systems reveals that the purchase of stock on a "25-day breakout" does, on balance, prove profitable. This period is one of the stronger periods for channel reversal systems. You will find, however, from time to time, that such breakouts do occur at market tops, constituting what is often referred to as a "bull trap"—a false breakout to new highs, followed by an immediate market decline. These are among the

FIGURE 12–4

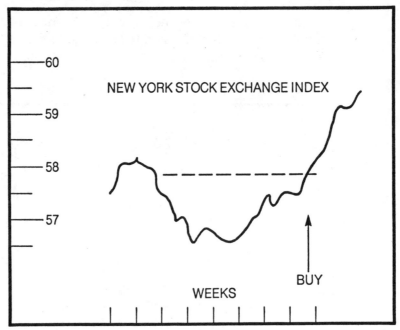

A Code 2 buy occurs when the NYSE Index surpasses its highest price reached during the previous 25 trading sessions (this buy occurred during July 1978).

most treacherous of stock market formations. Fortunately, the sell signals generated by the Time-Trend-Momentum Trading System rapidly become operative when these false breakout signals take place; your losses should remain relatively minor.

If you do suspect that an upside breakout may be false, you may, at your discretion, give the market an extra day or so before entering the market. False breakouts generally reverse very quickly, with no more than a day or two of follow-through before prices once again turn down. In assessing the results of the trading system, we have assumed that all signals, including the "25-day breakout signal," have been employed automatically.

Buy Rule 3 (a special additional condition)

If the 12-day rate of change oscillator has fallen to below −3.00, you must wait for at least three and a half to four weeks before buying, and then you may buy only if the oscillator shows a pattern of higher lows (Figure 12–5). The waiting period is measured from the day that the oscillator reaches its lowest reading, and is restarted each time the 12-day rate of change rises above and then falls below −3.00.

Rationales

You may recall that overbought and/or oversold conditions reflect likely areas for market turning points, *provided they do not reflect too strong a*

FIGURE 12-5

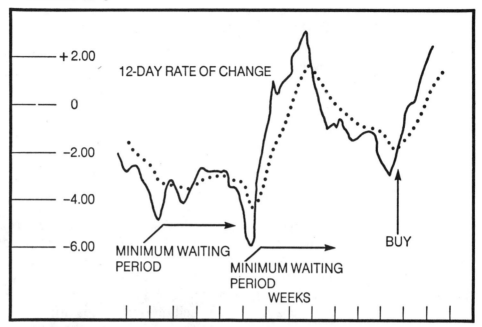

Should the 12-day rate of change oscillator fall to below −3.00, a 3½–4-week waiting period is required before you can act on upside reversals in the oscillator; the waiting period starts anew with each new low made. (the above pattern took place in mid-1970.)

momentum in one direction or the other. Periods of market weakness powerful enough to carry the 12-day rate of change indicator to regions as low as −3.00 are periods of severe weakness and are unlikely to reverse immediately into periods of strength. Given evidence of such market weakness, you should be in no hurry to reenter the stock market. Give the market time to recover, to repair technical damage, to build the base formations required for strong price recovery.

From time to time, by waiting, you may miss the actual lows of the stock market. Nothing, after all, comes to investors for nothing. You will, in exchange, receive much greater assurance that you are not entering into premature long positions within a serious bear market. A great deal of money is lost during bear markets by investors who do not recognize that severely oversold conditions represent market weakness—investors who attempt to "bargain hunt" as prices fall rather than to await evidence of price reversal. This mandatory waiting period will almost always provide ample time for you to profit from subsequent market rises, while keeping you out of stocks should prices continue to tumble.

The three- to four-week length of the waiting period, of course, hearkens back to our three-week trading cycle. If, following a severe decline, rates of change do not show any acceleration in downside momentum for a period of from three to four weeks, we can generally assume that downside momentum is ebbing and that the market may be safely reentered. As we review the history of signals generated by the Time-Trend-Momentum Trading System, you will see that, even with the mandatory waiting period, your purchases will often coincide with *actual price lows,* lows that often occur a few weeks following peaks in downside momentum.

Buy Rule 4

BUY on any buy signal that occurs immediately following a sell signal generated by a violation of the 0.04 exponential average, even if the 12-day rate of change oscillator falls to −3.00 in the interim. This rule will only rarely be triggered in the absence of other strong and valid buy signals.

Rationales

Sell signals based on the violation of the 0.04 exponential average are likely to occur, as we shall see, only following periods of very strong intermediate market strength. At other times, more rapidly triggered sell signals will be employed. Such market sells, occurring almost always during the initial stages of bull markets or late stages of very strong intermediate advances, are generally followed by rapid price recovery, even if the sell-offs prove sharp. (A sharp sell-off is not necessarily a long-lasting sell-off.) Therefore, you should be prepared to reenter the market quickly as soon as initial profit taking has been spent. Major market tops do take several months to form.

Rules for selling and for selling short

The above rules cover all of the *buy* situations; no buy signal occurs that will not be activated by at least one (and sometimes more) of the four buy signals. No market rise of any length can occur, mathematically, in the absence of at least one buy signal, which will trigger your entry into the stock market.

Following are the sell and sell-short triggering rules, at least one of which will be mathematically triggered before the stock market has progressed very far on a downward path. You sell on the first activation of a pertinent sell rule; however, you do not sell until at least one sell rule has been activated.

Sell Rule 1

SELL if the 12-day rate of change oscillator rises to above +3.00, but not to as high as +3.80, if the 0.15 exponential average of the NYSE Index is breached by the Index and starts to turn down (Figure 12–6).

Rationales

We stated above that The Time-Trend-Momentum Trading System automatically reverts from an excessive swing trading system to a trend following system when evidence exists that a strong trend has been set in motion. Such evidence is presented when the 12-day rate of change oscillator has been able to generate sufficient momentum to rise to the area of +3.00, a strong overbought area.

FIGURE 12–6

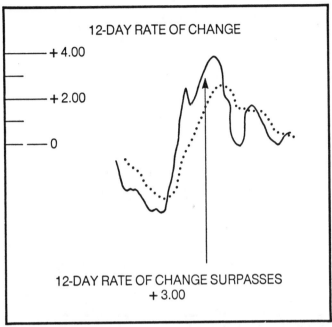

12-DAY RATE OF CHANGE

+ 4.00

+ 2.00

0

12-DAY RATE OF CHANGE SURPASSES
+ 3.00

If the 12-day rate of change oscillator surpasses +3.00, but does not reach +3.80, you switch to a downside crossing of the NYSE Index 0.15 exponential average as your next sell signal. (the above pattern developed during August 1971).

You will often find that, following such overbought readings, the market will continue to rise even while the indicator traces out a series of declining peaks. The appearance of these declining peaks in themselves often entices investors unfamiliar with the behavior of overbought-oversold oscillators to sell prematurely. Actually, the stock market frequently continues to rise—albeit at a slower rate—following high peaks in overbought-oversold oscillators. A peak reading as high as +3.00 usually indicates that the advance in question is a stronger than average market advance, and that investors need be in no immediate hurry to sell. The 0.15 exponential average serves, according to our research, as an excellent market trigger for selling, given the above conditions.

Sell Rule 2

SELL if the 12-day rate of change oscillator rises to above +3.80, if the 0.04 exponential average of the NYSE Index is breached by the Index and starts to turn down (Figure 12–7).

Rationales

Readings of +3.00 in the 12-day rate of change oscillator indicate the likelihood that the advance in motion is likely to be an above average market advance. Readings of +3.80 occur relatively infrequently and indicate that the advance in question is likely to be well above average in strength. Such

FIGURE 12–7

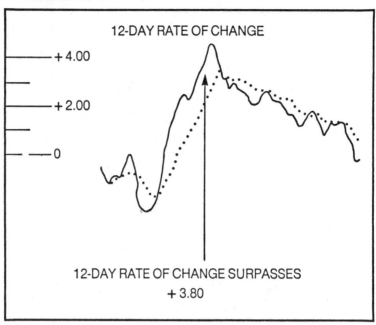

12-DAY RATE OF CHANGE

+ 4.00

+ 2.00

0

12-DAY RATE OF CHANGE SURPASSES
+ 3.80

Should the 12-day rate of change surpass +3.80, switch your sell signal to a downwards crossing of the .04 exponential average of the NYSE Index; do not sell short, however, on such a crossing (this pattern developed during December 1971).

readings tend to occur near the onset of market rallies that, in the end, are usually measurable in months rather than in weeks. You may see only one or two such market advances during each major bull market cycle.

Inasmuch as the evidence of a +3.80 reading indicates the promise of a very strong advance, our strategy will lie in attempting to ride with that market advance for as long as possible—in holding our stock positions for maximum gain, even through minor market corrections. We have therefore slowed our selling trigger, employing the 0.04 exponential average (the equivalent of a weighted 49-day or roughly 10-week moving average) as our sell trigger instead of the 0.15 exponential average.

You are likely to find, incidentally, that the first such sell signal, activated by a 0.04 exponential average penetration following a reading of +3.80, is generally followed by a resumption of market advance within a few days or weeks. In general, the conditions we have described tend to occur at the onset of major bull markets. During such periods, whereas declines may prove sharp, they are generally rapid, and price recoveries lead to either new highs in the market averages or a broadening of top formations prior to subsequent market declines.

Many investors may prefer to avoid selling on the first violation of the 0.04 exponential average, following a reading of +3.80 in the 12-day rate of change trading oscillator. Many such sell signals *will,* in the end, prove false. We have to leave this to you. For maximum safety, we do suggest that the signal be followed and that sales be made in accordance with the violation of the 0.04 exponential average. We do not, however, suggest that short sales be placed on such sell signals, *unless the market, in violating its 0.04 exponential average, either simultaneously or subsequently violates the lowest price recorded during the previous 25 trading sessions.* The violation of the 25-day trading channel often indicates serious weakness, weakness of sufficient magnitude to try a short sale or two. Under no other circumstance should you sell short on sell signals immediately following the sequence of a +3.80 reading in the 12-day rate of change oscillator and a sell signal triggered by activation of the 0.04 exponential average selling rule.

Remember that you repurchase on any buy signals generated subsequent to such sell signals *immediately,* even if the 12-day rate of change oscillator declines to −3.00. No waiting period is required on repurchases following the activation of the 0.04 exponential average sell rules.

Sell Rule 3 (for short term traders only)

You may SELL if the 12-day rate of change indicator turns down by 1.00 from a peak reading or traces out a series of declining low points, even if the low points are spaced very closely together in days. You do *not* sell short on such signals unless at least one sell-short rule, to be described, is activated. An example is shown in Figure 12–8.

Rationales

This rule should be applied only by short term traders, trading in very low or no-commission vehicles. The employment of this rule will help you exit from the market, often profitably, following very weak market advances but will often trigger you prematurely near the onsets of strong market moves, in which case you will probably have to reenter as the market moves to new 25-day high readings.

If you do opt to follow this sell rule, you will probably gain more total points over the years, but you will incur additional trades and additional commissions. In general, we do not advise investors other than very active traders to follow this rule, although some may employ it optionally, using it during dubious market periods but ignoring it when they suspect that the market carries good strength. In assessing our trading results, we have excluded sales based on Rule 3, although our research indicates that this is a very valid rule for shorter term operations.

Sell Rule 4

Sell when the following sequence of events occurs: the 12-day rate of change oscillator rises to a reading of +2.00 but not as high as +3.00. The indicator dips to a level below +2.00, but the market fails to activate any other sell signal. The indicator then rises once again but *fails to reach a level as high as +2.00. Sell* and *sell short* as soon as the 12-day rate of change oscillator falls by 1.00 from its secondary peak and/or if (1) a descending double top is made and/or if (2) the 0.20 exponential average of the oscillator turns down, especially if the turndown occurs at a point in time approximately three weeks from the previous peak. An example is shown in Figure 12–9.

FIGURE 12-8

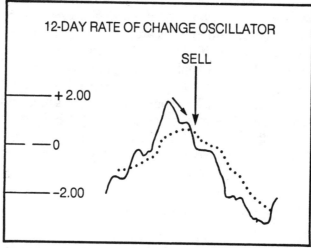

Short term traders may sell (but not sell short) whenever the 12-day rate of change oscillator either declines by 1.00 or etches out a declining double top formation. Both conditions are met in the above example.

Rationales

The above conditions present clear evidence that upside market momentum has diminished, following a stock market advance that promised no greater than average gains to begin with. You will often find that prices peak with the secondary (but lower) peak in the 12-day rate of change oscillator— the combination, a new high in price coupled with decreasing momentum,

FIGURE 12-9

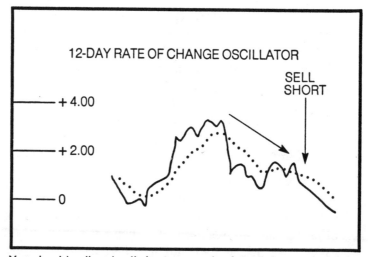

You should sell and sell short on a pair of declining peaks in the 12-day rate of change oscillator when the first peak surpasses +2.00 but the second peak fails to do so; this presumes that no .15 exponential or .04 exponential sell rules are in effect (the above pattern developed during May 1975).

provides the "top divergence" pattern described previously, a pattern that very frequently foretells market tops.

Rule 4 sell and sell-short signals are generally very effective and useful in protecting profits during trading range market periods. Do notice that Rule 4 sell signals are based on excessive swing techniques. Inasmuch as no greater than average upside momentum has been generated—the 12-day rate of change oscillator failing to surpass 13.00—we have *not* reverted to a trend-following sell trigger.

Sell Rule 5

SELL and sell short when the NYSE Index falls below the lowest level recorded during the previous 25 trading sessions (Figure 12–10). Closing levels are employed.

Rationales

This rule is likely to prove only marginally, if at all, profitable during bull market periods. However, it will often move you into short sales at very opportune moments following bear market rallies, which are often sharp—sharp enough to raise trading oscillators rapidly. If you suspect that you are in a good bull market, you may opt to employ Sell Rule 5 in conjunction with Sell Rule 6, awaiting a sequence of Rule 5 followed by Rule 6.

Sell Rule 6

SELL and sell short if the market, following a decline and then the onset of a new market rally, fails to reach a price level above the previous 25-day high (Figure 12–11). You sell and sell short as soon as the 12-day rate of change oscillator starts to turn down—either declining by 1.00 from its high reading, creating a double top, or falling below its own 0.20 exponential average.

Rationales

The failure of the stock market to achieve new highs within a 25-day period from previous high readings generally represents a sign of weakness and an indication that the 5–6-week trading cycle has turned down. Many significant intermediate double top formations are indicated in this manner.

A more bearish configuration takes place when the following sequence of events occurs.

1. The market falls to a reading below the lowest reading of the previous 25 trading sessions. This development, in itself, is a sign that the 5–6-week trading cycle has turned down. However, the attainment of new lows is frequently followed by at least some price recovery, so better short sale levels are often attainable if you await
2. the market's failure to reach new 25-day highs on the subsequent market rally. Given this failure, you may discern a pattern of lower lows, fol-

FIGURE 12–10

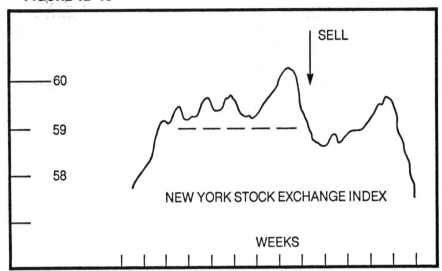

Sell and sell short whenever the NYSE Index falls below the lowest level reached over the previous 25 days. (The above example, September 1978, ultimately produced excellent short sale profits.)

lowed by lower highs, a clear downtrend in prices. Such a pattern developed in October 1978, an excellent short selling juncture.

The above trading rules encompass virtually every contingency you are likely to encounter and, as we have noted, will automatically trigger your entry into and out of the market before any significant price reversal can take place. They are designed to maintain long and short positions during periods of either extreme market strength or weakness, but to move you more rapidly in and out of stocks during more neutral market periods.

Let's summarize the signals now and the market conditions under which they are activated.

1. *Extremely strong stock market periods—12-day rate of change oscillator reaches +3.80.* You sell but do not sell short when the 0.04 exponential average of the NYSE Index is violated.
2. *Strong market periods—12-day rate of change oscillator reaches +3.00.* You sell but do not necessarily sell short when the 0.15 exponential average of the NYSE Index is violated. You sell short if the 12-day rate of change oscillator traces out a series of descending peaks, the last of which falls below +2.00.
3. *Neutral market periods—12-day rate of change oscillator fluctuates between −3.00 and +3.00.* You buy on double bottoms or on rises of +1.00 from the lows of the oscillator. You sell on minor double tops or on falls of +1.00 in the oscillator (short term traders). Intermediate traders will sell and sell short when the oscillator traces out a clear pattern of 3–6-week double tops, the second peak of which fails to reach a level of +2.00.

FIGURE 12-11

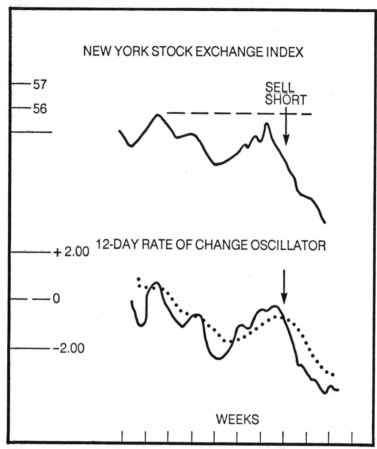

NEW YORK STOCK EXCHANGE INDEX

SELL
SHORT

12-DAY RATE OF CHANGE OSCILLATOR

WEEKS

Sell and sell short on a turndown in the 12-day rate of change oscillator if the NYSE Index turns down after failing to make a new 25-day high. (This pattern developed in October 1971, initiating a serious market decline.)

4. *Very weak market periods—12-day rate of change oscillator falls to below −3.00.* You wait at least 3–4 weeks from the latest low in the oscillator in the area below −3.00 and then buy if the oscillator's 0.20 exponential average turns up, if a double bottom is created, or if the oscillator rises by 1.00 from a secondary bottom.

Fail-safe signals

You buy if the market rises above the highest level it has attained over the previous 25 trading sessions. You sell if the market falls below the lowest level reached during the previous 25 trading sessions. You also sell short should the market fall beneath the lowest level recorded during the previous 25 trading sessions, unless you believe that a bull market is in effect, in which case you await a rally and sell short if the market turns down without moving to a level above the highest level achieved during the previous 25 trading sessions.

**How to maintain the
daily postings
required for tracking
the market
with the Time-
Trend-Momentum
Trading System**

The actual computations required each day for the posting of the oscillators and exponential averages involved in the Time-Trend-Momentum Trading System should involve no more than a few minutes. You will require some ledger sheets with columns and some graph paper. On the graph, you plot each day the closing level of the NYSE Index, the 12-day rate of change oscillator and the 0.20 exponential average of the 12-day rate of change oscillator. Your ledger worksheet should be laid out as follows:

Date (1978)	Closing level, NYSE Index	.15 exponential avg., NYSE Index	.04 exponential avg., NYSE Index	12-day rate of change, NYSE Index	.20 exponential avg., 12-day rate of change
4/13	50.91	50.27	49.91	+0.95	+0.54
4/14	51.85	50.50	49.99	+1.79	+0.79
4/17	52.69	50.83	50.10	+2.75	+1.18
4/18	52.16	51.03	50.18	+2.31	+1.41
4/19	52.35	51.23	50.27	+2.91	+1.71
4/20	52.73	51.45	50.37	+3.07*	+1.98
4/21	52.64	51.63	50.46	+2.55	+2.10
4/24	53.10	51.85	50.56	+2.91	+2.26
4/25	53.81	52.15	50.69	+3.40	+2.49

* Note: +3.00 surpassed, switch to .15 exponential signal.

In maintaining your daily worksheets, we suggest that you might find it useful to allow an extra column for notes, such as the one we placed on this sheet following the trading day 4/20/78. Such notes may be useful as reminders. In the example given, the note reminds you to switch from excessive system sell signals to a trend following sell signal, in this case the 0.15 exponential average. Had a reading of +3.80 been achieved during this series, you would have added an additional note, "3.80 reached, switch to 0.04 sell signal." As it turned out, the maximum reading of the 12-day rate of change oscillator achieved during this period came to +3.47 on April 28, so the 0.15 sell signal remained in effect. This sell signal became activated on May 24, 1978, at a New York Stock Exchange Index level of 54.36; the market subsequently fell to an intermediate low point at 53.00, achieved on July 5, 1978.

Other notations you may find useful will include notes such as the following: "−3.00 reached, wait four weeks before buying," "−3.00 reached once again, wait 4 weeks before buying," "−3.28 reached, new low, start four-week wait once again," "new five-week high in averages just attained," "new 25-day low just made, sell short," "peak reading in 12-day oscillator at 2.81, sell if it falls to 1.81," and so forth. These again are reminder notes that should be entered on your daily worksheet.

Just one more word regarding the worksheet: if you will refer once again to our example, you may notice that the daily readings of the 12-day rate of change oscillator demonstrated sharp declines on April 18 and again on April 21, 1978. *However, the 0.20 exponential average of the daily rates of change continued to rise, even on both of those days, indicating that the trend of momentum remained nicely up during the period.* You will find that the 0.20 exponential average of daily readings of the 12-day rate of change oscillator does smooth the data and does provide an extra and valuable ingredient in your measurement of market momentum. Do take the trouble to plot this exponential average.

Tracking the Time-Trend-Momentum Trading System over a nine-year period

Table 12–1 shows all the signals rendered by the Time-Trend-Momentum Trading System between April 1970 and February 1979. Buy signals are those signals described previously. No sell signal was employed unless it was also a signal to sell short, so certain signals that might have been acted on by shorter term traders are not reflected in this table.

Table 12–2 shows all of the results of sell-short signals that would have been activated between April 1970 and February 1979. Sell signals in Table 12–1 appear as sell-short signals in Table 12–2. Buy signals in Table 12–1 appear as cover-short signals in Table 12–2. You can see the summary of results for buy signals only in Table 12–1 and for sell-short signals only in Table 12–2.

The codes that appear on the tables correspond to the codes for the various signals presented earlier in this chapter. Each signal appears in sequence. Buy signals are identified by numbers, sell signals are identified by letters. Figures 12–12 to 12–20 show the NYSE Index for the years 1970–78, the 12-day and 25-day rate of change oscillators, their respective 0.20 exponential averages, and all the buy and sell signals that appear in Tables 12–1 and 12–2. Downward-pointed arrows identify sell signals; rising arrows identify buy signals. Each arrow is numbered, and the code of the activating signal is presented. You should be able to follow all the transactions that would have, at least hypothetically, been made during this period, and should be able to familiarize yourself with the chart patterns involved.

Let's consider some of the more significant signals that were rendered during this period.

Sell Signal A

The first sell and sell-short signal in our series, April 1970, developed when the NYSE Index and its 12-day rate of change oscillator both turned down after failing to make new highs within a 25-day period. Notice how the 0.20 exponential average of the oscillator more clearly rendered a sign of the turndown than the raw oscillator readings themselves.

Buy signal 1

This was a classic bear market bottom buy signal. The 12-day rate of change oscillator plummeted during the selling climax, May 1970, to the area

TABLE 12-1
Results of buy signals employing the Time-Trend-Momentum Trading System, 1970–1979*

Buy signals				Sell Signals				Point change	Percent change
Date, buy	Signal number	Action code	Price level, NYSE Index	Date, sell	Signal number	Action code	Price level, NYSE Index		
7/9/70	1	1A	40.26	11/13/70	B	4	45.38	+ 5.12	+12.72%
11/23	2	1B	45.73	5/17/71	C	2–5	55.48	+ 9.75	+21.32
5/26/71	3	1A–4	54.86	6/17	D	6	55.46	+ .60	+ 1.09
6/29	4	1A	54.48	7/13	E	6	55.12	+ .64	+ 1.17
8/17	5	2	55.27	9/24	F	5	54.26	−1.01	−1.83%
9/30	6	1B	54.33	10/14	G	6	54.27	− .06	− .11
11/26	7	1B	50.57	5/2	H	5	59.12	+ 8.55	+16.91
5/5	8	1A	59.30	6/28	I	5	59.20	− .10	− .17
7/5	9	1B	59.85	7/11	J	6	59.40	− .45	− .75
7/18	10	1A	58.45	9/8	K	5	60.53	+ 2.08	+ 3.56
10/20	11	1A	59.77	1/29/73	L	5	62.79	+ 3.02	+ 5.05
5/2/73	12	1A	57.46	5/14	M	5	56.20	−1.26	−2.19
6/29	13	1A	54.84	8/16	N	5	54.57	− .27	− .49
9/19	14	1A–1A,2	56.90	10/31	O	5	58.28	+ 1.38	+ 2.43
12/26	15	1A	50.80	1/31/74	P	4	51.64	+ .84	+ 1.65
3/15	16	2	52.17	3/29	Q	5	50.21	−1.96	−3.76
5/24	17	1A	46.59	6/27	R	5	45.13	−1.46	−3.13
10/7	18	1A	34.19	11/5	S	4	39.54	+ 5.35	+15.65
11/7	19	2	39.63	11/18	T	5	36.76	−2.87	−7.24
12/23	20	1A	34.72	6/9/75	U	4	48.54	+13.82	+39.80
6/20	21	2	49.39	7/25	V	5	47.87	−1.52	−3.08
9/4	22	1A	45.86	9/15	W	5	44.01	−1.85	−4.03
9/18	23	1A	44.53	11/21	X	4	47.38	+ 2.85	+ 6.40
12/10	24	1A	46.40	4/23/76	Y	6	54.54	+ 8.12	+17.50
6/2	25	1A	53.33	7/15	Z	4	56.23	+ 2.90	+ 5.54
9/1	26	1A	55.50	10/8	AA	5	54.85	− .65	−1.17
11/16	27	1A	53.52	1/4/77	BB	4	57.14	+ 3.62	+ 6.76
3/1/77	28	1A	54.64	3/25	CC	5	53.92	− .72	−1.32
4/6	29	1A	53.26	4/22	DD	5	53.67	+ .41	+ .77
5/5	30	1A	54.60	5/17	EE	5	54.33	− .27	− .49
6/20	31	2	54.90	7/25	FF	4	55.32	+ .42	+ .77
8/12	32	1A	53.61	8/25	GG	5	52.68	− .93	−1.73
9/28	33	1A	52.14	10/12	HH	5	51.57	− .57	−1.09
11/3	34	1A	49.80	1/3/78	II	5	51.82	+ 2.02	+ 4.06
1/20/78	35	1A	49.73	2/14	JJ	6	49.47	− .26	− .52
3/7	36	1A	48.62	5/24	KK	4	54.36	+ 5.74	+11.81
6/5	37	2	55.85	6/21	LL	5	53.85	−2.00	−3.58
7/26	38	2	55.62	9/18	MM	5	58.23	+ 2.61	+ 4.69
11/30	39	1A	52.89	1/31/79	NN	4	55.94	+ 3.05	+ 5.77
2/13	40	1B	55.46	2/27	OO	6	53.88	−1.58	−2.85

* Presuming that purchases of the NYSE Index were made on buy signals and held until sell short signals were received. (This record is hypothetical; no actual trading took place via this system for the period shown.)

Summary of results of signals shown in Table 12–1

Number of profitable transactions: 21
Number of unprofitable transactions: 19

Average point gain, profitable transactions: +3.95
Average point loss, unprofitable transactions: −1.04

Average percentage gain, profitable transactions: +8.82%
Average percentage loss, unprofitable transactions: −2.08%

TABLE 12-2
Results of short sale signals employing the Time-Trend-Momentum Trading System, 1970–1979*

Sell short signals				Cover short signals				Point change		Percent change	
Date, short sale	Signal number	Action code	Price level, NYSE Index	Date, cover	Signal number	Action code	Price level, NYSE Index				
4/10/70	A	6	48.86	7/9/70	1	1A	40.26	+ 8.60		+17.60%	
11/13	B	4	45.38	11/23	2	1B	45.73		− .35		− .77%
5/17/71	C	2–5	55.48	5/26/71	3	1A–4	54.86	+ .62		+ 1.12	
6/17	D	6	55.46	6/29	4	1A	54.48	+ .98		+ 1.77	
7/13	E	6	55.12	8/17	5	2	55.27		− .15		− .27
9/24	F	5	54.26	9/30	6	1B	54.33		− .07		− .13
10/14	G	6	54.27	11/26	7	1B	50.57	+ 3.70		+ 6.82	
5/2	H	5	59.12	5/5	8	1A	59.30		− .18		− .30
6/28	I	5	59.20	7/5	9	1B	59.85		− .65		−1.10
7/11	J	6	59.40	7/18	10	1A	58.45	+ .95		+ 1.60	
9/8	K	5	60.53	10/20	11	1A	59.77	+ .76		+ 1.26	
1/29/73	L	5	62.79	5/2/73	12	1A	57.46	+ 5.33		+ 8.49	
5/14	M	5	56.20	6/29	13	1A	54.84	+ 1.36		+ 2.42	
8/16	N	5	54.57	9/19	14	1A–1A,2	56.90		−2.33		−4.27
10/31	O	5	58.28	12/26	15	1A	50.80	+ 7.48		+12.83	
1/31/74	P	4	51.64	3/5	16	2	52.17		− .53		−1.03
3/29	Q	5	50.21	5/24	17	1A	46.59	+ 3.62		+ 7.21	
6/27	R	5	45.13	10/7	18	1A	34.19	+10.94		+24.24	
11/5	S	4	39.54	11/7	19	2	39.63		− .09		− .23
11/18	T	5	36.76	12/23	20	1A	34.72	+ 2.04		+ 5.55	
6/9/75	U	4	48.54	6/20	21	2	49.39		− .85		−1.75
7/25	V	5	47.87	9/4	22	1A	45.86	+ 2.01		+ 4.20	
9/15	W	5	44.01	9/18	23	1A	44.53		− .52		−1.18
11/21	X	4	47.38	12/10	24	1A	46.50	+ .88		+ 1.86	
4/23/76	Y	6	54.52	6/2	25	1A	53.33	+ 1.19		+ 2.18	
7/15	Z	4	56.23	9/1	26	1A	55.50	+ .70		+ 1.30	
10/8	AA	5	54.85	11/16	27	1A	53.52	+ 1.33		+ 2.42	
1/4/77	BB	4	57.14	3/1/77	28	1A	54.64	+ 2.50		+ 4.38	
3/25	CC	5	53.92	4/6	29	1A	53.26	+ .66		+ 1.22	
4/22	DD	5	53.67	5/5	30	1A	54.60		− .93		−1.73
5/17	EE	5	54.33	6/20	31	2	54.90		− .57		−1.05
7/25	FF	4	55.32	8/12	32	1A	53.61	+ 1.71		+ 3.09	
8/25	GG	5	52.68	9/28	33	1A	52.14	+ .54		+ 1.03	
10/12	HH	5	51.57	11/3	34	1A	49.80	+ 1.77		+ 3.43	
1/3/78	II	5	51.82	1/20/78	35	1A	49.73	+ 2.09		+ 4.03	
2/14	JJ	6	49.47	3/7	36	1A	48.62	+ .85		+ 1.72	
5/24	KK	4	54.36	6/5	37	2	55.85		−1.49		−2.74
6/21	LL	5	53.85	7/26	38	2	55.62		−1.77		−3.29
9/18	MM	5	58.23	11/30	39	1A	52.89	+ 5.34		+ 9.17	
1/31/79	OO	6	55.96	2/13	40	1B	55.46	+ .48		+ .86	

* Presuming that short sales of the NYSE Index were made on sell short signals and that short sales were covered on subsequent buy signals. The results shown in both Table 12–1 and Table 12–2 are hypothetical, based on retroactive study of the market. No trading took place based on the signals employed during this period, and no assumptions of equal performance should be necessarily made for the future.

Summary of results of signals shown in Table 12–2

Number of profitable transactions: 26
Number of unprofitable transactions: 14

Average point gain, profitable transactions: +2.63
Average point loss, unprofitable transactions: −0.75

Average percentage gain, profitable transactions: +5.07%
Average percentage loss, unprofitable transactions: −1.42%

of −6.00. This called for a four-week waiting period, measured from the low point. The buy signal, early in July, developed as the 12-day rate of change oscillator turned up from a clearly rising double bottom formation. The period between the May lows and the July lows was almost exactly six weeks—once again demonstrating the validity of the 6-week cyclical period.

Buy signal 7

The buy signal in November 1971, a very significant buy, developed just 4 weeks from a −3.00 reading—once again, evidence of the 3–4-week trading cycle. You can see how the 0.20 exponential average of the 12-day rate of change readings etched out a clearly rising double bottom formation.

The trading oscillator reached +4.00 during December 1971, so we would have switched to a trend following system, requiring in this case a violation by the NYSE Index of its 0.04 exponential average before selling.

Buy signal 14

In this case, August 1973, the 3–4 week waiting period following a decline in the 12-day rate of change to −3.00 did not help. Buy Signal 14 had to await the market's rising to a new 25-day high. Sell Signal O, on the other hand, triggered by a violation of a 25-day low, did prove quite timely.

Buy signal 15

Here the four-week waiting period once again would have kept you out of the market until the completion of the December 1973 bottom formation. The nicely rising pattern of the 12-day rate of change oscillator confirmed the existence of at least a temporary market bottom. The entire December 1973–April 1974 period was difficult, however, and befuddled just about all trading systems.

Sell signal R

There will be many occasions when it will not pay to sell short on violations of the 25-day channel, when prices fall to a new 25-day low. There will be many other occasions when this signal will place you properly on the short side in time to profit from major market declines, particularly during the most severe phases of bear markets.

During 1973 there were two periods when the four-week waiting period from low points in the 12-day rate of change oscillator, in the area below −3.00, did not help—the August and the December periods. The reason for the waiting period, however, becomes clear during such periods as the May 1974–September 1974 span of time. Refer to the June 1974 period. Were it not for the imposition of the four-week rule, you would probably have been a buyer during June and July—just in time to become whipsawed as the market entered into its final selling wave, the worst of the bear market.

Buy signal 18

This was an excellent buy signal, right at the bear market low point, triggered by a clear turnup in the trading oscillator, following a mandatory four-week waiting period from oscillator lows in the area below −3.00. Sell Signal "T", of no particular help of course, was rapidly canceled by Buy Signal 20 in December 1974. The oscillator surpassed the 13.80 line during January 1975, and so the market went onto its long-term 0.04 sell signal basis.

Sell signal U

The period between May and September 1975 was difficult for the trading system, although final losses proved, in the end, to be minor. The final market run to new highs during July proved to be a bull trap. The 12-day rate of change oscillator lay in a downtrend as the market advanced to new highs but, according to the rules of the trading system, no selling or short selling could take place until a 25-day low was violated. This occurred on July 25, still early enough to avoid approximately half of the total market decline of the period.

We have presumed, in calculating our results, that signals would have been operated on in accordance with all codified rules. However, as we have mentioned, thrusts to new highs in the face of declining upside momentum often constitute traps. If you suspect at all this is taking place, give the market an extra two or three days before reentry on the long side. False upside moves generally give way very quickly.

The sell signal at W, based on a violation of a 25-day low, is followed for the record in our tabulations, but here too you may have given the market the benefit of the doubt before actually selling, inasmuch as the rising pattern of the 12-day rate of change oscillator, following an extreme oversold reading, promised eventual price recovery. Relatively little was lost, however, as Buy Signal 23 led you back into the market fairly quickly.

The Time-Trend-Momentum Trading System is obviously not perfect: there will be periods of false signals, some of which you may be able to recognize via other technical tools. The system does prevent you, however, from remaining on the wrong side of the stock market for very long periods of time.

The 1976 period

The 12-day rate of change trading oscillator reached +3.80 during January 1976, and so no sell-short signals were rendered until April, when the market failed to make a new five-week high.

Our system operated very well during this period, a period when trend following systems fared less well, befuddled by the price oscillations that took place between February and April.

The year as a whole proved relatively uneventful for the stock market; the sysem caught the two trading opportunities that did develop during the year, one in June and one in November.

The 1977 period

We discovered in our research that 1977 was a particularly difficult year for the majority of our trading systems. Almost all systems produce their best results during strongly trended markets, which 1977 was not. You will generally find that gradual downtrends produce the greatest problems, since it takes little in the way of a rally to trigger buy signals but few buy signals during such periods result in profit.

The year did prove profitable on balance, however, particularly if you operated with short signals as well as long signals, and if you operated with issues that conform to the NYSE Index, heavily capitalized issues. The years 1977 and 1978 were unusual in the degree of disparity that existed between the institutional sector of the market (downtrended) and the secondary sector (strongly uptrended). Had your purchases been confined to secondary issues, buy signals would have produced superior results; short sale signals, however, would have proved less profitable.

Buy signal 38

Buy signal 38, in July 1978, developed late; our system was fooled somewhat by the mandatory four-week wait following a decline in the 12-day rate of change trading oscillator during June 1978. The oscillator actually reached a low point of −3.01, so many of you (and ourselves) might have been tempted to ignore the mandatory four-week waiting period as the market started its July rise.

Sell signal MM

Sell signal MM, triggered by a decline to a 25-day low, proved particularly propitious. The 12-day rate of change trading oscillator fell to −3.00 during the initial phase of the decline, and the subsequent market advance lacked vigor—volume declining during the move, and the advance-decline line falling far short in its recovery of the Dow Industrial Average.

The early October period witnessed ideal conditions for aggressive short selling. A new 25-day low had just been made. The subsequent price recovery failed to reach a new 25-day high. Volume during the advance proved low; breadth was weak. Aggressive short selling should have been undertaken as soon as the market turned down.

Buy signal 39

You can almost always be certain that a significant intermediate bottom will soon be at hand when the 12-day rate of change oscillator declines to the −6.00 region. You cannot, however, be certain that further declines will not take place, just because that extreme level has been reached. That is why we impose the four-week waiting rule—a rule that sometimes delays action unnecessarily, but at other times prevents premature buying action.

Buy Signal 39 developed, as such signals often do, at the conclusion of the basing period that preceded the 1979 market advances, early enough for full participation but delayed sufficiently to minimize the chances of your being whipsawed as the basing activity developed.

The 25-day rate of change oscillator

We have placed within the charts a plotting of the 25-day rate of change oscillator and its 0.20 exponential average, as a useful adjunct to the 12-day rate of change oscillator. Our work has indicated that the 25-day rate of change oscillator tends not to produce as timely a set of signals as the 12-day rate of change oscillator. However, you may find the 25-day oscillator useful, as we do, as a confirming indicator, which often reaches low and high points more coincidentally with the market averages than the 12-day rate of change oscillator.

Top and bottom divergent patterns do tend to appear with greater clarity in the shorter term rate of change indicator.

Top and bottom divergences

We have drawn, in Figures 12–12 through 12–20, some of the significant top and bottom divergent patterns that appeared at significant market junctures during the 1970–78 period.

A top divergence develops when the market makes new highs, but the 12-day and 25-day rate of change oscillators fail to follow suit. Such conditions almost always shortly precede market declines, except when the initial upside momentum has been very strong (+3.80 in the 12-day rate of change oscillator).

Bottom divergences occur when market levels fall to new lows, while downside momentum decreases, evidenced by a rising pattern in the 12-day and/or 25-day rate of change trading oscillators. Such conditions generally precede imminent market advances.

Divergences are shown on the chart by arrows pointing, within a time frame, in divergent directions.

FIGURE 12-12
Action signals generated by Time-Trend-Momentum, 1970

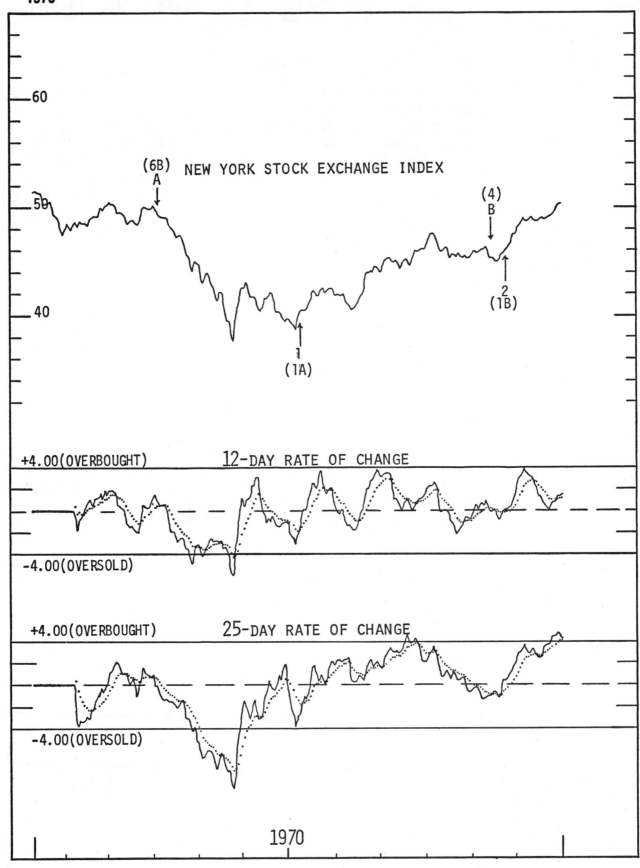

FIGURE 12–13
Action signals generated by Time-Trend-Momentum,
1971

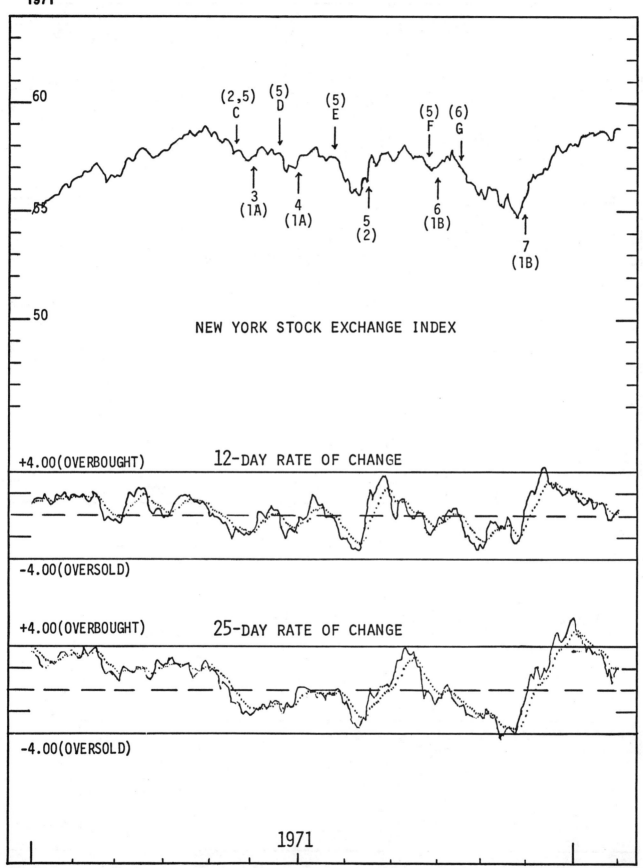

FIGURE 12-14
Action signals generated by Time-Trend-Momentum,
1972-1973

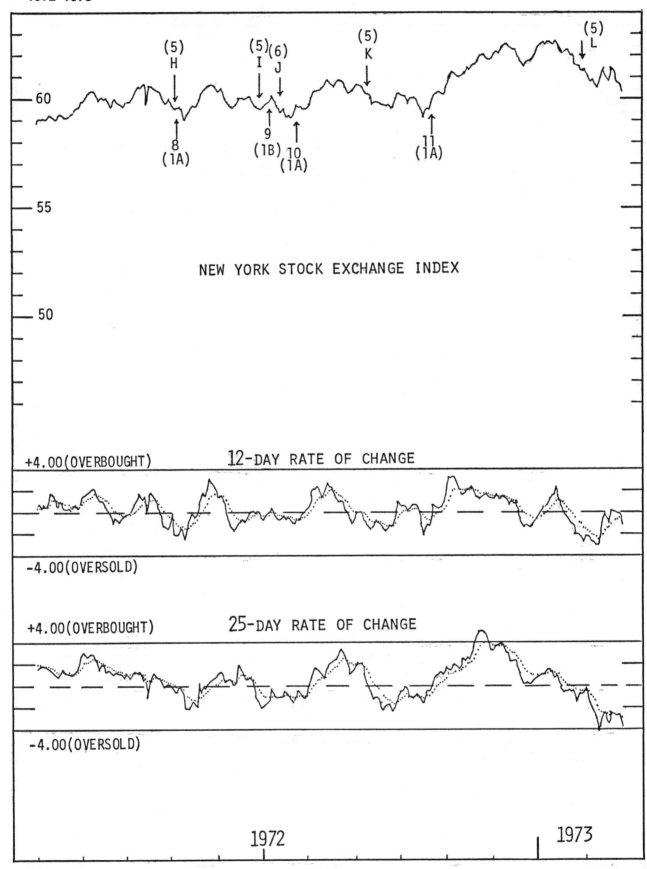

FIGURE 12–15
Action signals generated by Time-Trend-Momentum,
1973–1974

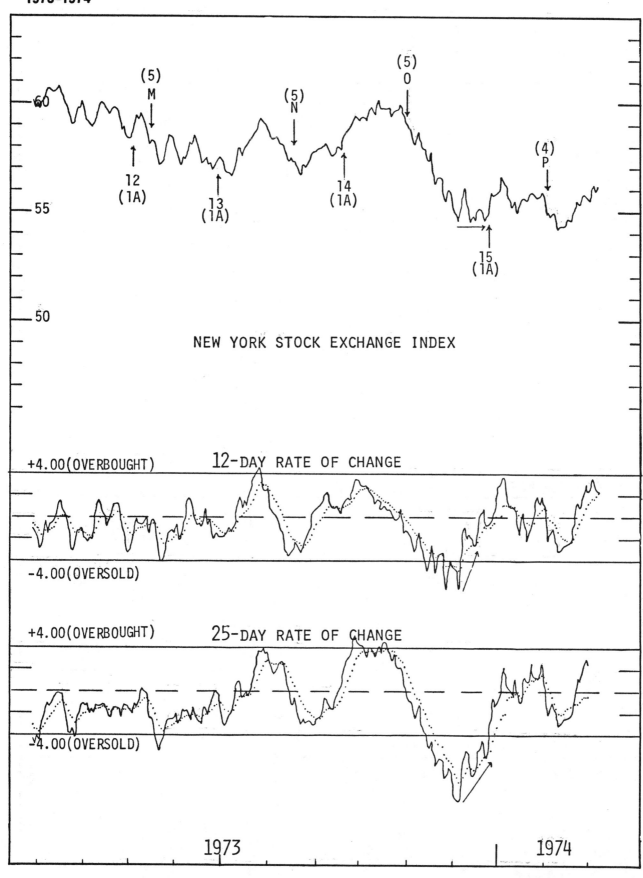

NEW YORK STOCK EXCHANGE INDEX

FIGURE 12–16
Action signals generated by Time-Trend-Momentum,
1974

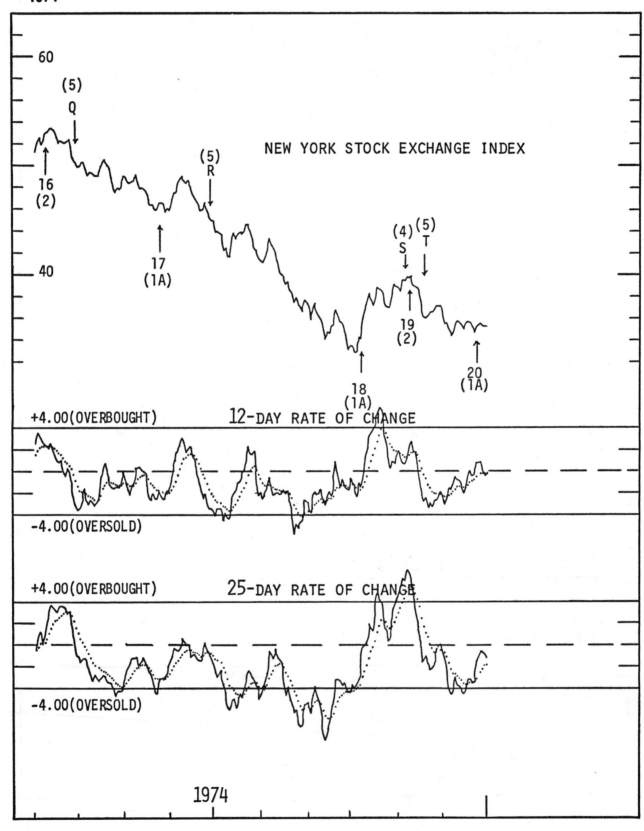

FIGURE 12–17
Action signals generated by Time-Trend-Momentum,
1975

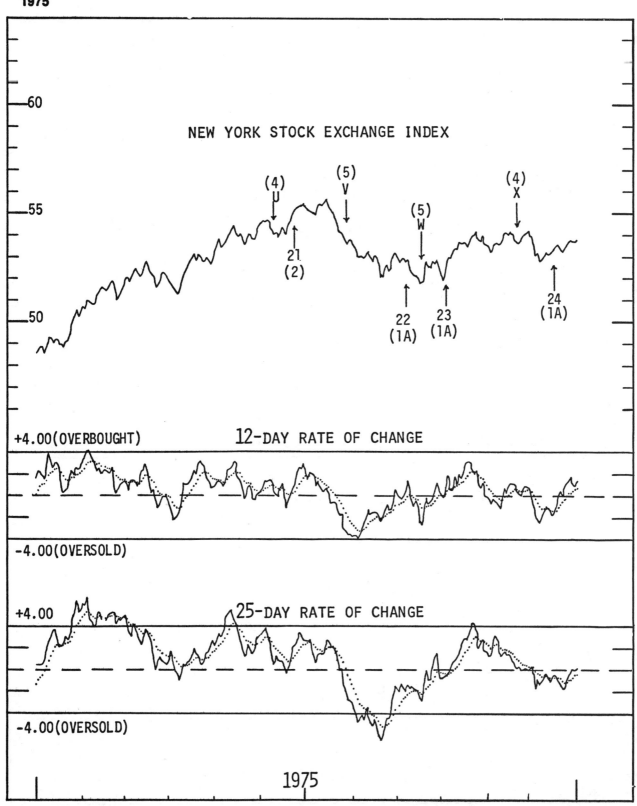

FIGURE 12–18
Action signals generated by Time-Trend-Momentum,
1976

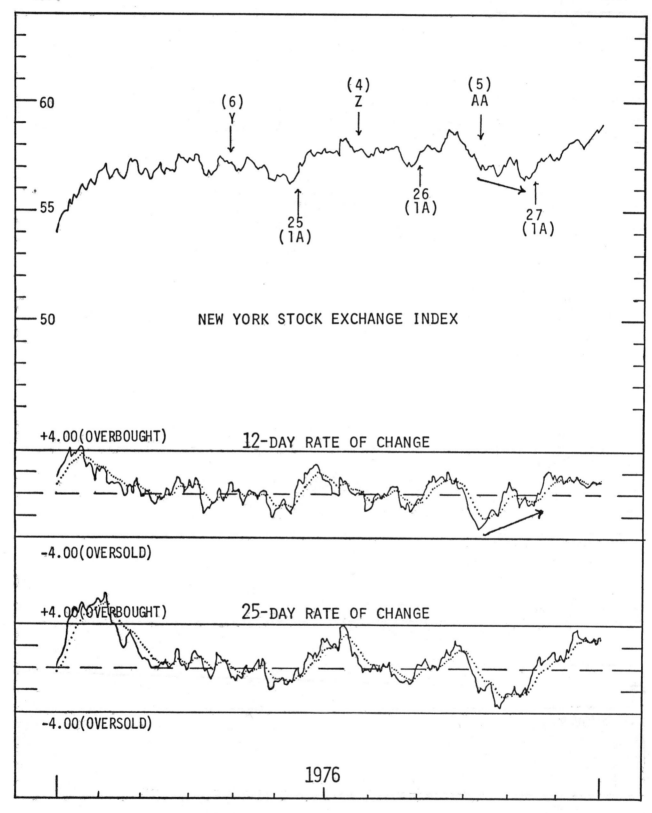

FIGURE 12–19
Action signals generated by Time-Trend-Momentum,
1977

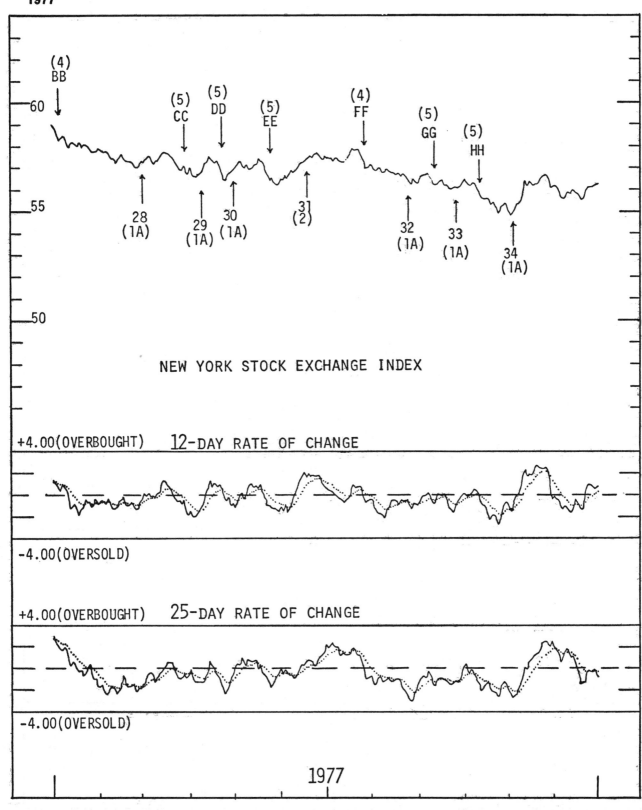

FIGURE 12–20
Action signals generated by Time-Trend-Momentum,
1978

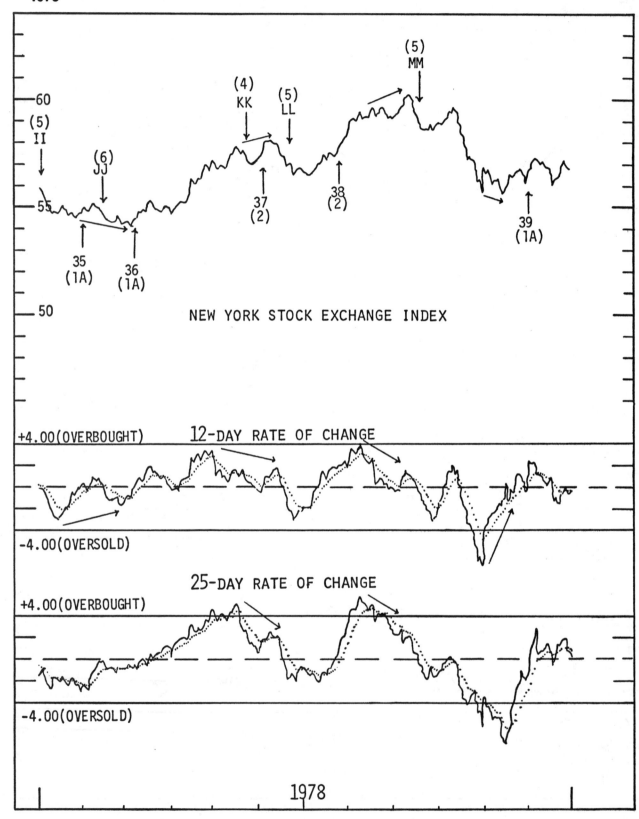

NEW YORK STOCK EXCHANGE INDEX

+4.00(OVERBOUGHT)   12-DAY RATE OF CHANGE

−4.00(OVERSOLD)

25-DAY RATE OF CHANGE
+4.00(OVERBOUGHT)

−4.00(OVERSOLD)

1978

13

The enormous profit potential
and the application of
the Time-Trend-Momentum
Trading System

We have now covered the mechanics and what we believe would have proved to be the essential hypothetical buy and sell short signals generated by the Time-Trend-Momentum Trading System for the 1970–79 period. It is time now to evaluate further the implications of these signals and the profit potential implicit in the close tracking and trading of stocks on signals generated by this trading system.

You may, at this point, refer back to Tables 12–1 and 12–2 in Chapter 12, which list the transaction signals and results for the above period. Right here, however, let's restate the summary of the results derived from these tables.

Magnitude of profits compared to magnitude of losses

1. *On the buy side, only slightly more than half of your trades would have proved to be profitable.* There were 21 profitable transactions (commission costs and dividends excluded) and 19 unprofitable transactions. In this regard, the time-trend-momentum trading system fares only slightly better than many other automatic trading systems. You must learn to accept small losses if you are going to employ this trading system.

2. *However, your winning trades would theoretically have proved to be nearly four times the magnitude per trade in relation to the size of your losing trades.* The average gain per winning buy transaction amounted in our study, to 3.95 points on the NYSE Index per trade. The average loss came to only 1.04 points. The greatest single profit came to 13.82 points on the NYSE Index. The greatest single loss came to only 2.87 points. In total, you would have

gained 82.89 points on winning transactions in 1970–79 and lost only 19.79 points during losing transactions—a net gain of 63.1 points. Between the time of the first buy signal and the last sell signal, a buy and hold approach to the NYSE Index would have shown a gain of only 13.62 points.

The average percentage gain per profitable signal came to 8.82 percent. The average percentage loss per unprofitable signal came to only 2.08 percent.

You can see, in short, that while your signals would have proved profitable on the buy side only slightly more than half the time, your total results would have proved very favorable. This system keeps you in profitable transactions for as long as the market behaves favorably; it removes you very quickly when the market turns against you.

3. *On the sell short side, 65 percent of the trades in our hypothetical study proved profitable!* It is often said that the most difficult part of stock trading is knowing when to sell. These results should certainly help your market timing in that regard, not to mention the losses avoided by not buying in right near market tops.

The magnitude of profit on the average profitable short sale is approximately 3.5 times the magnitude of the average loss on the unprofitable short sale. In this regard, the record of short sales is similar to the record of buy signals. However, the average price change shown per short sale is less than the average price change shown per buy action.

4. *The total points gained, long and short, in 1970–79 would have come to 121.05 points on the NYSE Index—or to nearly nine times the point gain achieved via a buy and hold approach!* That is something to think about, isn't it?

Caveat

Before we proceed any further, we do want to emphasize that the above results were secured by retroactive and hypothetical study, and we do not mean to imply any guarantees of similar profit, any profit, or equal results in the future. Furthermore, it is possible that your judgment may differ from ours as to when signals will and would have been rendered. Nor are commission costs and/or dividends included in the above tabulations.

That's the bad news. On a more favorable note, you will almost certainly find, as we have, that as you become familiar with the patterns generated by the Time-Trend-Momentum Trading System, you will be able, in actual usage, to anticipate signals frequently, thereby improving results considerably. Signal results are based, in our work, on closing market prices. There will be many occasions when you will be able to act intra-day at more favorable levels, as you see signals developing.

Transaction costs represent no problem at all if you trade no-load mutual funds. We will list in Chapter 15 a number of brokerage houses where you can trade stocks and stock options at very minimal commissions.

And finally, we make no allowance for interest received while in cash (if you do not sell short on sell signals), for dividend payouts and for taxes (a debit, unfortunately). This is not a system for the generation of long term capital gains; you will have to look elsewhere if minimum taxation is of prime importance.

The profit potential of compounding via the Time-Trend-Momentum Trading System

Figure 13–1 shows the results of compounding $10,000 hypothetically invested in "shares of the NYSE Index," presuming in the top scale that you had operated by buying on all buy and selling short on all sell-short signals shown in Table 13–1, reinvesting all proceeds of the previous transaction, and the results had you operated similarly, employing buy signals only and selling but not selling short on sell signals. The period covered is from July 9, 1970 (NYSE Index at 48.86) to February 29, 1979 (NYSE Index at 53.88). A buy and hold approach would have seen your original $10,000 grow to $13,383. Buying the NYSE Index shares on buy signals and selling on sell signals—moving into cash—would have theoretically resulted in your original $10,000 growing to $36,854 between the first buy signal, July 9, 1970, and the last sell signal, February 27, 1979. A buy and hold approach through this period, again, would have shown a final value for an original $10,000 of $13,383.

Had you acted on all buy and sell-short signals, your final value, February 27, 1979, would have come to $91,264! Bear markets would appear to offer opportunity, not necessarily adversity. Do notice in Figure 13–1, however, that neither approach—buy and sell, buy and sell short—resulted in losses of any magnitude during bear markets.

Your compounded rate of return, buy and hold, would have come to 3.42 percent for the period shown. It would have amounted to 16.24 percent for the buy and sell strategy. By buying and selling short on sell-short signals, compounding your capital, you could have theoretically achieved an annualized rate of return of 29.05 percent! (Commission costs, dividends and taxes are excluded in all cases.) Other caveats obviously pertain as well. Just for a pleasant flight into fantasy, $25,000 compounded at a rate of 29.05 percent per year would amount to $1,146,331.28 at the end of 15 years. If you could compound at that rate for 20 years, your $25,000 would grow to $4,102,987.43! This, we guess, is one way to beat inflation. You will, we are afraid, be faced with some tax problems along the way.

How to apply The Time-Trend-Momentum Trading System to a portfolio of securities

At this point, the issue naturally once again arises whether market-based timing signals can be applied to individual securities, or whether individual issues require individual tracking as well.

According to our research, a well-diversified (approximately 6–10 issues) portfolio of stocks should perform very closely in tune to market-based timing signals. We have already illustrated this point, but will illustrate it once again. Portfolios of mutual funds will almost certainly do so. If your mutual funds are typically more volatile than the stock market as a whole, you

FIGURE 13–1
Hypothetical results achieved by compounding, trading
"shares of the NYSE Index" according to signals generated by
The Time-Trend-Momentum Trading System, 1970–1979
(no actual trading took place with this method during the time shown)

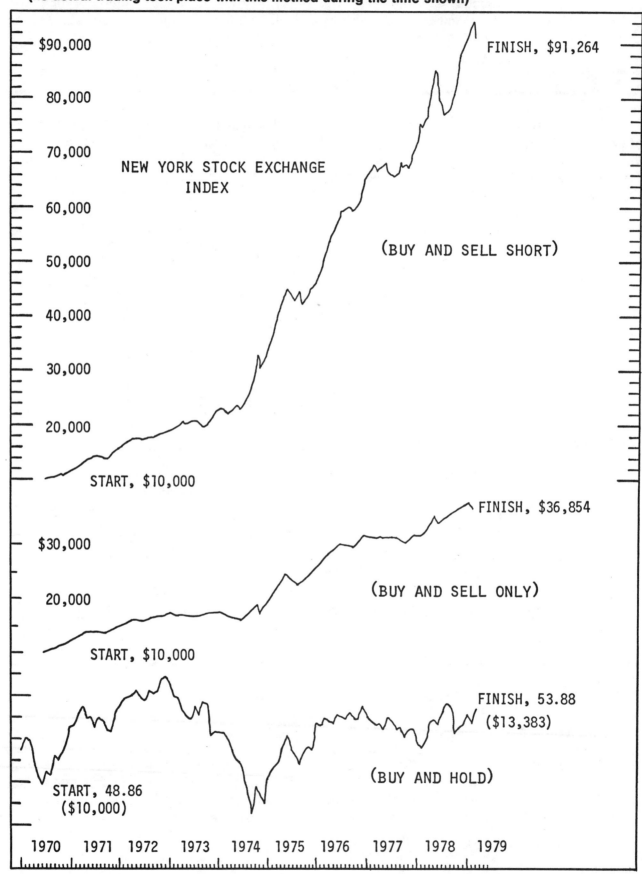

NEW YORK STOCK EXCHANGE
INDEX

(BUY AND SELL SHORT)

FINISH, $91,264

START, $10,000

FINISH, $36,854

(BUY AND SELL ONLY)

$30,000

20,000

START, $10,000

FINISH, 53.88
($13,383)

(BUY AND HOLD)

START, 48.86
($10,000)

1970 1971 1972 1973 1974 1975 1976 1977 1978 1979

$90,000

80,000

70,000

60,000

50,000

40,000

30,000

20,000

should achieve performance, in terms of total profit, superior to what we compute for our hypothetical trading of the NYSE Index shares, although this cannot be guaranteed. During 1972, for example, the Standard & Poor's 500 Index outperformed the majority of mutual funds. During 1977 and 1978, the reverse was true.

Institutional grade issues will generally conform most closely, as a group, to the NYSE Index, the index employed in our tracking. We have obviously not evaluated any number of stock selection systems that have been purported to "beat the market," but, according to other research, issues that demonstrate superior strength relative to the market averages appear to offer some promise of continuing to outperform the market. Issues favored by insider buying appear to provide superior opportunities on the long side during rising market periods. Some research seems to indicate the advisability of selling short issues that have been subject to heavy insider selling. More volatile issues should provide greater price fluctuation—and potentially greater profit (and risk)—than issues of lower volatility.

Data concerning insider transactions, relative strength and such have been available from a variety of sources, including but not limited to *The Value Line Investment Survey* and *The Zweig Securities Screen,* both of which advertise regularly in such publications as *Barron's Financial Weekly.*

Let's return to our basic assumption, however, that you can operate with a simple but diversified portfolio of issues. How would such a portfolio have fared over the years had its components been traded according to market signals generated by the Time-Trend-Momentum Trading System? Table 13–1 should provide some clues.

Discussion

You can see the very close correlation between the results of trading individual issues according to market signals based on time-trend-momentum generated buy and sell signals and the hypothetical results we achieved by trading "shares of the NYSE Index." Individual issues do tend to be more volatile than market averages, and so swings per issue tend to run somewhat larger than swings of the NYSE Index itself.

The above group of issues was selected as representative of institutional quality issues we believed would track well along with the system. Of the group, only Atlantic Richfield failed to perform well. Some of these issues were stronger than the total marketplace during the 1970–79 period; some were not. If relative strength biased the results for long side purchases, then these issues should have performed poorly via-à-vis the total marketplace on our short sale signals. Table 13–2, which compares short sale results for the NYSE Index and for this group of stocks, should provide some additional clues to whether you can simply purchase and sell short a diversified group of stocks based on signals generated by a market average, in this case the NYSE Index.

Individual issues tracked very closely on the short side as well as the long side in terms of conformity to the total market, insofar as the frequencies of profitable and unprofitable trading signals were concerned. The trading of

TABLE 13–1
Comparative results of trading the NYSE Index via the Time-Trend-Momentum Trading System and trading a selected portfolio of issues via market signals generated by this system, 1970/1979*

Issue	Number of profitable trades	Number of unprofitable trades	Average percent gain per profitable trade	Average percent loss per unprofitable trade
NYSE Index	21	19	+ 8.82%	−2.08%
Honeywell	18	20	+19.75	−5.61
IBM	23	17	+ 9.32	−3.64
Avon	20	18	+13.17	−6.10
Dupont	25	15	+ 8.23	−3.69
Boeing...............	25	15	+17.40	−6.20
Atlantic Richfield	21	19	+ 0.88	−0.54
Hewlett Packard	24	16	+15.81	−4.08
Teledyne	21	18	+16.23	−7.81
Digital Equipment	20	19	+16.64	−7.05
Minnesota Mining	23	16	+ 8.36	−2.73
Aetna Life & Casual. ..	24	14	+11.37	−6.60
Burroughs	17	22	+14.20	−4.30
Texas Instruments	24	15	+14.46	−6.99
Schlumberger	26	14	+12.10	−4.57
Corning Glass	26	14	+15.13	−6.47
Halliburton	23	17	+12.73	−4.66
Raytheon	18	21	+18.65	−5.91

* The presumption is made that purchases of components in the portfolio are made on market buy signals and held until sell short signals are generated, but that sales, not short sales, are executed at those times.

Averages (individual stocks only):
  Average number of profitable trades: 22.23
  Average number of unprofitable trades: 17.06
  Average percent gain per profitable trade: 13.20%
  Average percent loss per unprofitable trade: 5.11%

the NYSE Index on Time-Trend-Momentum trading signals produced 26 profitable short sales and 14 unprofitable short sales. The trading of individual issues on the same signal dates would have produced an average of 22.70 profitable signals and 16.41 unprofitable signals. (Unchanged results were disregarded.) Of the seventeen issues in our hypothetical portfolio, only three—Schlumberger, Halliburton, and Atlantic Richfield—would have produced more losing than profitable transactions.

Only two issues—Boeing and Atlantic Richfield—showed a higher magnitude of percentage change for unprofitable short sales than for profitable short sales. Only two issues—Atlantic Richfield and Schlumberger—would

TABLE 13–2
Comparative results of selling the NYSE Index short on Time-Trend-Momentum Trading System sell short signals and selling short a diversified group of issues on sell short signals generated by this system, 1970–1979*

Issue	Number of profitable trades	Number of unprofitable trades	Average percent gain per profitable trade	Average percent loss per unprofitable trade
NYSE Index	26	14	+ 5.07	− 1.42
Honeywell	24	15	+ 9.95	− 4.58
IBM	27	13	+ 5.10	− 1.86
Avon	21	19	+ 9.39	− 3.31
DuPont	27	12	+ 5.76	− 2.96
Atlantic Richfield	17	22	+ 4.16	− 4.34
Hewlett Packard	21	19	+ 9.85	− 3.37
Teledyne	24	16	+ 8.17	− 7.17
Digital Equipment	20	18	+ 6.74	− 5.50
Minnesota Mining	22	18	+ 7.48	− 2.49
Aetna Life & Cas.	21	16	+ 6.96	− 5.54
Burroughs	22	17	+ 8.00	− 4.41
Texas Instruments	27	12	+ 7.05	− 5.95
Schlumberger	16	24	+ 5.76	− 5.08
Corning Glass	30	10	+ 7.99	− 4.76
Boeing	27	12	+ 7.20	−10.30
Halliburton	19	20	+ 5.84	− 5.50
Raytheon	21	16	+12.00	− 5.26

* The presumption is made that short sales of each issue in the portfolio are made upon sell short signals generated for the NYSE Index and that short sales are held until the first cover short signal that follows.

Averages (individual stocks only):
  Average number of profitable short sales: 22.70
  Average number of unprofitable short sales: 16.41
  Average percent gain per profitable short sale: 7.49%
  Average percent loss per unprofitable short sale: 4.85%

have shown an average loss per short sale transaction if all short sale transactions were averaged together. None of these issues would have shown a loss if all long purchases, reflected in Table 13–1, were averaged together.

All told, individual issues in our sample did not produce as high a profit as a group as the NYSE Index did in terms of short selling, but nonetheless, as a group, would have proved profitable short selling vehicles in terms of selling short via Time-Trend-Momentum short selling signals. Schlumberger, a poor performer on the short side, rose from a price of 10 in 1970 to over 98 in 1979, so that short sales made against the issue opposed a pronounced major long term uptrend. Boeing, another poor performer on the short side, rose during the 1970–79 period from a price of 7 to a price of 71. Halliburton rose, during the same period, from a price of 12 to a price of 63. The major uptrends in these issues, on the other hand, did help in their performance on the long side, as reflected in Table 13–1.

It does, indeed, appear that results of trading stocks via the Time-Trend-Momentum Trading System can be greatly improved if you select for purchase issues showing greater than average long term strength relative to the total marketplace and if you select for short sales issues showing weaker than average long term strength compared to the total marketplace. "Market stocks" such as IBM and DuPont have conformed very closely to the NYSE Index in results achieved through trading these securities on market-based timing signals.

We would like to emphasize once again, however, that the Time-Trend-Momentum Trading System does, in our research, appear profitable even in the absence of any particular attempt to select stocks, as long as you diversify your portfolio. Total return for a diversified portfolio is likely to prove more related to volatility than anything else, providing that the issues in your portfolio, as a group, show relative strength similar to the market averages.

How trading the volatile swingers can really pay off big

For a comparison of the effects of volatility on results, let us consider the results of trading Honeywell, a higher than average issue in terms of volatility, with IBM, a lower than average issue in terms of volatility. Both issues tracked very well, on the long side and on the short side, in terms of the Time-Trend-Momentum Trading System, but Honeywell showed much broader fluctuations in price between 1970 and 1979.

Figure 13–2 shows the results of a buy and hold approach to IBM in 1970–79, the results of a buy and sell approach based on time-trend-momentum, and the results of buying long and selling short on sell signals. An initial investment of $10,000 is presumed; no adjustments have been made for dividends, commission costs and/or taxes.

We see that IBM started the period at a price of 203½ and finished at a price of 299⅛. A $10,000 investment on July 9, 1970 would have grown to $14,699 as of February 27, 1979 had the issue simply been purchased and held.

By comparison, had you purchased IBM on buy signals and sold the issue on sell signals, reinvesting proceeds on subsequent buy signals, your initial $10,000 investment would have grown to $38,629.75. Had you purchased the issue on buy signals, selling shares short on sell-short signals, your initial $10,000 investment would have compounded up to $93,056.71—an annualized compounded rate of return of 29.34 percent—almost exactly what would have been theoretically achieved by trading "shares of the NYSE Index" for the same period on the same market dates.

Honeywell is among the more volatile of institutional grade issues, is actively traded and, in addition, features both put and call options on the CBOE for traders who prefer to employ the utmost in leverage. The results of simply

FIGURE 13–2
Hypothetical results derived by trading IBM on market signals generated by the Time-Trend-Momentum Trading System, presuming the compounding of all capital, 1970–1979

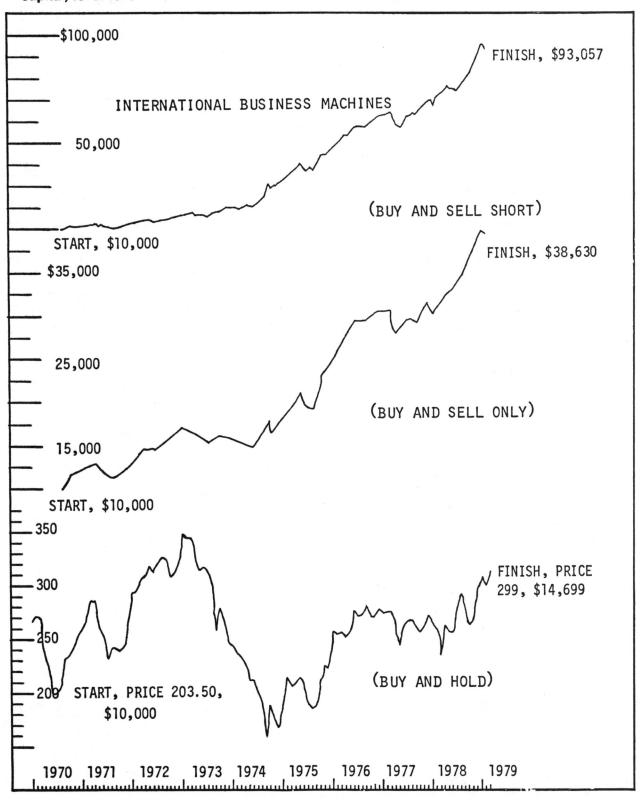

buying and holding Honeywell from July 9, 1970 through February 27, 1979 would have proved quite disappointing (see Figure 13–3). The issue declined in price over the period from a price of 70 to a price of 63¾; an initial $10,000 investment would have declined to $9,107.14 had the shares been purchased and held—hardly an inflation fighter, even if we do throw back in the dividends paid throughout the years.

Purchased and sold in accordance with market signals developed via the Time-Trend-Momentum Trading System, the stock would have produced a profit of $48,342.27 during the July 9, 1970 to February 27, 1979 period—a final value for the $10,000 originally invested of $58,342.27. This represents a compounded rate of return of 22.56 percent per year—very creditable. Results of buy-sell trading of Honeywell are reflected in Figure 13–3.

For really exciting results, however, refer to Figure 13–4, which reflects the results of buying Honeywell on Time-Trend-Momentum buy signals and selling the issue short on sell-short signals, compounding the proceeds of each transaction. Your original $10,000 calculates as having grown—from July 9, 1970, to February 27, 1979—to $195,119.77, an annualized compounded growth rate of 40.87 percent! These results exclude the effects of commission costs, dividends, and taxes, of course.

We have no desire to mislead any investor. Honeywell has been among the best tracking issues for almost all of the trading systems we have tested. The stock has, over the past decade, proved to be a strongly trended, market reliable issue, with above average volatility—in short, the ideal candidate for the Time-Trend-Momentum Trading System and for just about any trading system we tested. Nonetheless, the results of trading the issue do reflect the potential of the Time-Trend-Momentum Trading System and, if possible, you should search out issues with similar characteristics.

You should, we presume, have the idea by now; the Time-Trend-Momentum Trading System is by no means perfect, but it certainly does appear to offer considerable potential for profit. There may be periods, nonetheless, when you might opt to ignore certain of its signals. Let's move along now to Chapter 14, where we will encounter two useful backup trading systems, systems you may employ to clarify the direction of major market trends. The Time-Trend-Momentum Trading System does happen to be a very powerful market tool. However, even this system has periods of ambiguity, some of which may be resolved by recourse to one or the other of the backup systems we will be discussing.

FIGURE 13–3
Hypothetical results derived by buying and selling
Honeywell on market signals generated by the
Time-Trend-Momentum Trading System, presuming
the compounding of all capital, 1970–1979

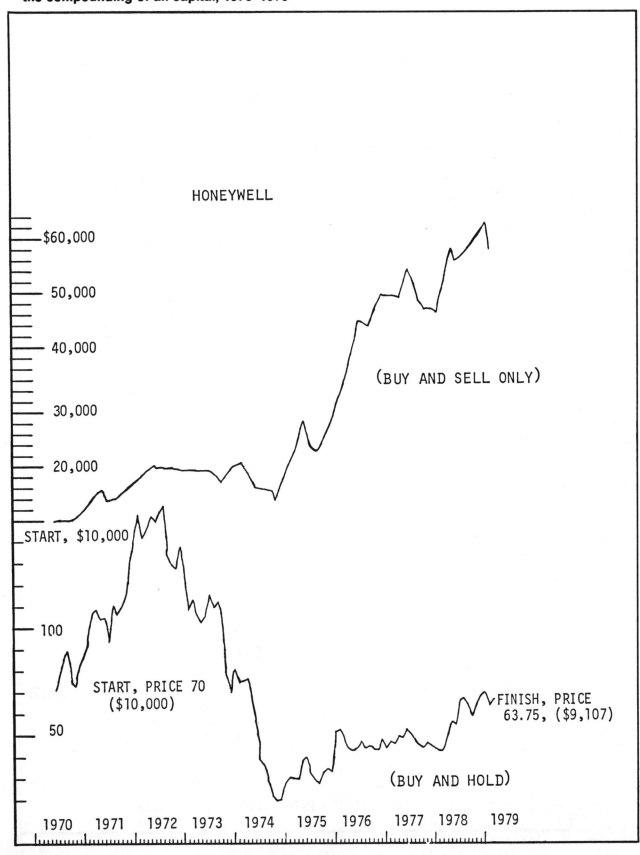

FIGURE 13–4
**Hypothetical results derived by buying and selling
Honeywell short on market signals generated by the
Time-Trend-Momentum Trading System, presuming
the compounding of all capital, 1970–1979**

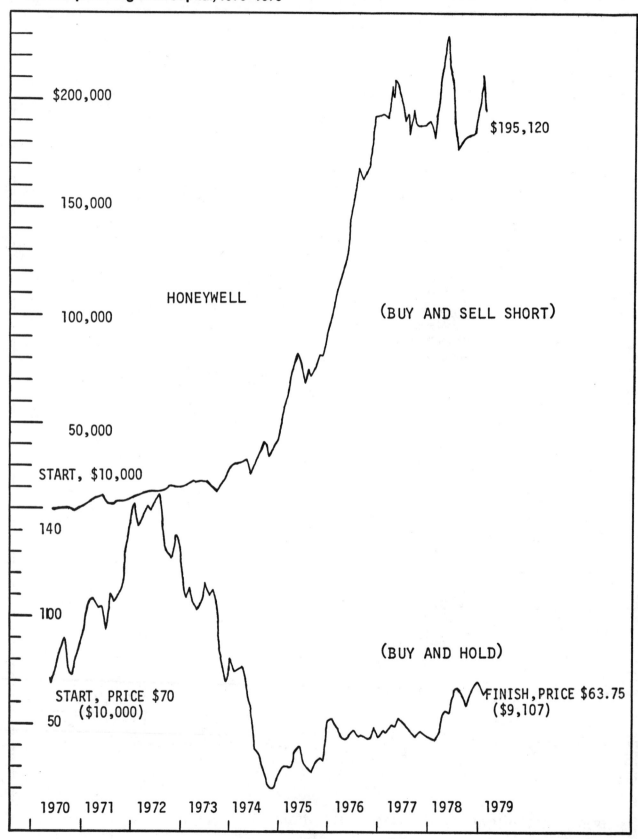

Two trading systems for
the determination of
the major trends of the stock
market—the "cats and dogs relative
strength major trend indicator"
and the "zero balance major
trend trading system"

The majority of trading systems that we have so far discussed relate to the shorter and intermediate term trends of the stock market and are designed to be more or less followed on a fully automatic basis. Nonetheless, there will be many occasions when you may prefer to disregard shorter term buy and sell signals, particularly when such signals fail to conform with the major trends of stock prices.

A number of means of determining major trends have already been discussed, including the employment of longer term moving and exponential averages, which do reflect longer term market trends. However, as we have also seen, such moving averages frequently lag the market, changing direction only after some considerable market movement has already taken place. This lag is likely to result in missed profits and perhaps some losses along the way, if you await confirmation of shorter term moving averages by changes in direction of longer term moving averages. Therefore, we did explore other means of determining major market trends, methods that are likely to trigger in advance of moving average systems but that still provide the advantages of virtually automatic signaling. In this chapter, we will discuss two methods for determining the major market trend, both providing excellent results over the years, and both bypassing many of the limitations of longer term moving average systems.

The cats and dogs relative strength major trend indicator

One of the so-called truisms of Wall Street involves the theory that the stock market is more likely to rise when the quality of market leadership is high—when higher-grade (and usually higher-priced) issues show strong relative strength compared to the secondary tier of stocks. In theory, purchases of higher-quality issues are more likely to be made by institutional or other heavily capitalized investors, supposedly the "smart money," while purchases of secondary, speculative issues are assumed to be made by the "public investor," supposedly the little guy, who is more likely to be incorrect in his assessment of market conditions.

Given these assumptions, popular theory has it that excess speculation—reflected in higher relative strength among the secondary issues—represents a forerunner of market decline. In other words, if the smaller investor is running up "his" stocks while the larger investor is failing to run up "his" stocks, time is running out for any bullish trend in motion.

This is the popular theory. As we shall shortly see, the myth that the institutional investor is smarter than the public investor turns out to be just that—a myth.

How to compute the cats and dogs relative strength indicator

We tested the assumptions, employing the following procedure:

1. A relative strength ratio was calculated at the end of each trading week by dividing the closing level of the Over-the-Counter (OTC) Composite Index by the closing level of the NYSE Index.

    The OTC Composite Index was employed as a measure of the strength of the secondary market. Although the NYSE Index includes all listed issues on the New York Stock Exchange, it is weighted by capitalization and is therefore more reflective of the primary sector of the stock market. The Dow Industrial Average and/or the Standard & Poor's 500 may have been employed as alternatives. We did not test these but assume that results would have proved similar to those obtained by employing the NYSE Index.

    Given our procedure, you would secure rising results from the division during periods when the OTC Composite showed greater strength than the NYSE Index, and descending results during periods when the over-the-counter segment of the stock market manifested declining strength compared to the New York Stock Exchange.

2. A .20 exponential average was maintained of the relative strength ratio secured each week by dividing the closing level of the OTC Composite Index by the closing level of the NYSE Index.

3. A buy signal is rendered when the relative strength ratio secured by dividing the level of the OTC Composite by the NYSE Index crosses from below to above its .20 exponential average. All figures are rounded to two decimal places. In the event of a tie, the current signal remains in effect.

4. A sell (and, if you choose, sell short) signal is rendered when the relative strength ratio secured by dividing the level of the OTC Composite by the NYSE Index crosses from above to below its .20 exponential average.

Assumptions

As you can see, our assumptions have run counter to the assumptions generally made. We have assumed, implicitly in the nature of our signals, that the market is likely to show greater strength when the more volatile OTC Composite outperforms the less volatile NYSE Index. Therefore, buy signals are rendered during periods of mounting OTC relative strength and sell signals are rendered when the more volatile OTC Composite declines relative to the NYSE Index.

Results

Table 14–1 shows the results of hypothetical trading, 1972–79, based on the signals generated by the cats and dogs relative strength major trend indicator.

Assessment of results

This system produced excellent signals during 1972 and 1973, fair signals between 1974 and 1976, and excellent signals once again between 1977 and 1979. Had you employed these signals on the buy side only, between 1972 and 1979, you would have achieved a compounded annualized rate of return, by the Value Line (VL) Composite, of approximately 6.9 percent per year on your capital. This presumes that all proceeds from sales were reinvested upon buy signals, but excludes dividends, commissions and interest received on your capital while you were in a cash position.

While a 6.9 percent return may not exactly result in instant wealth, in assessing these results you should keep in mind that a buy and hold approach over the same period would have resulted in a loss of approximately .95 percent per year. This system certainly did outperform a buy and hold approach to the market for the period shown.

Had you sold short, instead of simply selling, on sell signals, your original $10,000 would have grown to approximately $22,298—a compounded rate of return of 11.3 percent per year, exclusive of dividends, taxes and commissions.

How to improve the results

Inasmuch as our results were based on the VL Composite, a broad market average, you should be able to improve results by trading high "beta" issues or mutual funds, stocks and/or funds that rise and fall more rapidly than the typical stock. Your average profit per trade should increase. Lower volatility issues will show a lower rate of return. Had we employed the NYSE Index

TABLE 14-1
Buy when the results of dividing the level of the OTC composite by the NYSE Index rise above the .20 exponential average of the results, computed weekly; sell when the .20 exponential average is violated to the downside

Date, buy	Price level, Value Line Composite Index*	Date, sell	Price level, Value Line Composite Index	Points gained (lost)		Percentage gained (lost)		Market value of initial $10,000 investment†
1/2/72	116.38	6/23/72	116.90	+ 0.52		+ 0.4%		$10,044.68
6/30/72	115.75	7/21/72	112.93		−2.82		− 2.4%	9,799.96
10/13/72	107.97	11/3/72	111.98	+ 4.01		+ 3.7%		10,163.93
7/20/73	88.55	10/12/73	96.58	+ 8.03		+ 9.1%		11,085.63
1/11/74	76.66	2/24/74	79.13	+ 2.47		+ 3.2%		11,442.81
3/29/74	78.45	4/19/74	77.40		−1.05		− 1.3%	11,289.66
9/27/74	51.44	10/11/74	55.73	+ 4.29		+ 8.3%		12,231.20
10/25/74	54.63	12/13/74	48.50		−6.13		−11.2%	10,858.74
1/17/75	56.75	3/7/75	66.55	+ 9.80		+17.3%		12,733.91
3/14/75	68.65	5/2/75	70.44	+ 1.79		+ 2.6%		13,065.93
5/9/75	72.25	6/27/75	77.77	+ 5.52		+ 7.6%		14,064.19
7/18/75	79.78	8/15/75	70.69		−9.09		−11.4%	12,461.74
1/9/76	79.26	1/23/76	80.94	+ 1.68		+ 2.1%		12,725.88
2/6/76	83.66	3/26/76	88.78	+ 5.12		+ 6.1%		13,504.70
7/16/76	89.39	8/27/76	84.75		−4.64		− 5.2%	12,803.71
10/15/76	83.16	8/4/78	112.32	+29.16		+35.1%		17,293.32
8/11/78	114.16	10/20/78	104.80		−9.36		− 8.2%	15,875.44
		Through						
1/12/79	104.73	5/18/79	108.45	+ 3.72		+ 3.6%		16,439.33

* The Value Line (VL) Composite Index, an unweighted average of approximately 1,500 stocks, was employed as representative of the total marketplace, more likely to reflect mutual fund performance, for example, than the NYSE Index, which is weighted by capitalization. Had the NYSE Index been employed as the average of record, the same signals would have proved profitable and unprofitable on the same dates. However, the magnitude of price change would have been approximately one third less because of volatility differences.

† Market value is computed by hypothetically starting with 85.93 shares of the VL Composite ($10,000 divided by starting price of 116.38) and then reinvesting the full proceeds of the previous sale upon buy signals. Commission costs, dividends, taxes and interest received while out of the market are not included in the above computation. A buy and hold approach would have resulted in a final holding of 85.93 shares with a market value of $9,319. Only buy signals were included in the above computations. A cash holding was presumed following sell signals.

Total points gained, profitable trades: +76.11
Total points lost, unprofitable trades: −33.09
Average percent gain: +8.26%
Average percent loss: −6.62%

instead of the more volatile VL Composite, returns would have been approximately two thirds the size of the results shown.

All told, we consider the results of this system rather excellent, particularly since they are based on a system that produces only slightly more than two buy and two sell signals per year.

You may employ this system in and of itself, if you are a longer term trader, or you may employ it in conjunction with shorter term trading systems, operating on the latter only when the signals generated conform to the major trends as indicated by the cats and dogs relative strength trading system.

We did not test but do assume that results could be improved if you maintain a daily posting of the relative strength of the OTC Composite compared to the NYSE Index and act on signals that are generated intra-week rather than at week's end. We have found this to be true for the clear majority of trading systems tested, since in weeks the market moves sharply, weekly based signals often lag to some degree. For example, the signal generated on October 20, 1978, a late sell signal, would have been generated earlier in the week had daily postings been maintained.

The zero balance trading system— anticipating trend changes before they actually take place

The "zero balance" trading system is actually rather an unusual, though surprisingly effective, long term trading system. If the truth be told—and it will be right here and now—we did not discover this system ourselves. Rather, we found it published almost simultaneously in two publications, *Professional Timing Service* (P. O. Box 7483, Missoula, Montana 59807), a market advisory edited by Larry Williams, and *Systems and Searches* (Institute for Technical Trading Research and Education, 1420A Southern National Center, Charlotte, N.C. 28202), edited by Lynn McIver and Gresham Northcott. Since the system seemed fairly interesting, even at first glance, we entered into a process of consideration and evaluation, finding in the end that zero balance is among the most effective of the longer term trading methods we have ever encountered.

What zero balance can do for you

The zero balance trading method *anticipates* significant market junctures, showing, often in advance of major and intermediate turning points, when the current trend is weakening and about to change direction. Signals are rendered fairly infrequently—this is a true longer term intermediate trading indicator—but a very high percentage of signals prove accurate. Annualized rates of return compute very favorably, particularly when compared to other systems that trade so infrequently (perhaps two buy and two sell signals per year, on average).

You have to maintain little data for zero balance, and, believe it or not, you have to make only one calculation every five to six weeks to determine buy and sell points. Obviously this is a trading system for the man who has everything but some extra time on his hands.

How to compute the zero balance points that are used to determine when the market is about to reverse its major trend

Your first step in computing zero balance points is the determination of significant cyclical market juncture points. Although zero balance can be adapted to shorter term as well as longer term market movements, we suggest its primary use will lie in its ability to determine significant rather than minor market junctures. Therefore, we suggest the 10–12-week market cycle be employed.

To employ this cycle, first locate on a stock market chart a significant market bottom that has occurred approximately 9–12 weeks past a prior, clearly defined market bottom. This low point will define your first 10-week cyclical low. Inasmuch as a 10-week market cycle will tend to consist, on average, of 5–6 rising weeks and then 5–6 weeks of decline, you will locate your first point at the market low then project your second point 5–6 weeks ahead, where you may anticipate the next intermediate market top.

This projection will tell you *when* to anticipate the forthcoming zero balance reversal points, but will *not* tell you at what level they are likely to occur. Figure 14–1 illustrates the location of zero balance points at 5–6-week intervals of time.

Second, number each zero balance reversal point. The actual market levels at which reversals take place should be numbered as they occur—1, 2, 3 and so forth. Your projected zero balance reversal points are placed on the same time frame, usually computed weeks in advance, and are numbered 1', 2', 3' and so forth. In other words, the zero balance point that corresponds in point of time to Market Reversal Number 2 would be labeled 2'.

Third, calculate where on the price scale to place your zero balance points (Remember, these are projected in advance of actual market prices for the time period in question.) by using the following formula:

$$\text{Projected zero balance level}' = (N - 2) + (N - 3) - (N - 5)$$

where

N' = The sequential number of the new zero balance reversal point to be projected.

$(N - 2)$ = That number minus 2.

You employ for your calculations the exact market level at point $(N - 2)$.

Example

We wish to calculate the zero balance point at Point 8, to compute Point 8'.

The Standard & Poor's 500 at Point 6 $(N - 2)$ came to 100. The Standard & Poor's 500 at Point 5 $(N - 3)$ came to 90. The Standard & Poor's 500 at Point 3 $(N - 5)$ came to 95. By applying the formula shown above, we secure our projection of Point 8'.

$$
\begin{aligned}
\text{Point } 8' &= (N - 2) + (N - 3) - (N - 5) \\
&= \quad 100 \quad + \quad 90 \quad - \quad 95 \\
&= \qquad\qquad 95.
\end{aligned}
$$

FIGURE 14–1
**In projecting zero balance points, make use
of the 9–10 week market cycle**

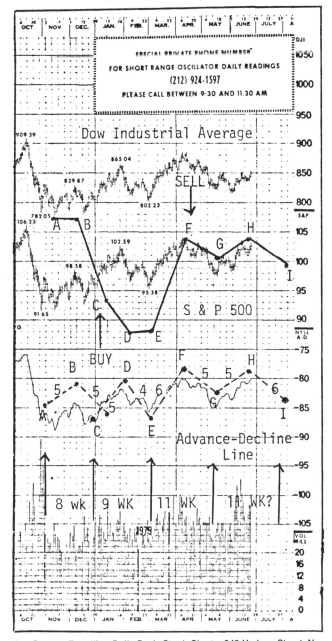

Source: *Trendline Daily Basis Stock Charts,* 345 Hudson Street, New
York, NY 10014.

188

FIGURE 14–2

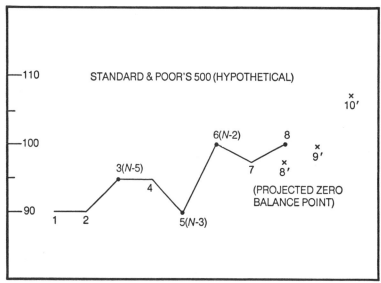

The computation and projection of zero balance points. Presuming that Point 4 stands at 95, Point 5 at 90, Point 6 at 100, Point 7 at 97.50 and Point 8 at 100, try to determine how we arrived at our projections for Point 9′ and Point 10′; with the actual market (Point 8) above the projection at 8′, a buy signal is in effect.

You would project Point 8′ on the Standard & Poor's 500 at a level of 95. Figure 14–2 illustrates the method.

Second example

Let's presume that we know that the Standard & Poor's 500 at Point 7 stood at 105, that at Point 6 it stood at 106 and that at Point 4 it stood at 94. At what level, Standard & Poor's 500, would we project Point 9′?

Try to work out the answer before proceeding any further.

If your result came to "117," you should be in pretty good shape for future computations of zero balance. The answer 117 was secured by adding $(N - 2)$, Point 7 to $(N - 3)$, Point 6 then subtracting 94, the price level at Point $(N - 5)$, Point 4.

How to interpret zero balance to predict the future trend of the market

Your first step is simply to draw lines that will connect the zero balance points you have projected. The line so drawn is referred to as the "zero balance line." *You may consider the major trend bullish for as long as the actual price levels of the market remain above the zero balance line.* If you are considering the purchase of stock, make your purchases at scheduled 10-week cyclical low points, providing that the actual market lows at those junctures remain above their corresponding zero balance projection points.

The major trend should be considered to have turned bearish when market levels at reversal points fall below their projected zero balance points or when

FIGURE 14–3

The zero balance line, 1977–79

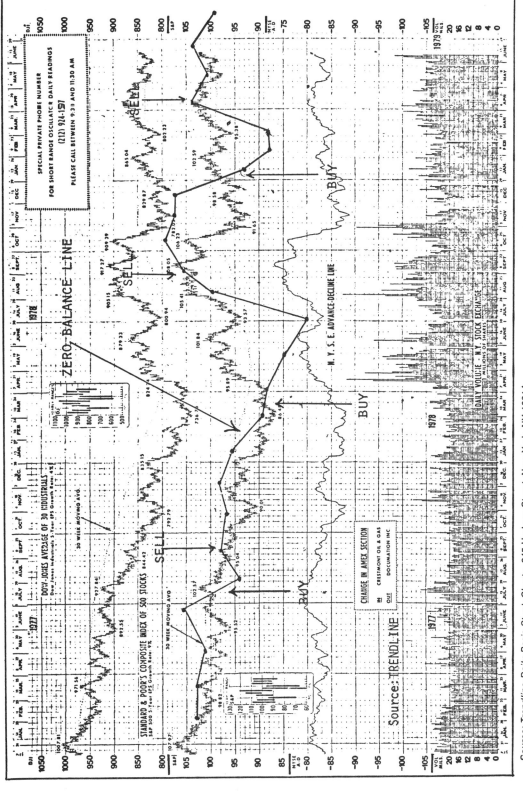

Source: *Trendline Daily Basis Stock Charts*, 345 Hudson Street, New York, NY 10014.

the price level of the market falls below its zero balance line. Should either of these events transpire, sell (and, if you are so inclined, sell short) either immediately, if the zero balance line is violated to the downside, or at the next projected 10-week top reversal point, presuming that the market falls short of reaching the zero balance projection at that point of time.

Figure 14–3 shows the zero balance line and related buy and sell signals for the period 1977–79. An excellent sell signal was rendered in September 1977, followed by a very excellent buy signal during March of 1978. The March buy was followed in turn by a fine sell signal, right at the true market top, in August 1978. You can see how zero balance pointed the way, weeks in advance, to the decline that took place during October of 1978. The January 1979 buy signal proved timely as well.

Not all zero balance buy and sell signals are profitable, of course, and our backtracking of this method has been hypothetical. Nonetheless, results have been quite satisfactory. Table 14–2 signals we have hypothetically derived via this method for the period 1971–79.

Discussion of results

The clear majority of both buy and sell signals would have hypothetically proved profitable during the period of time covered in our study. Zero balance produces few whipsaws, and commission costs are kept to a minimum when this system is employed.

Buy signals alone, all capital proceeds from sales reinvested, would have produced an annualized rate of return of approximately 7.0 percent a year,

TABLE 14–2
**Hypothetical results of trading the Standard & Poor's 500
average via zero balance**

Trading signals, 1971–1979				Sell short signals			
Date, buy	Level, S&P 500	Percent gain	Percent loss	Date, sell	Level, S&P 500	Percent gain	Percent loss
				Jul. '71	99	+ 1.0%	
Aug. '71	98		−2.0%	Oct. '71	96		−3.1%
Dec. '71	99	+ 8.1%		Mar. '72	107	0	
Jul. '72	107	+ 0.9		Sep. '72	108		−3.7
Oct. '72	112	+ 6.3		Jan. '73	119	+14.3	
Jul. '73	102	+ 2.0		Nov. '73	104	+10.6	
Feb. '74	93		−7.5	May '74	86	+14.0	
Oct. '74	74	+21.6		Jun. '75	90	+ 2.2	
Nov. '75	88	+13.6		Apr. '76	100		−4.0
Aug. '76	104	0		Oct. '76	104	+ 3.8	
Jul. '77	100		−4.0	Sep. '77	96	+ 6.3	
Mar. '78	90	+14.4		Aug. '78	103	+ 4.9	
Jan. '79	98	+ 4.1		Apr. '79	102		
Averages:		+ 8.9	−4.5			+ 7.1	−3.6

had the Standard & Poor's 500 Average been traded according to zero balance buy and sell signals. This result does not include the effects of commissions, dividends, taxes or interest on your capital while you were in a cash position. A buy and hold approach to the Standard & Poor's 500 Average over the same period would have resulted in an annualized rate of return of only 0.5 percent per year, so zero balance outperformed a buy and hold by 14 times.

Had you purchased the Standard & Poor's 500 on buy signals and had you sold the average short on sell signals, reinvesting all capital proceeds on both the long and the short side, you would have achieved an annualized rate of return of approximately 13.9 percent per year—nearly 14 times the rate of return of a buy and hold strategy over the years. (Dividends, commissions and taxes excluded, of course.)

This system may be employed in and of itself, as a longer term trading system, or in conjunction with shorter term trading systems, in which case it would be employed as a confirming signal. Readers are invited to experiment with short term zero balance signals, but frankly, for shorter term purposes, we prefer The Time-Trend-Momentum Trading System.

Some further tips on using zero balance—recognizing when there are changes in trend and when the market is simply continuing in its present direction

Your zero balance line is capable of showing you when the current market trend appears to be weakening or strengthening. It is not necessarily capable of showing you when prices are actually going to change direction, although, for the most part, changes in the thrust of trends are shortly followed by significant price reversals. For so long as trends are consistent, zero balance will remain in a neutral configuration—even, in some cases, if the prevailing trend is bullish or bearish. In this regard, zero balance can sometimes prove a bit deceptive.

To illustrate this point, let's consider the behavior of zero balance during three different hypothetical market climates.

Climate 1: A neutral market

Figure 14–4 illustrates a neutral stock, ranging evenly in price from 10 to 20, swinging at regular intervals. The zero balance line for that stock, plotted, remains exactly on the price line of the issue. So far, so good. We would expect zero balance to continue to render neutral readings given a neutral market condition. Let's move along, however, to a stock in a clearly defined uptrend.

Climate 2: An orderly uptrend

Figure 14–5 illustrates an issue in a clearly defined and orderly uptrend, rising two points on each upwards swing then declining by one point on the downlegs. The zero balance line, in this case, is also rising, reflecting the uptrend. However, as in the case above, the price of the issue on both uplegs

FIGURE 14–4
**If a stock is neutrally trended, zero balance will
remain neutral, protecting a contribution of trend**

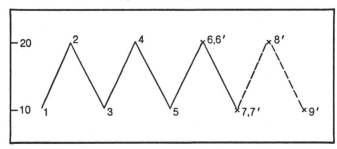

and downlegs parallels the zero line, reflecting a trend that is neither increasing nor decreasing in strength. Such patterns occur only infrequently, but when they do, signals based upon penetrations of the zero balance line alone may occur very late. In such cases, where both price and zero balance appear to move jointly in clearly defined trends, employ the direction of trend as your deciding factor, even if no penetration of zero balance occurs.

Climate 3: An orderly downtrend

Figure 14–6 illustrates the reverse situation: an issue in an orderly downtrend. Here, too, the price of the issue does not move away from its zero balance line, at least not until the downtrend is reversed, but here, too, the direction of price movement and the trend of the zero balance line prove decisive in your interpretation of events.

Do keep in mind, however, that the ability of an issue finally to rise above its zero balance line represents a bullish development despite the fact that

FIGURE 14–5
**If a stock rises in an orderly pattern, its zero balance
line will rise in conformity, but may render no other
buy signal**

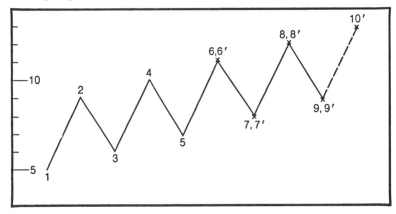

FIGURE 14–6
Should a stock decline in a very orderly downtrend, its zero balance line will trend downwards in conformity, but may render no additional sell signal

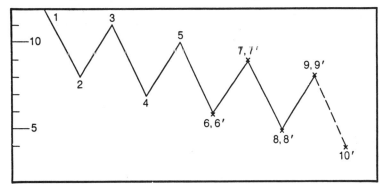

zero balance at the juncture of penetration remains in a downtrend. There are times in actual market behavior when this takes place, mid-1978 for example, and such occasions almost always provide excellent buying opportunities. In general, divergences between price action and zero balance action prove significant, and, in general, divergences are the rule rather than the exception. It is only when price action and zero balance action coincide that the trends in the direction of both will be decisive.

15

Some portfolio management
techniques that should improve
your odds and provide even
better returns from the trading
systems you have learned—one
final trading tip

By this time, we have covered a considerable amount of ground. We have explored short-term, intermediate-term and longer-term trading systems. We have examined moving average systems, channel reversal systems, momentum trading systems, excessive swing trading systems and, in Chapter 14, "zero balance" and the "cats and dogs relative strength" major trend indicators. Some of these systems, according to our research, figure to produce sufficient profit to cover commission costs. Others are more adapted to very low or no-commission vehicles such as no-load mutual funds. Let's consider now some strategies that should help you increase your returns from any of the trading systems we have discussed.

How you should be able to make nearly forty-eight percent on your money by buying call options on a stock that declines by 14.3 percent!

The purchase of listed put and call options, particularly the latter, has, in our opinion, been greatly misunderstood as an investment strategy. The general consensus is that the purchase of a listed call represents a highly speculative venture, suitable only for gamblers, plungers and investors with plenty of risk capital to spare.

This is only partially true, if at all, and in fact, with proper portfolio management, the purchase of listed call options can represent a far more conservative approach to the stock market than the purchase of common stock. For example, suppose that you had taken advantage of high recent interest rate periods to purchase a portfolio of high-grade corporate or treasury bonds, with a current yield of 10 percent. And let us suppose that with the proceeds of that 10 percent yield—nothing more—you purchased listed put and call options from time to time in accordance with market signals generated by one of our trading systems. You would probably find that with the use of 10 percent of your initial capital—the interest return from your bond holdings—you could control an amount of common stock, via options, in the total value of your cash assets, if not more. Should the market move in your direction while you hold your options, you could very possibly produce as great a return as if you had held or sold the underlying common short properly. If, on the other hand, the market moved against you, your total portfolio loss could be no greater than the equivalent of the interest you received from your bonds. No actual reduction in your starting portfolio would occur, even if all of your options expired worthless, providing that you refrained from ever investing an amount greater than the interest you received from your bonds. In this case, a strategy of combining option purchases with the holding of long term, high grade debt instruments is a far more conservative, but potentially as profitable, strategy than employing your capital to purchase shares of stock.

This postulation has been supported by serious academic research. For example, a working paper, "A Simulation of the Returns and Risk of Alternative Option Portfolio Investment Strategies," by Robert C. Merton, Myron S. Scholes and Mathew L. Gladstein (1976) suggested that this strategy was likely to outperform both the strategies of the outright purchase of securities and the strategy of the purchase of securities and the writing of covered call options. By and large, out-of-the-money call options produced the best results. One caveat: the writing of call options against existing holdings will perform best during periods when options trade at above normal value, as determined by the widely employed Black-Scholes option valuation formula. (You can secure normal option valuations through the use of the Texas Instruments TI–59 hand calculator, combined with TI's Securities Packet.) The purchase of options should be confined to periods when options trade at or below calculated normal values.

The purchase of options as opposed to the purchase of common stock provides many advantages: lower commission costs, lower capital requirements, limited loss and favorable leverage. With some care, even the most conservative of investors should find option trading a suitable enterprise. This brings us to a significant capital management strategy: the scale trading of call options.

Scale trading: making the leverage in options work on your side

Option scale trading is not basically a new strategy, but rather a variation of the basic dollar cost average strategy commonly applied to the investment in mutual funds. Risks and potential rewards, however, are both much greater when you scale trade options.

The scale trading of options is a particularly good strategy because of the favorable leverage inherent in stock options. Given a 10 percent move in the underlying common, for example, listed at-the-money calls are likely, roughly, to double in price if the stock rises by 10 percent, but are likely to lose only about 50 percent of their value if the issue declines by 10 percent. These ratios hold, of course, for only relatively short periods of time, perhaps six to eight weeks for an option originally purchased with six months of life remaining in the option. Nonetheless, these leverage relationships for such periods of time are very real and very advantageous to the option buyer.

The strategy of scale trading is particularly suitable for the purchase of call options when your trading systems indicate that the stock market is probing for an intermediate bottom. Through the use of scale trading, you should be able to profit even if you take your long positions prematurely.

How scale trading is carried out

The technique is simple and will, of course, lend itself to certain variations, if you so choose.

1. You purchase an amount of options (calls if bullish, or puts if you are bearish) on your trading selection, preferably a stock with at least normal and preferably above normal volatility.

    Let's presume that you will start with an at-the-money option, six months of life remaining. With a presumed price of 35 for the underlying common, we may assume that a call option of this nature will trade at 3¼ or for 9.3 percent of the price of the underlying common.

    Should the issue immediately rise in price, or stand still and then rise in price, you have no problem. You simply cash in your option at the appropriate moment and collect your profits. But what if the stock drops in price instead? Well, in that case, move along to Step 2 in your scale trading program.

2. If the stock declines by approximately 15 percent or so (we are presuming a 14.3 percent decline in price, from 35 to 30), you purchase *an equal dollar amount of the same option.*

    Had you purchased two options with a strike price of 35, we are presuming, from normal option valuation formulae, that you would pay 3¼ for each option at your initial purchase: a total investment of $681, including commission costs. Were the stock to decline to 30, the 35-strike options figure would sell at a price of ¾ each, which would allow you to purchase eight additional options for an additional investment of $670, including commissions.

    Should the stock now return to a price of 35 within two months of your initial investment, the ten options you now hold calculate to sell at 2½ apiece, or for a total of $2,395 after commission costs. Your net profit would come to $1,044, or to 77.3 percent of your investment.

    So far, still so good. We profit if the underlying common rises in price, and we profit if it declines in price then recovers to its starting point. Suppose, however, that the stock continues to decline, say to a price of 25—28.6 percent below its starting price. Well, in that unhappy event you have to move along to Step 3.

3. If the stock, instead of recovering to its initial price, drops one further level—this time by 16.7 percent, from 30 to 25—you purchase an *equal dollar amount of the intermediate strike option,* in this case, the 30s. As

you can see in the workout shown in Figure 15–1, you will, by this time, end up with 10 35-strike options and 16 30-strike options. Should the underlying common retrace only 50 percent of its drop from 35 to 25—recovering to 30, a normal retracement—you would figure to net approximately 48 percent in profit after all costs. These projections are based on normal option valuations; the implied assumptions cannot, of course, be guaranteed.

Risks

The major risk lies in the possibility that the underlying common does *not* show any price recovery at all, that it declines in price then remains in a

FIGURE 15–1
Scale trading can prove a profitable strategy

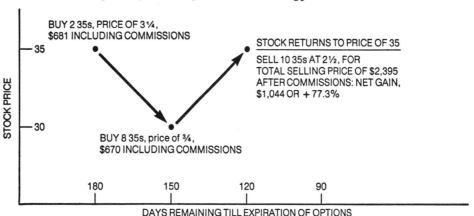

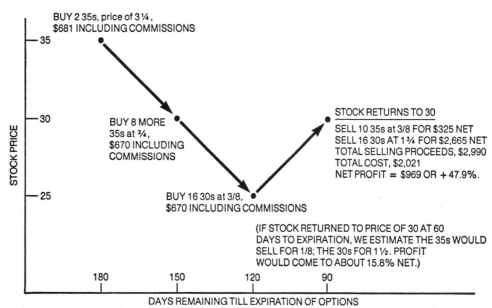

Projected workouts are based upon normal values for call options for stocks of average volatility (no dividends) generated by use of the Black-Scholes option valuation formula.

narrow trading range. In that event, all options held may lose value considerably, even expiring worthless if held until maturity. This technique is more suited for volatile than for flat market periods, although the movement required to show a profit is well within ranges generally seen in the stock market.

You must, of course, retain sufficient capital at the time of your initial purchase to make the secondary purchases, if necessary. And, of course, this sort of program should be entered into only with speculative capital.

Caveats aside, scale trading of options should prove to be an excellent strategy, and quite profitable over the long run.

Trade at the deep discount brokerage houses

It goes without saying that the lower your transaction costs, the higher will be your total return, particularly on an actively traded portfolio. With round trip commission costs lying in the area of 3 percent of the price of common shares at fixed brokerage rates at major houses, you will find it difficult indeed to outperform a simple buy and hold strategy. For example, if we presume that you make four trades per year—a small number for an active trader—you must outperform a buy and hold strategy by 12 percent per year to offset a 3 percent transaction cost per transaction. With the assumption of commission costs of such magnitude, many academicians have concluded that no trading system can significantly outperform a buy and hold strategy.

There is, however, no reason for you to be locked into transaction costs of such magnitude. Many discount brokerages provide virtually full service to investors while charging minimum commission rates. For example, at one firm, R. F. Lafferty & Co., it is possible to trade shares in stock in 500 share lots for a total commission cost, round trip, of $25 per 100 shares. Presuming that you are trading shares priced at $70 per share, your total round trip commission cost would come to 0.36 percent, sufficiently low to render many of our trading systems highly profitable. Commissions for stock options at Lafferty can run to as low as $10 round trip per option, regardless of the price of the option, providing that you transact in lots of ten.

Other firms provide similar discounts, and if you are an active trader, you should be able to negotiate even greater reductions. We present a list of discount brokerages that do offer sizable discounts from regular brokerage rates. This list is far from complete; new firms are being formed frequently. *Barron's* usually carries advertisements and further information.

Discount brokerage firms that offer sizable reductions in standard commission rates

Source Securities Corp., 70 Pine Street, New York NY 10005

Fidelity Brokerage Services, Inc., P. O. Box 2698, Dept. FB 061179, The Fidelity Building, 82 Devonshire Street, Boston MA 02208

Kennedy, Cabot & Co., 9465 Wilshire Boulevard, Beverly Hills CA 90212

Icahn & Co., 25 Broadway, New York NY 10004

R. F. Lafferty & Co., 50 Broad Street, New York NY 10004

W. T. Cabe & Co., Inc., 1270 Avenue of the Americas, New York NY 10020

Parker, Alexander & Co., Inc., 200 Park Avenue, New York NY 10017
Stock & Trade, 580 Fifth Avenue, New York NY 10036
Charles Schwab & Co., Inc., 134 South LaSalle Street, Chicago IL 60603
Ovest Securities, Inc., Seven Hanover Street, New York NY 10005
StockCross, One Washington Mall, Boston MA 02108

Trade no-load mutual funds, particularly telephone switch funds

We have made allusion to this strategy at several previous points within this book, but we do believe the point is well worth the repetition. The trading of stock options does offer the advantages, as we have seen, of limited risk, favorable leverage and reduced commission costs vis-à-vis the underlying common shares. However, if stock options are traded upon market timing signals, a diversified portfolio of at least six to eight such options should be created if you hope that your selections will reliably follow the market. Furthermore, option liquidity is often limited, particularly during rapidly moving markets. Finally, unless you have both the time and inclination to secure and act upon frequent intra-day price quotations, you may find that the options in which you deal change very rapidly in price during the course of any given trading day. The inability to stay close to events can sometimes prove very costly.

In comparison to stock options, and to trading the underlying common shares of such options, no-load mutual funds provide the following advantages:

1. In trading such vehicles, you pay no direct commission costs. For practical purposes, you can trade virtually free of any transaction costs, thereby reaping the full benefit of your timing signals.
2. Your portfolio becomes fully diversified automatically. Sudden shocks and surprises are virtually eliminated. The vast majority of mutual funds follow the market averages closely; differences among them are mainly a function of the funds' volatility, at least on a trade-by-trade basis.
3. The majority of mutual funds will provide execution at the fund price at the close of the day in which your order is received, providing that your order arrives at the fund prior to the close of the market on that day. Your liquidity is virtually fully guaranteed.
4. Certain mutual funds will allow you to make purchases and redemption by telephone, and certain funds will allow a telephone transfer of assets from an equity mutual fund to a money market instrument fund and back via telephone exchange. This allows you to place your capital rapidly into an interest-bearing vehicle when you leave the equity markets. Such funds are ideal vehicles for shorter term market timing signals.

Disadvantages

The major disadvantage in trading mutual funds as opposed to individual options or stock selections is that your profit potential does become somewhat limited by the very diversification that represents a major advantage of mutual funds. Investors who happen to excel at stock selection may prefer to select their own; the majority of investors will probably benefit from the diversification provided by mutual funds.

If you do trade mutual funds, as opposed to options or stocks, you may find some change in your perspectives regarding price movement. Whereas a 10 percent gain on the part of a stock is not unusual, even in a moderately changing market, and whereas a 50 percent gain in an option is common when your timing is correct, mutual funds rise and fall by much smaller amounts over short periods of time. A 10 percent gain in a mutual fund transaction will probably represent a trade that is well above average. On the other hand, losses will accrue at much slower rates when you trade mutual funds—funds rarely declining by more than 1 to 2 percent on any given day. Over an entire year, differences in volatility will tend to balance out.

Switch funds

Since mid-1975, the mutual fund industry has been offering so-called "switch privileges" in "switch funds," funds, as we have mentioned, that allow you to transact via telephone (or sometimes only by mail) and to "switch" your assets from equity funds to money market instrument funds, usually but not always within the same management family.

These funds, as we have also mentioned, are ideal vehicles for short term market timing signals—so ideal, as it has turned out, that investors' use, and perhaps overexploitation, of the switch privilege grew greatly within the first years of its introduction. As a result, the industry seems to have entered into something of a state of flux regarding switch privileges, with various restrictions and/or charges for the use of switching placed on some funds. Telephone switching for other funds has been eliminated altogether because of disruptions to their portfolios created by rapidly moving investors. It is possible that switching may soon disappear from the mutual fund scene altogether.

On the other hand, whereas many funds are restricting the use of switching, other funds have been introducing the privilege for their shareholders. As we said, the position of the mutual fund industry regarding switching does seem to lie, at the time of this writing at least, in a state of flux.

Mutual funds will probably remain a viable instrument for market trading, even should switching disappear altogether. Many no-load funds will accept telephone orders for purchase, although relatively few, apart from the switch funds, will accept telephone orders for redemption, requiring bank guaranteed letters of instruction for such action. Our research indicates to us that relatively little is likely to be lost if all but the shortest term market signals are acted upon one day late. You should be able to get by if, on the day of sell signals, you write to your fund, employing the post office's twenty-four-hour delivery service. Signal delays of one day should occur only on the sell side. If you reside in a major metropolitan area such as Boston or New York, where many funds are located, a messenger service should be able to transmit your letters reliably and rapidly, reducing delays even further.

The following mutual fund families have been providing switch privileges to shareholders. Stipulations as to the cost and limits of frequency of switching have been changing, so we do suggest you secure the most recent prospectus of any fund in which you have interest before placing an investment into that fund. We also suggest you telephone management of these funds to ascertain the attitude of management to active traders. We have found that in many cases management, in practice, is more restrictive than its prospecti indicate and that, in other cases, management is actually less restrictive. Mutual funds do retain the right to refuse to accept purchase orders from overly active traders, but only in the rarest of cases will they refuse to honor a properly submitted redemption request.

Caveat

Whereas stock brokerage firms are geared to accept a heavy volume of transaction orders, the majority of switch funds tend to become overloaded during climactic market periods, when many traders are moving into and out of the funds. Errors in execution are fairly common. To protect yourself in the event of any dispute, we suggest that you tape (letting the fund know) your transaction orders. You can secure the necessary equipment at minimal cost at electronic outlets. All that is required are a standard cassette recorder and a telephone microphone.

Funds that allow telephone switching

Dreyfus Number Nine—Dreyfus Third Century—Dreyfus Daily Liquid Assets, 600 Madison Avenue, New York NY 10022. Dreyfus Number Nine and Dreyfus Third Century are equity funds, more volatile than the typical fund. Dreyfus Daily Liquid Assets is a related money market fund. Both equity funds appear to have been reliable performers when traded according to market timing signals.

Pennsylvania Mutual Fund, 127 John Street, New York NY 10038. A much more volatile fund than most, which has allowed switching with money market funds sponsored by the Scudder organization. The fund, in mid-1979, charged a $1/10$ percent levy on all switch redemptions.

Price Growth—Price New Horizons—Price Prime Reserves, 100 East Pratt Street, Baltimore MD 21202. Price Growth is a fairly staid equity fund, not as volatile as the Price New Horizons fund. Prime Reserves is the related money market fund. Management charges no fee for switching but has limited such transactions to one per calendar quarter.

Nicholas Fund—Bank Account at First Wisconsin Trust, 312 East Wisconsin Avenue, Milwaukee WI 53202. Nicholas is a very volatile mutual fund, with no restrictions on the frequency of trading. However, the fund has been charging a $1/2$ percent redemption fee on sales made within 30 days of purchase. You may switch between the fund and an interest-bearing bank account at First Wisconsin Trust.

The 44 Wall Street Fund, 150 Broadway, New York NY 10038. Among the most volatile of mutual funds, a fund that employs margin leverage frequently and invests in only a relatively small portfolio of stocks. No restrictions on frequency of trading, but does charge a ¼ percent redemption fee on all sales. The fund has provided switch arrangements with the Reserve Fund, an unaffiliated money market fund.

Energy Fund—Guardian Fund—Partners Fund, 522 Fifth Avenue, New York NY 10036. A more conservative family of funds, which allows commission free switching among any of the family's equity funds or to an unrelated money market fund.

Fidelity Contrafund—Fidelity Equity Income—Fidelity Daily Income Trust, 82 Devonshire Street, Boston MA 02109. Contrafund and Equity Income are moderately volatile funds. The Daily Income Trust is the money market fund into which proceeds may be switched. The fund imposes minimal charges for switching.

Financial Dynamics—Financial Industrial—Financial Industrial Income— Financial Daily Income Shares, P. O. Box 2040, Denver CO 80201. Financial Dynamics is the most volatile of the equity funds in this family; Financial Industrial Income is the least volatile. As a group, this is a fairly conservative group of funds, and we consider Financial Industrial and Financial Industrial Income to be two funds that are very well suited for longer term system investors. Both funds have had a recent history of holding their prices well during market declines. The management company has been imposing no charges for trading, but will allow switching only approximately six times per year.

The Bull & Bear Group, 111 Broadway, New York NY 10006. This group consists of five funds—the Bull Fund (aggressive and very volatile), the Bear Fund (aggressive bearishly oriented investments), Capital Shares, Inc., (invests in small growth companies), Capamerica Fund, Inc. (a diversified fund) and Golconda Investors Ltd. (a fund that specializes in gold investments). Investors may switch among the funds or to a savings account. No restrictions on trading, but a ½ percent of asset charge is levied on redemptions made within sixty days of purchase.

In addition to the above, certain load funds, for example funds sponsored by Keystone, Dreyfus and American General managements, provide switch privileges. However, the initial load charge reduces the usefulness of such funds to any but the largest investors. True initial commission costs for such load funds can run to higher than 9 percent of your initial investment.

You should be able to make a suitable selection from among the above listed no-load mutual funds. Many funds advertise in *Barron's* and other sources that may be consulted for new fund listing.

And one final trading system . . .

A very useful daily composite indicator for calling the direction of the next day's market was published on June 1, 1979, by an advisory service, *Market Logic* (The Institute for Econometric Research, 3471 North Federal Highway, Fort Lauderdale FL 33306). The service evaluated the results of this system via computer, and with all due credit to *Market Logic*, we hereby present, with only a slight modification, its system for making daily predictions of the direction of stock price movement.

The Market Logic System for making daily predictions of stock market movement

To follow this trading system, you are required to take five readings pertaining to the stock market on a daily basis. These include:

1. *Change in level of market.* You may employ any of the broader-based major market averages such as the NYSE Index, but we suggest that the advance-decline line be employed. (*Market Logic* suggests that a "total return" index be employed, which includes dividend payouts.) If more issues advance on the New York Stock Exchange than decline, grade this variable "+". If more issues decline than advance, grade this indicator "0".

2. *Trend change.* If the daily reading of advances minus declines shows more favorable totals than the previous day, grade this indicator "+". If the daily reading is less favorable than the previous day's reading, grade this indicator "0".

   A "0" rating can be given even on a day when more issues advance then decline, if the plurality on such a day is less favorable than on the day previous. A "+" rating can be given on a day when more issues decline than advance if the net number of declining issues is less than on the previous day.

3. *Trin.* Trin is a measure of the relative amount of volume that enters advancing issues on the New York Stock Exchange as compared to the amount of volume that enters into declining issues each day. It is expressed in the following formula:

$$\frac{\text{Number of issues advancing}}{\text{Number of issues declining}} \div \frac{\text{Up volume}}{\text{Down volume}} = \text{TRIN}$$

   Readings below 1 are bullish and rate a "+" rating for the day. Readings of above 1 are bearish and rate a "0" rating for the day. Your stockbroker should be able to provide TRIN readings throughout the day from his quotation machine and should be able to provide final daily readings at market close.

4. *Tick.* This is a measure of the net amount of trades that have recently occurred on "upticks," at a price higher than the previous trade, compared to trades that have just occurred on "downticks," at a price lower than the previous trade. It is bullish ("+") if the day closes with a positive "tick" reading. It is bearish ("0") if the day closes with a plurality of downticks.

5. *Seasonality.* The stock market has a pronounced tendency to show strength during certain days of the week and month and just prior to certain holidays. Rate seasonality as "+" if the next trading day will occur on any of the following: (*a*) a Friday; (*b*) the last trading day of any month or one of the first four trading days of any month; (*c*) the two trading days prior to a market holiday.
All other days are graded "0."

Total up the results

After each day's trading, total up the number of "+" readings secured. According to *Market Logic,* the following probabilities are likely to be encountered:

Number of "+" readings	Probability of rising prices on the next market day
0	23%
1	29
2	50
3	66
4	78
5	90

On average, prices rise in the stock market approximately 55 percent of the time.

The *Market Logic* system is hardly a difficult trading system to apply. Employed in and of itself, it will probably not suffice for in and out trading. Employed in conjunction with one of our intermediate trading systems, the *Market Logic* system may well assist you in getting the jump on the gun, so to speak, to anticipate signals provided by intermediate indicators, thereby increasing the odds even further that your next trade will prove to be a profitable one.

Which is, we guess, what this book has been all about.

Index